020.973 Manley, Will,
MAN   1949-
         Uncensored thoughts.

$23.95

020.973
Man
   c.1

Books This One Is Not:

Unintellectual Freedoms (1991)

Unsolicited Advice (1992)

Unprofessional Behavior (1992)

For Library Directors Only/For Library Trustees Only (1993)

The Manley Art of Librarianship (1993)

Little House on the Prairie (1935)

020.973
Man
c.1

You Don't Have to Start Here Unless You're a Cataloger

THERE is no particular order to this book. It's designed for informal staff room browsing. You're supposed to be able to open it up anywhere and start reading. That's why we've boldfaced some of the print—to help you find words or phrases that might pique your interest and get you jump-started. I personally think there's something tyrannical about books that expect you to start on page 12 and plow yourself through to the bitter end. I think it's a lot more fun to start with whatever grabs your fancy. (For those of you manic enough to think you must have a table of contents it's provided on page 12—complete with page numbers.) So think of this book as verbal trail mix, and go from there. **IF** you're a cataloger, however, that's different. You ★★★**page 1**★★★

need bibliographic details and you need them now. I can relate to that. After all, I'm a library director and I certainly wouldn't want my catalogers wasting a lot of time hunting haphazardly through a book just to locate basic data. So out of deference to your needs, I'll give you the information you want in the appropriate order (CIP is on page 8).

Title

I suppose the first thing you want is a title, so let's get the formalities over with in a hurry. The title of this book is ***Uncensored Thoughts: Pot Shots from a Public Librarian.*** Originally this book wasn't going to have a title. My intention was to write a long rambling letter to the library profession with the covers of the book designed like an envelope, but I didn't have the discipline or the stamina to sustain a long rambling letter. I got about sixty-eight pages into it and gave up. Then I tried to reshape what I had into a book entitled "Unsubstantiated Rumors" but that was too gossipy so I gave that up also. Plus I didn't want to get sued.   **THEN** I was going to work something out under the title "Uncivil Liberties" but over lunch one day my friend Arnold, who by the way is a cataloger and knows all things (I realize that's redundant), told me that Calvin Trillin had already written a book with that title and that it would be foolhardy of me to try to compete with him since in Arnold's words: "Will, Calvin Trillin has more brains in his elbow than you have in your head." So then I decided that maybe I better write the book first and then title it later, and while I was writing the book I got fired from *The Wilson Library Bulletin* for writing a survey on the subject of librarians and sex and so I thought the title "Uncensored Thoughts" would be a nice backhanded slap at Wilson.

The Author

MY full name is William Laird Patrick Tecumseh Alexander Sylvester Manley—Will Manley for short. Here's my professional résumé: ***Work Experience***   **A.** Past Lives: 19950–19920 BC—Cave Painter, South of France; 9381–9347 BC—Ditch Digger, Central Babylon; 1290–1274 BC—Snake Charmer, Court of Ramses; 600–592 BC—Water Boy at Olympics in Greece; 173–177 AD—Spear Carrier in Roman Army; 889–917 AD—Alchemist, Paris; 1351–1403 AD—Royal Astrologer, Lisbon; 1881–1903 AD—Snake Oil Salesman, Mississippi River Valley. **B.** Present Life: 1967–1971— Philosopher, Various Park Benches; 1971 to the Present—Public Librarian.   ***Academic Achievements***   High School—Pitman (NJ) High—"Everybody Loves Pitman." **B.A.**—Notre Dame—Was used as live tackling dummy at Fightin' Irish football scrimmages. **M.L.S.**—University of Denver—#1 in Misanthropic Cataloging Professors. ★★★page 2★★★   **M.P.A.**—Arizona State University—#1 in Playboy

Party Poll. **D.L.S.** — Central Kansas School of Information Studies — found on matchbook cover at the bar of the Holiday Inn in Hutchinson, Kansas. **Consulting Experience** Bill Clinton and Elvis call every few weeks for advice. **Personal Data** 3 kids, 1 wife; no respect. **Publications** Wrote "Facing the Public" column for 12 years for the *Wilson Library Bulletin* but got canned for running a survey on "Librarians and Sex." Write "Will's World" column for *American Libraries* (have not yet gotten canned). Write "The Manley Arts" column for *Booklist* (not yet canned). **Career Objective** To get canned from the 3 major library publications. **Philosophy of Life** "Boolean Searching" is not the meaning of life. **Organizations** Corresponding Secretary of the American Library Association's Foolish Activities Round Table (F.A.R.T.).

The Illustrator

ONE thing that librarians have consistently said that they like about my books is that they have drawings. This I realize is a breakthrough for the library science genre. The credit goes to Richard Lee who in addition to being a cartoonist is also a branch librarian for the Las Vegas Public Library. He has contributed many cartoons to *American Libraries, Wilson Library Bulletin* (don't hold that against him), *Easy Rider, Velvet, Swank, Stag, Women's World,* and *Saturday Evening Post.* His professional goal is to do cartoons for *The New Yorker* and *Playboy.* He is the author/illustrator of the book *"You Can Tell Your Kid Will Grow Up to Be a Librarian When...",* which one reviewer called a "terrific treat."

The Publisher

THE publisher is McFarland & Company, Inc. Sure, they're not real big like Scribners or Macmillan, but they do publish well over a hundred books a year on subjects ranging from L.C. subject headings to the history of the condom industry, and unlike H.W. Wilson they would never fire anybody for writing a survey on sex and librarians. The next time you go to an A.L.A. conference you should stop at their booth. Nicer people you will find nowhere. **THE** only thing I don't like about McFarland is that they have a policy against dust jackets. That's why I wanted my picture in this book — so that you can get a look at me. I have always felt that it's very important for readers to know what the author looks like before they decide to invest time or money in a book. You wouldn't go on a blind date without looking at the person's photo and you certainly wouldn't want to read a cookbook written by an anorexic. **ANOTHER** reason I wanted my picture on page 1 was because I am really, really tired of librarians coming up to me at library conferences and saying "You can't be Will Manley. You're too young. Will Manley is an old stump of a man with coke bottle glasses, gray whiskers, male pattern

baldness, and a pot belly." Librarians have been saying this to me for the past fifteen years. I may not be young anymore but by God I'm not ready for a nursing home. The worst part about that experience is that when people realize I am Will Manley they lie and say, "I thought you were old because your writing reflects the wisdom of age." What that really means is that I write like an old fart. **THE** only good experience I ever had about my age was at the A.L.A. booth in New Orleans, where I was meeting and greeting people with my *Booklist* editor, Bill Ott. After seven or eight people told me that I was far too young to be Will Manley, Bill turned to me and said, "You know, Will, if people said that to me I'd really be upset because it means that they think you write like an old fart." Bill got his comeuppance five minutes later when a young library school student came up and said to me, "You're not really Will Manley, are you?" After proving my identity with my driver's license, I asked him what he thought Will Manley looked like. Pointing to Bill, he replied, "I thought that old fart over there was Will Manley."

Place and Date of Publication

McFARLAND is located in Jefferson, which is a small town (population 1,200) located somewhere in North Carolina, and London, which is a big city (population 6,700,000) located somewhere in England. Jefferson and London are two of my favorite towns, and some day I'd even like to visit them. **THIS** book was officially published in the fall of 1994, but it was written over about a six year period.

Cataloguing in Publication Data

I'M not going to give that to you right now because I really don't want you to catalog this book, not just yet anyway. First, some background. This book is the younger brother of an earlier book that I wrote entitled *Unintellectual Freedoms*, which was published three years ago. In that book I gave specific instructions not to catalog it, jacket it, stamp it, or hog-tie it with any other kind of bibliographic straitjacket. I simply wanted you catalogers to pick the book up, walk it over to the staff lounge, and quietly place it on top of the microwave oven so that it would be readily accessible to library staffers who were on break and were looking for something light to read while sipping soup or munching on a carrot stick. **UNFORTUNATELY** my instructions were largely ignored and so the book largely went unread. This makes me angry because I knew if the book went into its appropriate place in the collection, it would sit there ignored like a wallflower among geeks. Be honest, have you ever heard of anyone browsing through the library science section looking for a "good read?" **I** know that most of the libraries that acquired the book put it into their regular collection because I called a random sample of twenty-five libraries across the country. The flattering part of the survey was that nineteen of the libraries had gotten the book, but the frustrating part was that eighteen of them had catalogued, stamped, jacketed, and pocketed the book and the nineteenth simply hadn't gotten to it (they have a two and a half year backlog). My frustration increased when I discovered that in all eighteen libraries the book was sitting idly on the shelf. In not one of those libraries was it out in circulation when I made my call. **THIS** bothered me so much that I followed up my first survey with a second one in which I called the head catalogers in the eighteen libraries and asked them why they had decided to ignore my instructions on how the book should be handled. What follows is a listing of what they said to me: 1. I was afraid that the book would catch on fire on top of the microwave oven.   2. I didn't think you were serious.   3. You have no right to tell me what to do with your book.   4. I didn't want to block the air vents on top of our microwave oven.   5. Your suggestion violates every principle of bibliographic control.   6. Your suggestion would be the beginning of bibliographic anarchy in our library.   7. I just couldn't bring myself to do it.   8. I was afraid of being fired.   9. I didn't want to break policy.   10. Can you imagine what would happen if we gave special treatment to every author and every book?   11. I didn't want the book to be contaminated by microwave emissions.   12. It would be censorship not to put your book in the collection.   13. My supervisor told me that you were a crackpot.   14. Why should I follow your instructions when you've made a career out of ridiculing catalogers?   15. We had seven patron reserves on your book, all from your mother.   16. You're an idiot.   17. Whatever you told me to do, I'd do the opposite.   18. I didn't want our staff getting indigestion from reading your book during lunch time and coffee breaks. **THESE** responses were bad enough but the real insult came when I discovered that my own catalogers, my very own catalogers, had disregarded my written instructions. That's right. My own staff made the decision to stamp, catalog, pocket, and jacket my book. And to add insult to injury I found it one day standing **cheek by jowl** right next to that all time library bestseller, *The Matrices of Library Networks*. Talk about being condemned to oblivion. **NOW**, I could say a lot of nasty things about catalogers. I could say that catalogers constantly complain about being squeezed in our age of advancing technology and I could say the catalogers constantly grouse about original cataloging being a lost art. But I'm not going to do that. I'm not going to embarrass you catalogers by exposing your hypocrisy or your blind conformity to rules or your total lack of originality or your complete inability to do something not called for in AACR2. I'm not going to do that   ★★★page 5★★★

because quite frankly I don't want to offend you.   **ACTUALLY** I need to court your good graces. The truth is, I need your help. I need you to be my co-conspirator in this little enterprise. In short, I need you to somehow, someway, keep yourself from stamping, pocketing, jacketing, and cataloging this book. I know this is hard, very hard, for you to do, sort of like me turning down a carton of Ben and Jerry's Heath Bar Crunch ice cream, but I have some helpful news for you, news that is so new that it hasn't appeared in *Library Journal, American Libraries,* or even *Cataloging and Classification Quarterly.*   **VERY** recently, the Original Cataloging Task Force of CACTUS (the Committee on Alternative Cataloging Techniques in the United States) — recommended that catalogers seek new and innovative ways to process books so as to insure their fullest and most appropriate use. On page 37 of a December 1993 CACTUS report entitled, "Non-traditional Modes of Cataloging and Classifying the Traditional Monograph"

Tell me, are you a monograph, a serial, or a festschrift?

you will find a specific reference to my *Unintellectual Freedoms* preface. Here is what the CACTUS report said: "In our view, the request of an author to treat a book in an unorthodox manner should at least be considered. If, for instance, the author feels that the placement of his or her book will be more appropriate in a non-collection area (such as ★★★page 6★★★   the request of Will Manley to have his book,

Unintellectual Freedoms, placed in the staff lounge) the cataloger should give due consideration to such a possibility. Sometimes a book's exposure is actually enhanced by *not* relegating it to a place on the normal classification continuum. Each authorial request, therefore, should be evaluated on its own merits, and catalogers should be encouraged to exercise their creativity in making such an evaluation."   **SO**, catalogers, there you have it. Your own blasted committee has said it's okay to break a few rules once in awhile as long as it doesn't become a habit that will lead to bibliographical anarchy. And in that spirit I will now once again beg that you put this book unpocketed, unstamped, unjacketed, and uncataloged on top of the microwave oven in the staff lounge. Here are my reasons for this "unorthodox" but not "inappropriate" treatment: 1. If you catalog this book it will undoubtedly end up sitting unread next to *The Matrices of Library Networks Part II.*   2. There's no reason to make your shelves any more crowded than they already are.   3. You should be spending your time cataloging books that are in demand by patrons.   4. This book will make better lunchtime reading than old copies of *Cataloging and Classification Quarterly* for the non-catalogers on staff.   5. This book will give staff members who don't like to talk a good reason to keep quiet during lunchtime. 6. This book makes a good cooling pad for lunches that have been over-microwaved.   7. Insults and jokes about catalogers have been kept to a minimum in this book.   8. The Library of Congress never gives decent subject headings to my books anyway.   9. Librarians who don't like me can easily convert this book into a staff room dart board, thereby giving your employee a quality leisure time opportunity to get rid of job stress.   10. My mother won't be putting in any reserves for this book, because this time I sent her a personal copy (at a 20% discount).   11. By not entering the book into your data base you won't have to inter-library loan it.   12. You'll never have to worry about the book being overdue.   13. You won't have to worry about this book creating an embarrassing public censorship controversy for your library. 14. Your library board will be impressed that your staff spends its break time reading professional literature.   15. You won't have to do a retrospective conversion on this book when you get a new computer system.   16. You won't have to worry about having some idiotic patron waving this book in your director's face and saying, "Why did you waste taxpayer's money on this piece of garbage?"   17. If you're a cataloger in my library and you catalog this book you'd better get out the old résumé and dust it off because you'll be looking for a new job. 18. It's about time you did something to justify the title "original cataloger."   **OKAY**, okay, I know that you're still not convinced, and hey, that's what I really like about you catalogers. You're not easily conned. You are the backbone of integrity in the   ★★★page 7★★★

library profession. What you lack in humanity, you make up for in honesty. It's a trade off.   SO I've decided to offer you a deal, no not a deal exactly, more like a compromise. Yeah, that's the ticket. Here it is: You take this book and put it on the microwave oven in the staff room and leave it there for 18 months and I won't mind a bit if at the end of that 18 months you decide to catalog it, stamp it, jacket it, and pocket it. That way I will be happy and you will be happy, and neither of us will have to worry about the specter of bibliographic anarchy engulfing the libraries of America. So, just to show my good faith in this little bargain I will now provide you with cataloging in publication data (which, remember, you should not use for 18 months): ***Uncensored Thoughts: Pot Shots from a Public Librarian***—which is copyright ©1994 by **Will Manley** and which is caused by MCFARLAND & COMPANY, INC., PUBLISHERS, Box 611, Jefferson, North Carolina, and London, to be manufactured in the United States of America, and for which not only are British Library Cataloguing-in-Publication data available, but the Library of Congress Cataloguing-in-Publication Data as well (they actually read "Manley, Will, 1949—   Uncensored thoughts : pot shots from a public librarian / by Will Manley ; illustrations by Richard Lee. p. cm. Includes index. ISBN 0-89950-992-4 [lib. bdg. : 50# alk. paper] ∞   1. Library science—United States—Humor. I. Title. Z665.2.U6M37 1994 020'.97302'02—dc20   94-20155 CIP").

Other Books by the Author

Most books I have give a list of the author's previous books. To be honest, this is done for advertising purposes. The hope is that if you like this book you will like the other ones that I have written. Obviously I am no different from any other writer. Of course I hope that you will buy my other books, but not to the point where you feel exploited. As a librarian I believe in the importance of reviews. I don't think you should spend taxpayer monies on a book without first checking out what the critics have had to say about it. Therefore in addition to a list of my books I am going to give you excerpts of reviews (both positive and negative) that were done on each book.   1. **Snowballs in the Bookdrop** (Shoestring Press, 1982): *Booklist* (August 1982, p. 1506) "There is humor in these pages; Manley comes across as a warm, compassionate person who obviously enjoys what he does."   *Wilson Library Bulletin* (October 1982, p. 168)"...in content and style Manley is not in the same class as Edmund Lester Pearson, Sam Walter Foss, and some other librarians who wrote regular newspaper columns..."   2. **Unintellectual Freedoms: Opinions of a Public Librarian** (McFarland, 1991): *Library Journal* (March 1, 1991, p. 122) "Provocative and amusing, this is also the eloquent testimony of a writer passionate about his profession." *Australian Library*

Review (9:2 [1992]: Supplement, p. 42) "The book resembles a bad Woody Allen movie—therapeutic for the main actor and director, but tedious for the audience. It is repetitive, prejudiced, arrogant, exhibitionist, and hypocritical. Manley professes to be anti-intellectual but is oddly pedagogical, to be funny, but at the expense of women, children, yuppies, and employees of public libraries. His style is verbose and declamatory. The design and layout of the book—presumably meant to lighten its message—are a mess. It is a book trying not to be a book." 3. **Unprofessional Behavior: Confessions of a Public Librarian** (McFarland, 1992): *Canadian Library Journal* (August 1992, p. 317) "*Unprofessional Behavior* is the most irreverent book on library science this reviewer has ever read and is, therefore, a delight. Not only does Manley set out to break all the rules of library practice and decorum, but he also sets out to rend them and stomp on the pieces with hob-nail boots. I speak metaphorically, of course, having no personal knowledge of his footwear proclivities." *Australian Library Review* (9:4, 1992, p. 328) "It is practically impossible to review this book in a serious manner.... It's a great gallop through iconoclastic anecdotes if you enjoy rollicking, slapstick, verbose, all–American humour. It's deathly dull if you don't.... It invites ridicule, just as it ridicules.... The tall stories of library life, mixed indiscriminately with private peccadilloes, are narrated by a manic public library manager. The incidents are about as funny as a dinner-party clown who regales guests with drunken reminiscences of a never-ended, sour, egocentric adolescence." 4. **Unsolicited Advice: Observations of a Public Librarian** (McFarland, 1992): *Library Journal* (February 15, 1993, p. 204) "What he presents in this very large work is good stuff ... when it comes to library humor and helping this God-awful profession smile at itself, he has probably done as well as anyone." *Library Review* (42:4, pp. 58–9) "Will Manley is not Stephen Leacock or even James Thurber." 5. **For Library Directors Only/For Library Trustees Only** McFarland, 1993 (Bound together upside down and backwards). *Technicalities* (July 1993, pp. 13–14) "Buy this book with the money that you saved by canceling *Wilson Library Bulletin*." *Technicalities* (July 1993, pp. 13–14) "If you are a cataloger here's a chance for revenge for Manley's stale and offensive cataloger jokes—request this on ILL." 6. **The Manley Art of Librarianship** (McFarland, 1993): *College and Research Libraries News* (October 1993, p. 529) "A potent antidote to biblioangst, or the uncertainty felt at least once in a librarian's lifetime that lobster fisherman or shepherdess might have been a more appropriate career choice." *Library Association Record* (December 1993, p. 698) "The enforced humour becomes tedious. This is a nicely produced book in the American manner. Humour in print, however, does not always cross oceans." **YOU'VE** probably noticed that there's a "love 'em or hate 'em" aspect to the reviews of my books. The critics have a hard time treading a middle road with me. I can understand and sympathize with the plight of the reviewer. **Book** reviewing is a terribly difficult, often stressful task. I speak from the experience of having reviewed books about thirteen years ago for *School Library Journal.* Here are the hazards: 1. Other than indicating your preference for broad subject areas, you really have no control over the books that your journal sends you to review. 2. If you've got any sense of ethics at all, you really have to read the entire book before you review it. This can be excruciatingly painful if the book is long, verbose, and awful or even if the book is short, terse, and awful.   3. If the book is awful, unless you are a person who enjoys inflicting pain, it is fairly difficult to say that the book is awful because you know that the person who wrote the book devoted a good part of his or her life to writing the book and do you really want to be the one to tell an author publicly that he or she just wasted a good part of life, time that could have been better spent playing tennis or learning the two-step.   **THAT'S** why I admire a book reviewer like Graeme Johanson. Graeme cuts through this little ethical conundrum like a person chopping through an outback thicket with a Crocodile Dundee knife. Graeme, of course, is the person who reviewed *Unintellectual Freedoms* and *Unprofessional Behavior* for the *Australian Library Review.* It is interesting, though, to consider the observation of the British publication, the *Library Association Record,* that "humour in print does not always cross oceans." There must be something to this because in general my American and Canadian reviewers have been quite kind, while my Australian and British critics have been quite negative. I wish, therefore, that my publisher would stop sending review copies overseas.

Dedication

The truth is that book dedications can get a bit sticky. I don't know where the practice of dedicating a book got started but it's something that is sort of expected. If you don't dedicate your book, people think you're anti-social or that you don't have any friends or, worse yet, that you don't love your wife, parents or children. And if you do dedicate your book to someone, you end up making one person in your life happy and all the others unhappy. **Actually** over the years I've compiled some rules of thumb regarding book dedications: 1. Don't dedicate your book to dead people because they're not around to appreciate it and because **dead people don't buy books.**   2. When feasible try to dedicate your book to someone rich. This will result in better book sales.   3. Don't dedicate your book to people who are hated by the general public. Hitler, Nixon, and Saddam come to mind. People will think you're a misanthrope if you name these people, even if it's only for a joke.   4. Don't dedicate your book ★★★page 10★★★   to someone your spouse doesn't like. This will get you into trouble. For instance, I thought it would be nice to dedicate one of my books to an old friend named Gunner who also happens to be someone whom my wife thinks is a bad influence on me. She therefore went into a tizzy fit when she saw Gunner's name on the dedication page of the galley proofs. Needless to say, Gunner never made it to the final dedication page. Guess who did? That's right—my wife.   5. Don't dedicate your book to a secret lover. What would someone named Hillary say if someone named Bill dedicated a book to someone named Gennifer?   6. Don't dedicate a book to your pet boa constrictor with the words "to my best friend and lover." Some things are best left private.   7. Always dedicate a book to your parents before they die to ensure your rightful place in the will.   8. Don't dedicate your book to anyone in the Mafia. Rival families might come after you.   9. Don't dedicate your book to peace and harmony. They're nice concepts but they don't pay the rent and they make you sound very pretentious.   **HAVING** said all this, it suddenly occurs to me that there is another way around this dedication business. Where does it say that a book has to be dedicated to just one person? I mean think about it—if you really want to boost book sales why not dedicate it to a whole bunch of rich people? Yeah, that's the ticket.   **THIS** book is, therefore, officially dedicated to the following ten people who according to *Forbes Magazine* are the ten richest people in the United States: 1. Bill Gates—co-founder of Microsoft—net worth: $6.3 billion.   2. John Werner Kluge—founder of Metromedia—net worth: $5.5 billion.   3. The Waltons—not John Boy, stupid, Sam's widow and 4 children—net worth: $25.3 billion (shared).   4. Warren Edward Buffet—stock market genius—net worth: $4.4 billion.   5. Sam and Don Newhouse—publishing and teevee magnates—net worth: $7.7 billion (shared).   6. Sumner Murray Redstone—movie theater innovator—net worth: $3.25 billion.   7. Ronald Owen Perelman—leveraged buy-out king—net worth: $2.9 billion.   8. Ted Arison—Carnival Cruise Lines dude—net worth: $2.85 billion.   9. Paul Gardner Allen—co-founder of Microsoft—net worth: $2.8 billion.   10. Rupert Murdoch—Owns Fox Broadcasting—net worth: $2.6 billion.   **WITH** a dedication list like that how many sales do you think I can generate? Added up, the people I have dedicated this book to have a total net worth of $63.6 billion. But that's not all. There's someone else I would like to add to the list: 11. Stephen Manley—Baseball card collector—net worth: $1.2 thousand.   **OH,** one other thing, before we move on it occurs to me that there is still one more person that needs to be listed: 12. Graeme Johanson—Book Reviewer—net worth: beats me.   **GRAEME,** if this is what I have to do to get a good review out of you, I'm perfectly willing to do it. Now the ball's in your court, Graeme. I'm waiting. It's pay-back time, buddy. Either that or deal with my attorney, who happens to be a guy named Moe from New Jersey.

Acknowledgments

If dedications are hard, acknowledgments are even harder, but really every self-respecting author needs to acknowledge all those people who made the book possible. This is difficult because you're ghastly afraid of leaving someone out. There is, therefore, the greatest temptation to thank everyone in the world for their help, but this sounds a tad insincere. For credibility you really need to create a definitive list. **THE** first and only name on my acknowledgment list is—you guessed it—Graeme Johanson. This book would not have been possible without Graeme because truthfully the only thing that motivates me to write books is the challenge of trying to get a good review out of him/her. So Graeme, think about it. This gives you all the more incentive you need to give me a decent review. If you hate my books as much as you say, I promise I'll stop writing them if you can just be charitable to me this one time.

Table of Contents

THIS book contains the following: Preface *(page 12)*, New Jersey's Garbage *(page 13)*, Fish Story *(page 15)*, A Real Riot *(page 18)*, Trust Me *(page 21)*, From the Sublime to the Ridiculous to the Absurd—A Tour Guide to Southern California *(page 24)*, Pasadena Do-Gooders Do Bad *(page 32)*, Arizona Do-Gooder Does Bad *(page 36)*, Flying by the Seat of Your Pants *(page 36)*, How About Some Real World Research? *(page 42)*, Ahead of My Time *(page 48)*, Five Days in June *(page 52)*, Safe Sex the L.J. Way *(page 61)*, Mom, Mozelle, and Me *(page 65)*, Mr. Suspenders *(page 67)*, The Most Controversial Book in Library History *(page 71)*, Librarians and Food *(page 74)*, Art *(page 77)*, Shit Happens *(page 91)*, Of John Bobbitt's Penis and the New Information Age *(page 94)*, The Theory and Practice of Managing People *(page 96)*, Stopping World Hunger *(page 103)*, See, I Told You So *(page 110)*, Garbage In, Garbage Out *(page 114)*, Me and My Bookdrop *(page 116)*, Bibliotherapy *(page 121)*, The Death of the Book—A Case Study *(page 129)*, A.L.A. Not Allah *(page 133)*, Soft Pretzels with Mustard *(page 136)*, History *(page 147)*, Mr. Big *(page 151)*, P.C. and I.F. *(page 157)*, Bedtime Fables *(page 163)*, and the Index *(page 170)*.

Preface

DID I say preface? Yes, it's time for a preface. I for one have always loved a preface and have always been a bit skeptical of an author that eschews this literary nicety. The preface has an important purpose. It allows the author the opportunity to explain him or herself. This is an opportunity that should by all means be taken because every book should have a definite purpose: to make you laugh, to make you cry, to inform you, to educate you, to

★★★page 12★★★   make you a better person, to inspire you, or even to annoy you. This book's purpose is much more modest than all that. It is intended to give your mind something to munch on at break time. That's why the book is designed like a bag of trail mix. You open it up and just start snacking.   **IF** there's a theme running through the book (and there's not), it has something to do with me taking a pot shot or two at some of the things in the library profession that need a little zinging. Of course the risk that you run in engaging in the art of the pot shot is that when you miss the mark, more often than not your shot ricochets around the room and ends up hitting you right between the eyes. As a consequence I take my own fair share of self-inflicted hits.   **IN** attempting to understand the art of the pot shot it is important to appreciate how it differs from the cheap shot. A lot of people tend to get the two terms confused. A cheap shot is deceitful and destructive while a pot shot is up front and honest. A cheap shot is throwing a firecracker at someone's back; a pot shot is **lobbing a rotten tomato** at his face. The purpose of the cheap shot is to insult and injure, but the intent of the pot shot is to startle and sting.   **THE** cheap shot is destructive criticism, and the pot shot is constructive. The cheap shot is easy to deliver because there's no artistry to it. It's calling Robert Jones a jerk. A pot shot requires more skill. It's calling Robert Jones a jerk for **not taking a bath** for two weeks. I wrote this book with the staff lounge in mind because, let's face it, when librarians need to let off a little steam during the day, the staff room is the appropriate place to do it. You can't take pot shots at your boss and your patrons in a public area. That's the value of the staff lounge. It's a place where you can engage in pot shottery with impunity.

New Jersey's Garbage

"**SO,**" I said to the reference librarian who was there at the Newark Airport to pick me up and take me to the New Jersey Library Association Conference at the Meadowlands, "what are the big issues facing New Jersey librarians these days?" I was scheduled to be the keynote speaker at the opening session of the conference and was desperate for something relevant to talk about. "**GARBAGE,**" was his grimmaced reply.   "**GARBAGE?**" I responded quizzically.   "**YEAH,** garbage, it's a real problem for libraries."   "**I** don't get it."   "**NEW** Jersey," he explained, "has run out of places to dump its garbage, and so our cities and towns have to transport it to other places for disposal."   "I still don't get it."   "**IT'S** a very expensive way to get rid of garbage."   "**WHY?** How far away are they taking it?"   "**MOSTLY** to Indiana, Tennessee, and Kentucky. Our garbage is a big growth industry for those states."   "**YOU** mean to tell me that New Jersey has to dump its garbage halfway across the country." "**THAT'S** exactly right, and you can imagine what that has done to municipal budgets." "**IMAGINE** what it would be   ★★★page 13★★★

like," I marveled, "to be a New Jersey garbageman. You leave the house in the morning and say to your wife, 'Hey, honey, I'll be home in twenty-seven hours. We're making the Kentucky run today!'" **IMAGINE** what it's like for public librarians. **The temptation is great** for city and town councils to pay for the increased costs out of library funding."
"**BUT,** on the other hand," I said, "think of what it feels like to live in Indiana, Kentucky, or Tennessee. What does it do for your ego and sense of environmental safety to be the dumping grounds of New Jersey's garbage. No offense, but really what state could have worse garbage than New Jersey with all of its many heavy industries and oil refineries."
"**YES,** but do you know what it costs to export 8.5 million tons of garbage a month?" **"PROBABLY** millions of dollars." **"EXACTLY,** and that money has got to come from somewhere. Libraries are really being threatened by this garbage crisis." **PICKING** up on this point, I oriented my keynote address around the theme that we librarians need to start portraying our services as essential components of the country's educational and informational infrastructure rather than as nice, but non-essential quality of life enhancers. Although the phrase, "Putting books on New Jersey library shelves is more important than putting garbage into midwestern landfills," drew plenty of applause, I think everyone in the audience knew that my point was more rhetorical than realistic. **THE** fact of the matter is that in the pecking order of local governmental services, libraries are far below streets, sewers, sanitation, schools, and public safety and probably just a bit above parks, recreation, museums, and public art. No matter how much we squawk about being undervalued and misunderstood, the reality remains that libraries are not absolutely essential for sustaining community life. If, however, libraries are not necessary for sustaining life, we should not be hesitant to proclaim that they are absolutely necessary for making life worth living. It's a point that many of the New Jersey librarians sadly related to me after my speech that their local politicians "just don't get." **"YOU** wouldn't believe," said one public library director, "how much pressure my city manager is putting on me to put the library on a self-sustaining basis. He thinks all we need to do is charge people ten dollars for a library card and we will be rolling in money. Then he gets his calculator out and says twenty dollars would even be better!" **"THAT'S** nothing," said another administrator, "our city council had the gall to suggest that we needed to start holding weekly bake sales." **"OUR** mayor," said a third director, "thinks that we should investigate privatizing library services by contracting out to Waldenbooks or B. Dalton." **"I'VE** got you all beat," responded a fourth librarian. "Our County Board of Commissioners wants me to investigate the cost savings that would accrue from firing half the staff and replacing them with volunteers." **IT** doesn't matter what ★★★page 14★★★ term our politicians throw around—"cost recovery,"

"user fees," "revenue enhancements," "creative financing," "cost offsets," "downsizing," "rightsizing," or "privatizing"—the New Jersey garbage crisis had brought into focus what will probably develop all across the nation as *the* public library issue of the '90s: How will public libraries be funded? Will we continue to enjoy a bedrock of general tax support that will ensure free and open access to all or will we become institutions that cater to the privileged few who can afford the fees?   **IT'S** an issue that every library director and every library board need to reflect upon before they decide to implement, however modestly, fees on on-line searching, photocopying, program attendance, reserves and holds, and bestseller book rentals. Today's trickle can rage into tomorrow's deluge.

The Mayor says that if you shot a cannon through the library you wouldn't hurt anybody. I want to prove him wrong.

Fish Story

WHAT I hate most about being a librarian is settling into your seat on an airplane, getting all your carry-ons stowed in the overhead bins, buckling your seat belt, bringing your seat to its upright position, taking a deep breath in anticipation   ★★★page 15★★★

of take-off and having the well-dressed man sitting next to you tap you on the shoulder and say, "So, what do you do?" **YOU** say, "I'm a librarian." **HE** looks at you quizzically as though something is not quite right. He's probably surprised that librarians actually get out once in a while and on airplanes to boot. Finally he responds, "Well, that must be steady work." **"YES,** very steady," you say politely. **"AND,"** he adds, "you must get a chance to read plenty of books." **"YES,"** you agree, "last year I read over nine hundred books. My taxpayers really got their money's worth out of me." **"IT** must be nice quiet work," he responds ignoring the sarcasm of your last answer, "with little or no job stress." **AT** that last remark you cringe, grab the flight magazine in front of you, and pretend to start reading the article entitled "Fifteen **Fun Things to Do in Akron.**" He looks at you, smiles, and concludes with quiet amusement that yes, librarians are addicted. They will read anything, even airline periodicals. I love everything about being a librarian except for the idiotic notion that a good portion of our population seems to have that we librarians lead quiet, stress-free lives. If there is a librarian around who wakes up in the morning and says, "My life is too boring because I don't have enough tension in my daily routine and what I really need is a good crisis to get the blood running," I would be very shocked. **THE** reality is that librarianship is **a helter-skelter proposition**. We are expected to serve all of humanity—the rich and poor, the well educated and illiterate, and the young and old; we are charged with the responsibility of organizing and keeping track of the bibliographic details of all the world's publications; and we are expected to do all of this with skeletal staffing, marginal budgets, and substandard wages. Is a little bit of respect and understanding from the outside world too much to ask? **APPARENTLY** so. More and more, instead of garnering some gratitude and appreciation from those we serve, we are the recipients of our patrons' frustration, anger, and irrationality. "Eat garbage with a smile" is how one of my colleagues defines his job as a reference librarian in an urban public library, and that's often the challenge that we are faced with—how to stay nice, polite, and even personable in the face of patron rudeness and stupidity. When someone calls up and asks for "the best English translation of Hamlet," "a tape recording of live dinosaur sounds," "**the phone number for 911**," "a videotape of Abraham Lincoln delivering the Gettysburg Address," or "the correct technique for saying hello to someone in sign language over the telephone," there's the greatest temptation to respond by saying, "Congratulations, that question qualifies you for the dumbest reference patron of the year." I've always thought that David Letterman would get a lot more laughs if he would substitute "Stupid Reference Questions" for "Stupid Pet Tricks." **BUT** ★★★page 16★★★ that's not the half of it. Not only do we have to suffer this stupdity with good humor but we also have to cheerfully tolerate the insults that follow when we can't produce a tape recording of the original Gettysburg Address. "What kind of a library is this? You have a video of Bill Clinton but not of Abraham Lincoln." It's hard, almost impossible to stay calm when you're being **insulted by an absolute moron**. Sometimes these pea-brains even threaten to call the mayor or the city council to complain about your incompetence and you hope, you desperately hope, that they will.   **BUT** it's not always at the reference desk where this stupidity manifests itself. Boorish patrons often manage to find other library venues to vent their idiocy and insensitivity. The absolute living end for me came as a result of a special fishing program that the children's department put on as a part of their summer reading project. **BY** all accounts, the program was a big success. The staff had contracted with a local fishing expert to do two one-hour programs on the rudiments of using a rod, reel, and net at a local urban fishing lake. Attendance was heavy and a number of the participants even managed to catch a few fish.   **BUT** then I got a phone call from a Mr. E.J. Wennington. The name E.J. Wennington sent shivers up my spine. He was generally considered to be the community's most powerful and influential citizen. He was owner and president of the town's largest bank, and was said to have had the entire town council in his back pocket. He was a man who was used to pushing people around and getting what he wanted. So far I had escaped his bullying. The public library was fortunately not something he had much interest in. What, I wondered, was pulling his chain today.   **"ARE** you the library director, Mr. Manley?" he asked impatiently.   **"YES."   "WELL**, sir, then you have two very unhappy little boys on your conscience."   **"WHAT** exactly is the problem, Mr. Wennington?" I asked with genuine concern.   **"MY** two grandsons, Billy and Dick, didn't catch any fish at your Glen Lake fishing program."   **"THAT'S** a shame," I said with as much sympathy as I could muster.   **"YES**, a shame for you. Do you know who I am?"   **"YES**, Mr. Wennington, you're the owner and president of the First Bank and Trust located at the corner of Main and Oak."   **"DO** you know how heartbroken my grandsons are about not catching any fish?"   **"YES**, sir, I'm sure they're very disappointed, but I'm not sure what this has to do with me or the library. By all accounts our fishing program was very popular with those who attended. While some of the participants were lucky enough to catch fish, there were others who naturally came up empty. That's the way it is with fishing, a good lesson in itself."   **"IT'S** not right, Mr. Manley, to put on a program where some children catch fish and others don't. All should catch fish or none should."   **"WHAT** can I say?"   **"WELL**, Mr. Manley, you haven't heard the end of this. You don't put on a fishing program in which E.J. Wennington's grandsons do not catch fish!" With that pronouncement Wennington hung up. **I** wasn't sure if it would be five minutes or ten before Michael Redken called me. Redken was town manager. He was an okay guy most of the time, but when someone was pulling the town's political levers Redken could get—how do I put this diplomatically—somewhat unreasonable. I had underestimated. The phone rang in only three minutes. This apparently was being treated at town hall as a major crisis.   **"WILL,** we've got a problem," Redken said in the same tone of voice you might use to issue a tornado warning.   **"I** know, I know. Old Man Wennington's upset because Billy and Dickie didn't catch any fish, right?"   **"RIGHT.** How could you let something like that happen? Don't you have any political sensitivity at all?"   **"MICHAEL,** for God's sake, save your lecture for the fish. They're the ones who need a lesson in political correctness, not me."   **"WILL,** the mayor is pretty upset. He wants that fishing instructor to take those kids out separately and help them catch some fish."   **"YOU'RE** kidding?"   **"NO,** I'm serious."   **"OKAY,** okay. I'll make it happen, but this is the living end. I've seen everything now."   **"NO** you haven't," said Redken, "You haven't seen everything until you've seen the Parks and Recreation Department giving special swimming lessons to Wennington's dog!"

A Real Riot

IT'S almost a cliché that success at one rung of life's ladder does not necessarily guarantee success at the next rung. It does not automatically follow, for example, that a great violinist will become a great conductor any more than it follows that a great home run hitter will develop into a great manager. In fact the skill that it takes to be a great hitter—the singular and solitary ability to hit a hard, round ball traveling at your head at the speed of 90 miles an hour with a hard, round bat—has nothing to do with the qualities required to be a great manager—leadership, communication, and strategic thinking. **THE** same thing, of course, holds true for librarianship. Many of our finest catalogers, bibliographers, computer analysts, and youth specialists end up making the most horrible supervisors and administrators imaginable. It's almost tragic to watch someone who was absolutely superlative in providing frontline services to the public flounder and fail in the much different role of supervisor. You don't know whether to feel sorrier for the supervisor or those being supervised.   **"I** never knew how difficult it was to organize, motivate, evaluate, train, and direct a staff of highly diverse personalities," is the way Alfred put it to me several months after I had promoted him to head of the reference department. Alf, as everyone called him, was by anyone's measure the finest reference librarian in our library. He was the person that everyone turned to for help on difficult questions. **WHAT**

made Alf special was his range. He was as comfortable with the Congressional Record as he was with the periodic chart of elements. It didn't matter what subject area was involved, Alf always knew where to look for the answer. In addition to being knowledgeable, he was also tireless and determined. The five most hated words in Alf's vocabulary were "I can't find the answer."   **ALF** typically kept working on a reference challenge long after most **mere mortals** would have called the patron with sincerest regrets. Some people on staff felt that this doggedness was a bit neurotic. Was Alf an obsessive-compulsive in his inability to bring reference search to closure within a reasonable amount of time? No, I don't think that Alf was obsessive about reference work. I think his obsession had to do more with pleasing the patron.   **ALF** could not stand to disappoint people. He had an inordinate need to please, and I don't think this had anything to do with getting positive strokes in return. Alf simply could not bear telling people what they did not want to hear. So he worked until he found the

Hi, my name is Alf and I'll be your reference librarian tonight.

correct answer.   **PROBABLY** his most impressive reference search was a six hour marathon through business directories and data bases to find a company that fabricated H.O. scale models   ★★★page 19★★★

of the White House. Any normal person, of course, would have checked the Thomas Register and then called it quits, but not Alf. He tried phone books, classified ads in model railroading magazines, and even searched the yellow pages of the D.C. telephone directory. Finally either by luck or sheer thoroughness he came across the name of a small California company that made scale models of famous public buildings for the movie industry. A quick phone call verified that they had the White House model in their inventory. "It felt so good to not have to disappoint that little boy who needed the model," is what Alf said in recapping his finest hour as a reference librarian. **IT** was that sense of dedication that convinced me that Alf would succeed at whatever challenge he was faced with in a public library. That's why I promoted him to reference supervisor. What a role model he would make for his employees. His example of hard work in service of the patrons would serve him well with his staff. Respect flows from performance, right? **WRONG.** As a supervisor Alf was a disaster. No one who worked for him respected him. Everyone liked him. It wasn't a situation where Alf turned into a monster as soon as he was promoted. He never put on airs or suddenly started acting like a control freak. It was just the opposite. **ALF** stayed his simple, humble, hard working self. The problem was he was too humble. He simply could not assert any authority when the situation demanded it. Basically Alf was too nice a guy. He couldn't bear to make unpopular decisions, enforce rules, or offer constructive criticism. Alf wanted to be liked by everyone, and as a result he was respected by no one. The word quickly spread on the library grapevine that Alf could "be **rolled like a jelly doughnut.**" **IN** fact, Alf couldn't make the simplest decisions regarding staff scheduling. It's axiomatic that no employee, even the most dedicated librarian, ever wants to work nights or weekends. So how did Alf solve this problem in his own hassle-free, wimpy way? Yes, you guessed it. He ended up working every night and weekend himself. **"IT'S** not so bad," he told me. "It's better than having everybody mad at me, and I guess it's only fair that I should work extra hours." **"WHY** do you say that, Alf?" **"AS** a supervisor I'm being paid more," answered Alf, "so I should work harder." **"ALF,"** I responded, "you're being paid more to make decisions and direct your staff. It's pretty obvious that they're directing you. You need to get down there and get control of your people." **"HOW** do I do that?" **"I'D** start by reading them **the riot act**, Alf." **"THE riot act?** Are you serious about that?" **"YES,** Alf, I'm serious. I want you to go down there and read your librarians **the riot act** at your next staff meeting." **"WHY the riot act?" "BECAUSE** that will show them that you're no creampuff." **"YOU** really think that will do the trick?" **"YES,** Alf, ★★★page 20★★★   I really do. You need to show them that you're in charge. "**OKAY,** then that's what I'll do." A couple of days later I saw Alf in the library parking lot. He called me over and said, "Mr. Manley, that riot act that you told me to read to my staff, is it a municipal ordinance, a state statute, or a federal statute?" "**ALF,** what in heaven's name are you talking about?" "**REMEMBER** when I came up to your office last Wednesday and talked to you about the problems I was having with my staff." "**YES.**" "**WELL,** you told me to read the riot act to them. The problem is I can't find it anywhere in our law collection. I've scheduled some time to go over to the county law library tomorrow, but it would really help if you could tell me if it's a local, state, or federal regulation." "**ALF?**" "**YES,** Mr. Manley?" "**YOU'RE** hopeless."

Trust Me

TODAY in the 1990s when high schools resemble armed camps and car theft prevention devices constitute a major growth industry, the concept of the free and open public library seems startlingly naïve. Reckless might even be a better way to put it. What responsible person in this day and age, after all, would spend millions of dollars of taxpayers' money on books, tapes, magazines, and computer software, arrange them invitingly on open shelves, and invite the great unwashed public in to check them out and take them home? **WHEN** librarians get depressed about the future of their profession they usually end up talking about the obsolescence of the book. What they should be discussing, however, is the obsolescence of truth, justice, honesty, honor, and the willingness of library patrons to bring books back on time. Of all the institutions that comprise our great American civilization, none is more founded on trust than the public library, and none is more threatened by the current wave of crime and disorder. I can remember twentysome years ago when I was a student in library school engaging in longwinded debates about whether or not libraries should charge fines. Fresh from an undergraduate education overladen with philosophy and theology courses, I always tried to frame these debates in terms of a basic view of humankind (in those days it was called "mankind"). In my mind the "we should charge fines as a deterrent against patron irresponsibility" people held a Hobbesian view of the world (**humans are brutes**) and the "fines are a non-productive manifestation of mistrust" people held a Rousseauian perspective (humans are basically good when they are treated with dignity and respect). I was a self-righteous follower of Rousseau and always tried to paint my Hobbesian opponents in the dimmest personal light. "Of course," I would say to them, "you can't see the inherent goodness in your fellow man because you yourself are a darkly pessimistic person who always looks for the bad in any given situation. I hope you end up in cataloging because

someone with your view of humanity shouldn't be working with the public." **THIS** kind of an insufferably self-righteous attitude of course did nothing to endear me to my fellow students. "You're hopelessly naïve, Will," one of them said to me. "You've never really been out in the real world of public librarianship. I've worked circulation for five years and I've seen things that would make your head spin." **"LIKE** what?" **"LIKE a Roman Catholic priest** razor blading the twenty page entry for "Monasticism" out of *The Catholic Encyclopedia*." **"I'LL** bet he was an imposter," I said stubbornly, "and even if he wasn't I'll bet he had some higher purpose for what he did. Remember what Jesus said, 'if someone steals your cloak, give him your coat also'." **THE** only antidote to such an insufferable case of smugness, of course, was, as my fellow student had suggested, prolonged exposure to the real world, and oddly enough, my comeuppance came not in some gritty urban jungle but rather in a picturesque Carnegie Library located on the tree lined main street of a pleasantly sleepy midwestern town. It was the kind of community where locking your car, your house, or your office was considered aberrant behavior. In fact, it was exactly the kind of place that I thought Rousseau had in mind when he wrote about the perfectability of man. **ONE** evening ten minutes before closing time while I was working the reference desk a nicely dressed and very personable traveling salesman (**industrial bathroom fixtures**) from Chicago came into the library and asked me if he could borrow our regional business directory, which was a specialized and highly expensive ($120) locally produced reference book. It was also one of the most intensively used business tools in our reference collection. "Trust me," he said with great sincerity. "I promise to return the book first thing in the morning." **AT** first I hesitated to approve his request because he was from out of town, but when he gave me his name and the name of the motel where he was staying I felt better about his reliability and decided to give him the one night check-out. "Maybe, you'd feel better if I left my driver's license with you," he said. **"OH,** no," I replied embarrassed by the fact that I, a disciple of Rousseau, had created the impression that I had reservations about this polite and personable man. **"IT'S** no problem," he persisted, "maybe you'd feel more comfortable with one of my credit cards. Take your pick," he said reaching for his wallet. "I've got Visa, MasterCard, and American Express." **"OH,** no, no, no" I pleaded, "that's not necessary. I'm only too happy to accommodate you. We take pride in providing the best library services in the county. We are here to serve the patron." **"THANK** you very much," he said with a smile and was quickly out the door with the $120 book. **SEVERAL** minutes later while we were closing the library, I told my director,
★★★page 22★★★ Hilma, what I had done. "I suppose you had to

learn your lesson sometime," she said half annoyed and half amused. **"WHAT** do you mean?" I asked.   **"YOU'RE** too trusting," she said. **"ARE** you saying he's not going to bring the book back?"   **"THERE'S** not a snowball's chance."   **"I** disagree. This man was very respect-

Let me see that first one again.

able."   **"THEY'RE** the worst kind."   **"OKAY,** let's make a little wager. How about five dollars?"   **"NO,"** said Hilma, "let's do something a little more appropriate. If the book doesn't come back you have to stop fighting me about spending $50,000 for a Tattletape security system for the library."   **"AND** if the book does come in, you'll agree to spend the money on children's books?"   **"YOU'RE** on."   **HILMA** and I were, I suppose, the classical case of the wizened old war-weary veteran and the **wide-eyed know-it-all** young idealist. In retrospect, I realize now that her patience with me qualified her for sainthood. Although she was securely in charge of   ★★★**page 23**★★★

the library, she always kept an open mind about my sometimes rather cockeyed ideas. Our main bone of contention was the need for an electronic security system. Hilma, a native New Yorker, never really bought into the trustworthiness of our cozy little midwestern community. "Jack the Ripper," she was fond of saying, "came from a rural background." I, on the other hand, felt that spending money on security was tantamount to taking new books out of the hands of children.

THAT'S another area where Hilma and I never saw eye to eye. She hated kids and, while I didn't exactly love them, I saw them as the key to getting more political and financial support for the community. "If you support children's services," I used to say to Hilma, "you will end up getting adults interested in the library." She never bought my logic.

THE next morning, however, I was sure that Hilma would develop a new sense of respect for me and my ideas. "What are you waiting for?" she said to me as I stood by the front door waiting for my salesman to appear with the library's $120 book. **"I'M** waiting for the opportunity to prove you wrong. He'll be here any minute, I'm sure." **HILMA,** of course, was right—no salesman, no book. I called the motel and naturally there was no one registered there under that name. "You've been had," Hilma said nonchalantly at the end of the day. "We'll chalk the $120 up to training and continuing education. Meanwhile I want you to put out a request for proposals for an electronic security system." **THREE** months later just as a local contractor was putting the finishing touches on the installation of the system, a parcel from Chicago arrived. It was the book. No name, no message, just the book.

From the Sublime to the Ridiculous to the Absurd — A Tour Guide to Southern California

THE San Juan Capistrano Public Library is the only library I know of that is listed in the Mobil Travel Guide. Nestled unobtrusively between Interstate 5 and the Pacific Ocean, it is, however, a munchkin among giants when it comes to tourist attractions. With Los Angeles to its north and San Diego to its south, it's a place you're too harried to visit as you scurry quickly from Sea World to Disneyland with your restless kids in the back seat, unless, of course, you're on empty, which I was. **ACTUALLY** I planned it that way. If I had been honest and said, "We're stopping here briefly to visit a library," my wife and children would have mutinied. A long time ago they let me know that they had reached the zero tolerance level for my annoying habit of planning family vacations around library tours. **THE** trick I had learned was to make these stops seem purely accidental. So as I dutifully filled the tank of White Trash, my '82 predatory white Chevette with the paint peeling off, I casually mentioned that my traveler's bladder was, ah, acting up again and could everybody simply stretch their legs while I used the gas station facilities. It was one of those places where you have to ask a greasy-handed mechanic for a key that is invariably attached to a piece of wood so large that it would burn for two hours in your fireplace at home.   **WHEN** I returned two minutes later to announce to my impatient family that having unlocked the door to the bathroom I had found it impossible to proceed further what with the unspeakable condition of the floor area around the toilet, they, disgusted by what I might track into the car, readily agreed that I proceed to the local public library where presumably I might find more **appropriate bathroom accommodations.** That's how I weaseled my way into the San Juan Capistrano Public Library.   **IT** was well worth the effort because San Juan Capistrano is one of the few library buildings built in the last twenty years that actually has that uplifting bookish feeling that libraries used to have before librarians and architects jointly decided that the last thing a library should look like is a library. What do the purveyors of contemporary design excellence deem that a library should look like today? Take your pick: 1. The cockpit of the Starship Enterprise;   2. A Las Vegas casino;   3. The non-smoking section of a Kentucky Fried Chicken restaurant;   4. A fern bar;   5. A Toyota factory;   6. A semi-conductor plant;   7. An office building;   8. A shopping mall atrium;   9. A Blockbuster video store;   10. A minimum security prison.   **LIBRARY** architecture today, in a sense, no longer exists. Libraries derive their design coordinates from something else. The idea, I suppose, is that we should dare to be something fresh, new, and different. The irony is that in trying to create a new image for the library we're actually creating something quite old and tired—something that makes us feel like we've just been to the Sam Goody music store in the mall.   **SO** it's refreshing to find a library like the one in San Juan Capistrano that is quiet, dignified, classical, and daring in the sense that it wants to be more than a repository for CD-Roms and Harlequin romances. It's the kind of building where you want to read Stephen Hawking rather than Stephen King. And with its architectural references to ancient Greece and Egypt, it's a place that reminds you that there is more to Western civilization, thank God, than Oprah, Phil, Geraldo, and Donald Duck. **IT'S** also a place, dare I say it, where you are drawn to the sacred scriptures, and that's not just because it is across the street from the mission of swallow fame. With its vaulted ceilings, celestory windows, spires, towers, courtyards, and monkish reading cells, there is a temple-like feel to both the exterior and interior spaces of the library. This may be the building's biggest taboo—linking learning to religion. But, whether we like to admit it or not, there is a religiosity to our work. **We're monk-like,** aren't we, in the way that we stubbornly persist in our mission in the face of financial neglect and societal disrespect? **TODAY**, of course, the temptation is great to substitute our old-fashioned stubborn persistence with surrender. It's becoming increasingly fashionable to speak less of our educational mission and more of our informational and recreational functions, hence our architecture tends to careen between the look of a semi-conductor plant in St. Louis and the feel of a shopping mall videostore in Seattle. **THAT** is why San Juan Capistrano is important. Its architecture points to a more expansive purpose—reflection, education, enlightenment, even transcendence. Compared to it, the countless other public libraries in Southern California, those colorless cubes of plastic and steel that serve the area's blob-like sprawl of suburbs seem **depressingly plebeian**, which is unfortunately not a criticism because that's exactly the effect that the architects and librarians wanted to achieve—buildings that the common person is familiar and comfortable with—Kentucky Fried Library. Thank God, San Juan Capistrano dared to be different. **FORTY-FIVE** minutes later, White Trash stopped at a red light in front of a garish sign that proclaimed DISNEYLAND—THE HAPPIEST PLACE ON EARTH. It took me 43 years to finally get to Disneyland and as soon as I stepped into the Magic Kingdom I knew I was going to be desperately unhappy there. The place was filled with a lot of sweaty people grimly lugging around camcorders and pushing their way hither and thither to get just the right camera angle. I looked back longingly toward the parking lot and realized that I wouldn't see the inside of my car for at least twelve hours. My children had an ambitious agenda planned, and my job was to follow their instructions dutifully. Parenthood carries with it certain obligations, not the least of which is to feign happiness in unhappy circumstances. **THIS**, I heard one of the camcorder carriers say wearily, had already been officially declared as the fifth busiest day in the history of Disneyland. Even the human-sized puppet who cavorted around the grounds in the role of Scrooge McDuck seemed surprisingly lifeless and, should I say it, markedly unhappy, maybe even clinically depressed. Well, it was rather steamy and the duck outfit could only have been utterly unbearable. Mickey, Minnie, and Donald must have had a "hot, crowded day provision" in their contracts because they were nowhere to be seen, which must have added significantly to Scrooge's sense of despondency, but then again at least he was getting paid union scale which was more than I could say about myself. **OF** course, much of the unhappiness of those of us who paid large sums to get into this paradise of dreams stemmed from the uncomfortable frustration of standing in long lines all day. By the middle of the afternoon I felt as though I had been reduced to a small body part of a long, slow moving, slithering reptile whose natural habitat is fake

★★★page 26★★★

mountains, jungles, and seascapes. Actually the lines were a salvation in that they provided a welcome recovery period from the rides. **VERY** early on, my boys discovered that the best rides were those which came with the following warning: "Due to the nature of this attraction, expectant mothers should not ride." Although not pregnant, many of my internal organs, most notably my heart, my spleen, and my stomach did not respond well to being jerked around with such intensity, which was actually a blessing since the food at Disneyland is very stale, very bland, and very overpriced, although they do do some nice things with popcorn and lemonade.   **THE** other redeeming thing about the lines is that they were what you would call very multicultural. On this particular day, for instance, half of Asia, Africa, and Australia seemed to be in the park. This made for some interesting discussions and I quickly decided that the only thing worse than coming to Disneyland when it is crowded is to go there when it is empty. Not only would you have to submit to the torture of riding the Space Mountain roller coaster fifteen or sixteen times, but there wouldn't be anyone interesting to talk to.   **DURING** the two hour wait for the privilege of being soaked on something called Splash Mountain (where they strap you into a hollowed out log and send you hurtling down a fake waterfall) I met someone from Australia named Frank, a beer drinking rugby enthusiast—my kind of guy. As well as Frank and I hit it off, however, our conversation hit a downside when I mentioned to him that if Australia produced nothing but toaster biscuits it would still be tops in my book. Frank looked at me with bafflement and asked, "What's a toaster biscuit?"   **"WHAT'S** a toaster biscuit?" I replied in shock. "Don't pull my leg, Frank. You Aussies invented the toaster biscuit."   **"I'VE** never heard the term," bristled Frank frankly. **"WELL,** maybe you call them something else. Maybe the term 'toaster biscuit' is an Americanism."   **"WHAT** exactly is this biscuit?" asked Frank who now seemed more curious than puzzled. **"WELL,"** I said groping for words—food is never easy to describe, "it's like this—if a piece of Texas Toast could make love to an English Muffin, their child would be an Australian Toaster Biscuit, which is the way, I guess, I've always pictured Australia—a blend of Texas and England. Anyway, they make a great foundation for poached eggs. It's a new product from Orowheat and they come in plain, sourdough, and raisin."   **FRANK,** of course, had never heard or seen anything like what it was that I was describing, which simply crushed me because I always felt that by buying these toaster biscuits I was not only participating in the world economy but also enjoying an ethnic food, which was an important breakthrough for me because by definition I neither like nor trust ethnic foods, but with the toaster biscuits I could at least sound halfway sophisticated when all my   ★★★page 27★★★

pretentious little cataloger friends started talking about "this wonderful new Korean restaurant down the street" or "that exciting new Sonoran place across town."   **AND** really maybe that's why I ended up hating Disneyland. It was the place that took the word Australian out of my daily diet. But actually I think my dislike is even deeper than that. It has to do with what Disney has done to literature, to history, and to truth in the name of entertainment. I look at animated classics of Cinderella, Sleeping Beauty, Aladdin, the Little Mermaid, and it's not like I don't appreciate a splashy celebration of color, music, and art. Obviously they're brilliantly entertaining productions, but when the show is over this brilliance doesn't lead to anything but the movie theater gift shop to buy a Beauty and the Beast coffee mug.   **THAT'S** the key to understanding the dangers of Disney. The stories that they derail with animation were created not just to entertain but to educate and provoke young minds into thought, reflection, and yes, imagination. But Disney grabs the intellects and imaginations of young children and squeezes them dry.   **THEY** take a classic, ageless story like "Cinderella," kill it, dissect it, re-arrange the body parts, and then breathe new life into it. It's a process of reinvention called the Disney formula, and it's a very, very effective form of cultural imperialism. You cannot watch Cinderella and ever go back to the original sources (Grim, Perrault, etc.) without bringing to mind the Disney portrayals and interpretations, which is tragically sad when you realize that the Disney version simply doesn't deal with the revenge, retribution, and forgiveness issues of Grim and Perrault. By reducing a wonderful piece of children's literature into an hour and a half piece of entertainment, the Disney people are guilty not only of cultural brainwashing but also and more importantly of literary blasphemy.   **TO** understand this point, think for a moment what would happen if the Disney folks decided to animate the book of Genesis or even the crucifixion of Christ. The resulting movie production would become the new religious frame of reference for 200 million Americans, and clergymen everywhere would be screaming about the blasphemy of reducing God to a cartoon caricature, and I am completely convinced that this is the only reason why they don't do it.   **IF** you enjoyed the Disney/Robin Williams portrayal of Aladdin's genie, think about what these talented artists, directors, and producers could do with a Supreme Being that is not only polymorphous but also omniscient, omnipotent, omnipresent, culturally diverse, and bi-gendered. I read somewhere that Robin Williams did over a hundred different celebrity impersonations in his role as the genie. Think of what he could do in the role of God, as Big Guy/Big Gal. There would be **absolutely no limits.**   **ACTUALLY**, while the Disney version of God is probably a few years off. I really ★★★page 28★★★   wouldn't be a bit surprised if they didn't turn Jesus

Christ into an animatronic device. They've done it to everything else in this world. That's one of the first things that you notice about Disneyland—it's filled with mechanical things—pigs, elephants, pirates, tigers, Indians, pygmies, and birds. In fact when I saw a flock of real birds nibbling on some wayward pieces of pavement popcorn I had to look twice. How was this touch of authenticity allowed to intrude into our perfect world of make believe? Sure enough, within two minutes, one of those ubiquitous workers with the Disney uniform and the Disney smile (they do a wonderful job of turning their own staff into audio-animatronic machines too) not only swept up the popcorn but also shooed the birds away.   **BY** 11:30 at night (the park stays open until 1 AM in the summer) I expressed a fervent desire to sit down on a non-moving chair, and so my kids (in reward for the good behavior that I had shown all day) mercifully dragged me into something called the Disney Opera House to watch a machine built in the image and likeness of Abraham Lincoln give a speech about freedom, liberty, and independence. This machine is a computer programmed dummy that clears its throat, shifts its weight from foot to foot, and uses a diverse array of hand gestures that can best be described as herky jerky. It's actually quite a pathetic attempt to **duplicate a human being** and as I sat there and watched this grotesque spectacle I was able to bring to mind seven or eight human corpses that I had seen over the years that looked vibrant in comparison to this mechanical monstrosity.   **SINCE** the urge was great to laugh heartily and uncontrollably I turned my eyes away from Iron Abe and toward the other people in the room in an effort to maintain my composure, but to my horror I saw immediately that everybody else in that darkened theater was mesmerized by this thing. Okay, it was late, everyone was tired, their feet hurt, their heads ached but still that's no excuse to look gape-mouthed at a talking dummy.   **INSTANTLY**, I realized that they were all drugged. The Magic Kingdom had cast its spell upon them, and they were now no longer able to distinguish between fact and fantasy. All of those fake boats and trains and bears and spaceships and seaweed and glaciers and jungles and rivers and burning houses had worn them down. They were numb to reality. Their metaphysical bearings were off kilter. They were in Never-Never Land. Like the dummy on stage they themselves had become audioanimatronic.   **IT** made me feel like **the last sane man at Jonestown.** While, everyone else was obediently sipping cherry flavored cyanide, it was my job to get on the rooftop and sound a warning. Something in my emotional makeup snapped (I think it was when the dummy started talking about personal freedom) and I stood up and shouted: "WAKE UP YOU MORONS. THIS IS NOT ABRAHAM LINCOLN. THIS IS A TOY. DISNEY HAS REDUCED LINCOLN TO A TOY. THIS IS BLASPHEMY. THIS THING ON STAGE HAS NO SOUL.   ★★★page 29★★★

ABRAHAM LINCOLN WAS ALL SOUL. IF THIS THING IS LINCOLN THEN I'M JESUS CHRIST. IF YOU WANT TO GET TO KNOW LINCOLN GO TO YOUR PUBLIC LIBRARY AND CHECK OUT CARL SANDBURG'S BIOGRAPHY OF HIM. IT TAKES A GREAT POET, NOT A BUNCH OF MORONIC ENGINEERS, TO BRING A GREAT MAN LIKE LINCOLN TO LIFE." **AS** I sputtered on, a young woman approached me and tapped me on the shoulder. She had that smile, that audioanimatronic Disney smile, and in a very sweet voice advised me that there was a medical services facility just a block down on Main Street if I was feeling the effects of the day's warmth and excitement. Very quietly I sat down and thanked her for her kindness. **ONE** of my kids kicked me and whispered, "Get a hold on, Dad, you're lucky you didn't get kicked out." Getting kicked out, I thought to myself, what an interesting concept. What do you have to do to get **kicked out of Disneyland?** **TWO** days later I found out what it takes to get kicked out of a presidential library—specifically the one belonging to Ronald Reagan. The most interesting thing about the Ronald Reagan Presidential Library is getting there. Headquartered as we were at the San Clemente Econo Lodge we had to drive the entire length of metropolitan Los Angeles area to reach it. You take the Santa Ana Freeway north to where it intersects the Santa Monica Freeway. Then I strongly recommend that you get off at the Normandie Street exit and do some sightseeing in South Central L.A. It's really the best way to prepare yourself for the trip up Reagan's mountain. **NOT** only is this little side trip to the ground zero point of the Rodney King riots a much needed antidote to Disneyland's dummies but it is also a piece of urban geography that will always be inextricably linked to Simi Valley, the far northern suburban enclave where an all white jury found in favor of the four police thugs who seemed to mistake Rodney King's body for a Mexican piñata at a Christmas Eve fiesta. Simi Valley, appropriately enough, is also the location of the Ronald Reagan Presidential Library. **THE** difference between South Central and Simi Valley is the difference between black and white. While one is dirty, grimy, and burned out, the other is as fresh and clean as the bright beige stucco buildings that dot its streets and landscape. When you drive through South Central with your doors locked, your windows rolled up, and your teeth clinched you understand immediately why Simi exists. It is a mountain-protected enclave for scared white people who want to be located as far away from South Central as possible and still be within a reasonable commuting distance of Los Angeles, which is of course why it is a perfect location for the Reagan Library. **WHAT** happened in July of 1992 was basically a contemporary tale of two cities. The Simi Valley jury, by condoning the police brutality of a black motorist, was sending a definite message: We do not want black ★★★page 30★★★ people moving to Simi Valley. In response, the people of South Central sent back a message of their own: We're mad as Hell and we're not going to take it any longer.   **IT** is ironic that this rip in the social fabric of Southern California was in many respects caused by the divisive social policies of Ronald Reagan, a president whom the people of Simi Valley were only too happy to call their own. Undoubtedly, if the library had been built in South Central it would have been the first thing torched, but perched as it is, in the highlands surrounding Simi it looms as an impenetrable fortress safeguarding the artifacts that Reagan has chosen as being most representative of his life.   **WHILE** the building appears at first as a pleasant if unimaginative white stucco and red tile complex it is actually quite an unfriendly place. Granted the Rodney King riots were probably very threatening to the Reagans, but, really, did they have to hire so many armed guards to protect the place? Every time you turn around there's someone in a uniform with a gun telling you to keep your feet off the grass and your fingers off the exhibit cases.   **IT'S** a terribly unsettling experience for someone like me who had expected to find a quasi public library where you could browse at will. But it turns out that presidential libraries are not really libraries. They are museums. No, that's not correct either. They are monuments glorifying their subjects.   **ONE** of the few interesting things about the Reagan library is that you're never quite sure if it was built to honor Ronnie or Nancy, that's how prominent her presence seems to be. You get the feeling that Nancy had a lot to do with the design of the place. How else do you account for the fact that her red riding boots are on display? In what way do they qualify as historical artifacts and what exactly do they have to do with the Reagan presidency?   **THE** other interesting thing about this "library is that it sits atop the real library—the underground depository (closed to the public) that houses millions of documents from the Reagan administration. There is a symbolism over substance message here that seems quite fitting for our first Hollywood president. You breeze through the main floor exhibit rooms and photo galleries and you can only conclude that Reagan was the greatest president of all time. The great economic recovery, the Cold War victories over the Soviet Union, the restoration of American pride around the globe, and the great military build-up are all celebrated as precedent setting achievements. If anything bad happened during the Reagan presidency you find no hint of it here.   **BUT** as I breezed through the exhibits I couldn't repress the nagging thought that underground in the documents library a far different story was waiting to be told, a story that would be highlighted by the explosion of the federal debt, the proliferation of nuclear weapons, the collapse of the savings and loan industry, the decay of urban America, the decline of the middle class, the fall of American education, and the scandalization of

American foreign policy.   **THERE** is one artifact on that upper level that does manage, however, to rise above the level of the trivial. It's the four foot by ten foot section of the Berlin Wall that rises up awkwardly out of the back lawn of the library. This roughhewn, garishly spray-painted piece of concrete which has been jaggedly cut from its source is a much needed rock of reality in this presidential Disneyland. It was a welcome relief to Nancy's red riding boots, and I was immediately drawn to it because there is no other physical object that better represents the historical backdrop for the last fifty years of American life. It's the linking pin that bonds together World War II, the Cold War, the space race, the arms race, the Vietnam War, and the fall of Communism.   **YOU** look at the wall and you think instantly of what all of that means to you personally—nervously squatting in the school basement during an air raid drill at the time of the Cuban missile crisis, skittishly sweating out the draft in the late '60s, and bitterly watching a quarter of each paycheck going to the government to build bombs rather than to buy books for libraries.   **THE** wall is the perfect museum piece because of its indestructibility. Unlike most historical artifacts, it can be touched. In fact it begs to be touched. You can't look at the wall without wanting to touch it and make a physical connection with something that has been such a dominant force in your life. The wall is concrete. It is not a philosophical abstraction, a political ideology, or an economic theory. And most of all it is not a trinket, a replication, a model, or a toy. You simply have to grasp it in your hands.   **BUT** as soon as I did, one of Reagan's armed gestapos came running out of the back door of the library waving his arms wildly and screaming at me to get away from the wall.   **"WHY?"** I asked peevishly. "I can't hurt the wall."   **"NO,** but you're standing on the grass. Keep off the grass. Can't you read the signs? Keep off the grass. We're going to have to ask you to leave if you can't keep off the grass."   **IN** a way I'm sorry the guard didn't shoot me. The headlines would have been terrific: "Librarian Shot at Berlin Wall in Reagan Library."

Pasadena Do-Gooders Do Bad

I didn't know whether to laugh or cry or just get angry and start breaking some furniture. I decided to break some furniture. So I slammed my desk chair against a wall. Actually I'm glad I broke the chair. I always hated that chair. It squeaked. There's nothing worse than a chair that squeaks. You can't do anything in a chair that squeaks. You can't read or write or even listen to music. The squeak is too disconcerting. You can probably watch Beavis and Butthead from a squeaky chair, but I don't have cable.   **HOW** do you get rid of a squeak from a chair? You can try ★★★page 32★★★   to oil it, but usually all that happens is that you end up getting oil all over your clothes. You can try to ignore the squeak, but that makes you notice it even more. Finally, you can break the chair and get rid of the squeak that way. So I broke the chair. **FOR** that reason, I suppose I should thank the staff of the Pasadena Public Library. They're the ones who got me angry enough to break the chair. You may have noticed the article about the Pasadena Public Library in *American Libraries* magazine too. For me it was a landmark article because it's the first time that a piece of library literature got me mad enough to break a piece of furniture. Once a Rush Limbaugh newsletter incited me to break a footstool and another time a Pat Buchanan editorial motivated me to dent a coffee table, but nothing I had ever read in the somewhat oxymoronic field of library literature had ever made me want to so much as even chip an ashtray.   **THE** article in question was entitled "Pasadena Public Library Staffers Turn Down Pay Increases to Save Services." Yes, you read that right. With their library staring at the strong possibility of budget cuts of 10% or more, the employees at Pasadena Public voted to reject pay raises that averaged more than $100 per month. At a general meeting the staff debated the merits of accepting salary increases at a time when hours were being cut and book acquisitions were being slashed. Then after all the talking stopped 102 out of 110 employees nobly decided to forego their raises.   **SUCH** nobility should not go unpraised. What the library staff did was provide a very selfish world with a rare example of unselfishness. The *Los Angeles Times* called it "extreme devotion to the duty of supplying readers with books," and other city workers were reported to have been "astonished" by the librarians' generosity.   **THE** nobility of the situation aside, what the library staff did was also very stupid because it simply reinforced the old stereotype of the librarian as a person who is dedicated, selfless, and eager to live in poverty. One of the Pasadena staffers was quoted as saying, "This is not just a job. The library is an ideal. Most of the people who work here feel that way." **THAT'S** a very telling statement—that librarianship is an ideal and not a job. If the Pasadena staffers feel that librarianship is not a job, then why don't they get real jobs somewhere else to support themselves so that they can volunteer their services at the library for free? Haven't any of those people in Pasadena heard of Maslow's hierarchy of needs? Don't they know that it's great to have ideals, but that charity begins at home? How can we librarians expect to take care of other people when we can't take care of ourselves?   **NO** one makes me angrier than members of our profession who allow themselves to be rolled like jelly donuts by county boards and city councils in times of budgetary shortfalls. The other professions—engineers, accountants, fire fighters, police officers, personnel analysts, computer specialists, and public administrators—that comprise the Pasadena city work

> **We're librarians, Mr. Mayor. You can put us on food stamps, take away our lunch breaks, and cut our salaries, but please don't touch our book budget.**

force certainly didn't fold up like flimsy snack trays at the mere mention of the word "cuts." Why did the librarians have to be the ones to be so noble and unselfish?   **ACTUALLY**, come to think of it, maybe it wasn't unselfishness that motivated the librarians to be so noble. Maybe it was a lack of self-esteem. By refusing the raises, the librarians in essence were saying, "We're not worthy of raises. Books are more important than we are." With this kind of an attitude the librarians will inevitably fall farther and farther behind other occupational groups when it comes to salaries, benefits, and working conditions. If we ★★★page 34★★★   won't stand up for ourselves, who will?   **TO** add insult to injury the Pasadena librarians not only hurt themselves, they hurt the library. They may have thought that they were strengthening the collection and keeping the library intact by channeling their salary money into operational areas, but it's quite possible that their altruism will ultimately have a weakening effect. The next time the Pasadena City Council needs to make cuts won't they seize the library as an easy target? "If we cut the library," you can hear the councilmen thinking, "we can depend on the librarians to make more sacrifices on behalf of the public, so let's continue to cut the library."   **THE** most maddening thing about the Pasadena situation, however, is not the local impact it has in Pasadena but rather the damage it does to the profession as a whole. People reading the *Los Angeles Times* story undoubtedly drew certain conclusions about librarians in general. Too many people already picture librarians as members of some weird religious sect dedicated to silence, seriousness, and poverty. It's quite likely, therefore, that the Pasadena story simply confirmed their worst suspicions about us.   **IT'S** a shame, in conclusion, that the rest of the library profession, has to be victims of the Pasadena staff's benevolence. The biggest single threat to librarianship is low salaries. There is no way we can expect bright young people to enter our field at the levels of compensation that now prevail, and it absolutely burns me up to think that the employees of the Pasadena Public Library have consciously done their best to take these levels even lower.

Arizona Do-Gooder Does Bad

BUT my anger at the Pasadena librarians didn't last long. It was quickly replaced by a new object of scorn, an Arizona high school history teacher, who took it upon himself to stock the school's new library. "Drive Nets 25,000 Volumes" blared the headline in the Phoenix newspaper. Upon further reading I discovered that these 25,000 volumes were all used books that this history teacher had collected from individuals, businesses, and, gasp, retirement communities.   **CAN** you imagine stocking a new high school library with books collected from the residents of a retirement community? Was this a joke or a nightmare? A quick phone call to the school revealed that it was a nightmare. The shelves of the new library were in fact being filled with donations, the same kind of donations that your Friends of the Library organization collects and sells for five cents apiece.   **THIS** was outrageous, more outrageous than the Pasadena librarians sacrificing their pay raises. What was almost as bad as the fact that the school district would welcome this method of book acquisitions was the tone of the newspaper article. There was no suggestion in the story that maybe high school students in our rapidly changing world might deserve something   ★★★page 35★★★

better than unwanted hand-me-downs in their school library. In fact this history teacher was being applauded as a dedicated educator.
WHAT, I wondered, would the newspaper have to say about a police department that armed its officers with old handguns and rifles that had been discarded by the town's residents, or a fire department that stocked its fire engines with unwanted garden hoses that had been cleaned out of residential garages, or a street department that equipped itself with discarded brooms and mops? Obviously, the reaction would be disbelief followed by ridicule. But when some do-gooder runs a "clean out your attic and basement" book drive to stock a new library, the reaction is to nominate him for the humanitarian of the year award.   **PREDICTABLY**, the next day, another local newspaper picked up the story and the crescendo of praise for this teacher continued. It's hard to dislike someone who works so hard with the best of intentions, but I was by now having trouble resisting the temptation of putting this guy's picture on my dart board and firing away. Three times that morning I got phone calls from influential people in my community who wanted to sound me out about the feasibility of running a similar discard drive for our new public library. They too had the best of intentions and quoted freely from the morning paper. "Did you see," one of them said enthusiastically, "that this history teacher has saved his taxpayers half a million dollars?"   **"LET** me ask you this," I responded to the caller, "when Christmas rolls around this year are you going to give your children used books for their presents?"   **"OF** course not!" he responded with a touch of indignation.   **"MY** point exactly," was my response.

Flying by the Seat of Your Pants

IT'S the curse of all new library science graduates. You've just gotten your M.L.S. and you sadly discover that every professional job opening that pays above the poverty level requires a minimum of two years of experience. It's not fair you say to yourself. How am I going to get the necessary experience if no one will hire me because I don't have any experience?
THAT'S why newly minted librarians downplay the importance of experience and see it as an unreasonable job requirement. To the young, experience is not only unnecessary, it is also counterproductive because it often gets in the way of creativity, innovation, and enthusiasm.
TWENTY-THREE years ago I certainly felt that way too, but with each succeeding year as a librarian I came to value experience more and more. Let's face it, when you get to be a middle-aged codger like me, experience is one of the few things that you still have over youth. Recently I decided to write down everything that these twenty-three years of experience have taught me about

librarianship. None of these things are based on research. They are all things that I have learned from flying by the seat of my pants. **IF** I were you I wouldn't take them too seriously because one thing my experience has definitely taught me is that flying by the seat of your pants often results in a crash landing. With that in mind here are **Manley's Maxims:** 1. *You can tell your place in the organization by where you are on the routing slip for library periodicals.* I am constantly amazed when I write an article for say the January 1, 1994, *Booklist* and I get a letter the following November from a librarian who writes, "I just read your article on blah blah and I have to agree that blah blah is blah blah." There's no doubt that this person is way down on the organization's pecking order if it takes eleven months for a copy of *Booklist* to trickle down to him or her. You don't need to tell a librarian that information is power, so if you're last on the routing slip, that's a sure hint that you ought to either start getting on the ball or marry someone on the library board. 2. *Videotapes do not make readers out of non-readers. They make non-readers out of readers.* **THE** biggest justification that audio-visual librarians make for starting a video lending service in the library is that it will attract non-readers to the library and once they are in the door, they will graduate from "Rocky V" to *The Decline and Fall of the Roman Empire.* Actually the opposite occurs. An inner city branch librarian from Cleveland cornered me at a recent Ohio Library Association conference and confessed, "The worst thing I ever did was start a video collection. Now instead of heading for the new books shelf the first thing my patrons do is head for the new video collection." 3. *Adults will do things for their children that they will never do for themselves.* **THE** least cost effective thing that most librarians do is put money into adult programming. The dollars per participant ratio is dismal. Children's programming on the other hand is usually a big hit with both adults and children. Why? It's simple. Ninety-eight out of a hundred adults will not drag themselves away from Oprah to attend a book discussion on Plato's Dialogues, but they will abandon her to take their kids to library story hour. In the past ten years I have attended the world's worst band concert and the world's worst theatrical performance of "The Three Little Pigs" for the simple reason that my sons were involved. The point is if you want to draw adults to the library, put your programming money into youth services not adult. The child is the key to getting the adult community involved in its library. 4. *Don't underestimate the importance of food at library board meetings.* **THE** thing that you have to remember about library trustees is that they work for nothing. Not only do they receive no pay but they also receive little or no recognition. It's a thankless job that is done in anonymity except of course when there is a

You've got a heavy schedule today—breakfast with the trustees, brunch with the Friends, lunch with the Council, coffee with the Mayor, happy hour with the reference staff, and dinner with the chamber of commerce.

★★★page 38★★★

major censorship brouhaha. Then the thankless job is done under the white hot light of media scrutiny and in the middle of the sometimes deadly crossfire of various special interest groups. A plate of brownies or a dish of lemon bars is a good way to show your appreciation. Not only will your trustees appreciate the thought, but since board meetings often drone on for several hours they will also be grateful for the fortification. Always make sure, however, that your culinary offerings are homebaked. Sticking a box of Dunkin' Donuts on the board table doesn't exactly say, "I care."   5. **Patrons want books, not bibliographic records.**   IT'S a classic forest and trees kind of dilemma. We librarians are absolutely obsessed with creating bibliographical records and creating networks to share the records. That, after all, is our ultimate job—to bring order and control to the thousands of titles that are published each year. But in creating these records we need to remember that no patron has ever said "I go to Library X because it has the finest bibliographic records in our area." More likely the patron is going to say, "I go to Library X because it has the books I need." The point is, when it comes to budgetary priorities, cataloging still takes a backseat to collection development.   6. **Censors are also protected by the First Amendment.**   IT'S always open season on censors in the library profession. As defenders of the First Amendment, we librarians have fought hard over the years to combat the attempts of censors to take books off our shelves. Unfortunately our zeal for the principles of intellectual freedom has sometimes made us forget that censors are simply exercising their own First Amendment rights. When's the last time you actually read that often quoted but little understood law. Here's what it says, "Congress shall make no law respecting an establishment of religion, or prohibiting the free exercise thereof; or abridging the freedom of speech or of the press; or the right of the people peaceably to assemble and to petition the Government for a redress of grievances." What in essence is a censor but a citizen who is exercising his right to petition a governmental body (library board, city council, county board, etc.) for a redress of what he considers to be a grievance (the use of his tax money to buy harmful materials for the library)?   7. **Ask not what a politician can do for you but what you can do for the politician.**   THE goal of 99 out of 100 politicians is to get re-elected. The best way to develop political support for your library, therefore, is to demonstrate that library support equals votes. Never tell a politician what he or she should do, but rather explain that statistical studies show that people who use libraries are more likely to vote than people who do not use libraries.   8. **The more committees a library has, the less efficient it is.**   EVER wonder why A.L.A. conferences often resemble the theatre of the absurd. It's because A.L.A. has so many committees.   ★★★page 39★★★

In fact A.L.A. has so many committees that it had to form something called "the committee on committees" to keep track of everything. When you get too many committees turf battles arise, organizational infighting intensifies, and leadership erodes. On the other hand, committees do from time to time serve a purpose. Say your city council wants to institute a vigorous new program of user fees in your library. The best way to deep six the concept is to form a committee to explore it.   9. *The effectiveness of your meetings can be determined by the attendance at them.*   **MEETINGS**, meetings, meetings. Have you ever thought about the absurdity of pulling people off of service desks so that they can attend a meeting on how to improve service to the public? Every library I have ever worked in has meeting mania. The trouble is that half to three quarters of these meetings are worthless and wasteful. If your meetings fit this category it's easy to tell. Your staff will concoct the darnedest reasons to avoid them, like "The doctor says I have scarlet fever and should stay away from other people." Another sure sign that your meetings are stupid is when you hear three or four beepers go off five minutes into the meeting.   10. *There is an inverse relationship between the size of a library and how much work the director actually does.*   **NO** one works harder than the director of a small public library. This is a person who out of necessity must be an expert in all areas of librarianship—cataloging, circulation, reference work, children's services, personnel management, budgeting, and working with trustees and politicians. The director of the large public library, on the other hand, can delegate all of these duties to subordinates. He or she, therefore, only has to be an expert in drinking coffee, reading the local newspaper, and going to meetings with other directors to complain about the state library.   11. *Interlibrary cooperation retards local library growth.*   **ONE** of the cardinal rules of librarianship is "Always Cooperate." From library school to library retirement the importance of sharing resources is emphasized, and the librarian who is "uncooperative" faces a lifetime of the big chill from his or her colleagues. But in my working career, I've seen case after case where reciprocal borrowing agreements and interlibrary loan networks have relieved local politicians of the responsibility of developing their own library systems. Why build when you can mooch off others?   12. *Sometimes the public prefers closed stacks.*   **THE** concept of open stacks has always been seen as one of the great advancements of twentieth century librarianship, and for the most part it has been. There is no substitute when you are researching a particular subject to camp out in front of the books you need and browse to your heart's content. But I discovered that when it comes to back issues of periodicals, patrons often prefer closed shelving. "Why," I once asked a local college student, "do you use our periodical collection when the one at the university library down the street is fifteen times as large?" He responded, "Because your collection, small as it may be, is at least intact. At the university the magazines are either cut up or missing." What was the difference? Their shelves were open, ours were closed.   13. **When you're ready to build a new computer, don't call a library director for advice.**   LET'S say you're looking at computer system Z for your library. The company that markets this system gives you Harold Blodgett as a reference. Harold Blodgett is the director of the Dayspring Public Library and he bought system Z for his library last year. What's he going to say when you call him and ask him how he likes the system? If the system is a turkey is he going to admit it? Of course not. He's probably sunk a couple of million dollars into it and he's the last person in the world who would admit that the system stinks. Call his circulation staff instead. They'll know how good the system really is and they won't hesitate to tell you. Circ clerks have a flair for the truth.   14. **Your library board will not fire you for the first six months of your employment.**   THE library honeymoon is a much misunderstood phenomenon. Everybody thinks it's a period of voluntary good will and cooperation. It's not. The first thing that the average library board does after they hire you as their new director is call the local newspaper and brag about how they have, after spending hundreds of hours on recruiting, evaluating, and interviewing, come up with the greatest librarian in the country. After all that bragging, do you think they're going to fire you anytime soon? Of course not. Such a quick termination would expose them as a bunch of incompetent nincompoops. That means you can do virtually anything you want during those first six months with impunity.   15. **Libraries are more dependent on the economy than on federal funding.**   IT'S laughable. Everytime there's a new president elected, the library periodical editorialists try to tell us what it all means for us guys in the library trenches. The problem is they always get it wrong. They think that local library funding is largely determined by how much L.S.C.A. money is available from the federal government. The truth is federal funding accounts for anywhere from 1 to 3 percent of local library budgets. It doesn't matter a whit therefore what the new president thinks of L.S.C.A. What is important is the economy, stupid. If the new president's policies stimulate the economy, that's the best thing that can happen to libraries. If his policies depress the economy, say hello to downsizing.   16. **High technology does not always replace low technology.**   THE next time some doomsaying infodweeb tries to tell you that traditional book-oriented librarians are the blacksmiths of the 21st century, just point out to him that sales of bicycles, condoms, and no. 2 pencils are at an all-time   ★★★page 41★★★

high. The point is you don't take the space shuttle to get across town. The book is like the cockroach. Despite the emergence of new media, it lives, thrives, and multiplies.   17. ***The higher the public profile, the less effective the director.***   **THE** smart library director keeps a low profile. Whenever ribbons are to be cut, speeches are to be given, and photo ops to be staged, the director should always defer to his or her local politicians. The more public glory the politicians are given, the more they'll look at the library as a political asset. Directors who hog the limelight squander their political capital.   18. ***The desire to avoid censorship creates censorship.***   **THE** quickest way to lose peer respect in the library profession is to allow a censor to remove a book from the shelves of your library. Peer pressure dictates that you resign your job before you submit to the disgrace of caving in to censors. It's for that reason that many librarians will not take a chance on a potentially controversial book. But that's not censorship, that's selection.   19. ***Nothing is more permanent than a library service.*** **THE** idea of starting a pilot project in a library with a grant can sound innovative and exciting, but it's important to keep in mind that whenever you start a new program or build a new branch you also create a new client group, and if and when you ever want to terminate that program or close that branch you need to be prepared to fight that client group. Beware, therefore, of creating a Frankenstein's monster that will turn on you.   20. ***In dealing with censors the best defense is a good offense.***   **WHY** do we allow ourselves to be put into defensive corners by censors? Too often we are thrust in the position of having to prove that a particular book is not inherently harmful or inappropriate for the communities that we serve. It's much better to turn the issue around and put the burden of proof on the backs of the censors. Specifically, Mr. Falwell, how will this book endanger the moral life of our community and what research data do you have to prove your point?   21. ***One trustee carries more political power than 100 library directors.***   **THE** key to building a successful, well funded public library is to get the library board of trustees fully engaged in the political process. Too often the politicking is left to the director with tragic results. The reason is simple. When politicians see library directors they see a narrow professional agenda, but when they see trustees they see voters.

How About Some Real World Research?

IN many respects librarianship is a profession of sheep. Our shared values are so strong that only the most eccentric mavericks among us have the temerity to question the importance of electronic networking, intellec-
★★★page 42★★★   tual freedom, bibliographic control, resource

sharing, and intertype library cooperation. **SO** if you're planning a dinner party for your librarian friends and you want to create the opportunity for lively, interesting and spirited conversation what topic should you put on the table along with your garden salad, red snapper, and bottle of Chardonnay? My recommendation is library education. **IT'S** an issue that not only invokes a wide diversity of opinions, but also one that is in a considerable state of disarray, and nothing makes librarians—the organizers of the world's information base—more unsettled than something in a state of disarray. Basically our internecine squabble about library education roils around two points: 1) does it have a future? and 2) does it adequately prepare students to work in the real world of yuppie parents, **purple-headed skateboarders,** and right-wing dittoheads? **SO** much has been written about these points that they're not worth going into other than to offer the rather axiomatic perspective that the answer to question #1 weighs more toward the negative with the closing of each additional library school. There are now only about 50 A.L.A. accredited schools left. This means that entire cities and states are schooless, and this means that the residents of these locales who aspire to librarianship are stuck with a difficult dilemma—is it worth the money and disruption to one's life to go out of state to pursue a degree that will provide only a marginal salary? **ALTHOUGH** questions one and two are certainly the threshold questions concerning library education, there is a third, and in some regards, equally important issue—the question of research. The purpose of any graduate school, whether it be engineering, business, law, or librarianship, is always twofold: to teach students and to do research. Both purposes are critical to the growth and development of the field in question. Librarianship will not prosper without new practitioners and without new advancements to its knowledge base. Too often, however, we ignore the importance of the knowledge base, probably because at heart we know that librarianship is an applied trade, not a purely intellectual pursuit. There are no inherent laws in nature regarding the art of librarianship. **THIS** does not mean that there is any less validity for librarians to do research into their field than for political scientists, anthropologists, biologists, and sociologists to do research into theirs. The purpose of this research ultimately is to make observations about libraries and library use patterns that will support the practitioners in their efforts to refine and enhance their service to their clienteles. **IT'S** not that there isn't research being done, it's not that this research isn't being done accurately and precisely and it's not that much of this research isn't challenging and sophisticated. The problem is that very little of it is useful to the practitioner, especially the public library practitioner. If you're a working librarian and you don't believe me, simply open up the latest edition of *Dissertation Abstracts* and you'll see what I mean. **SO** what's the solution? What can be done to encourage research with a greater potential for usefulness in the field? My proposal is that library practitioners and library school theoreticians stop shouting at each

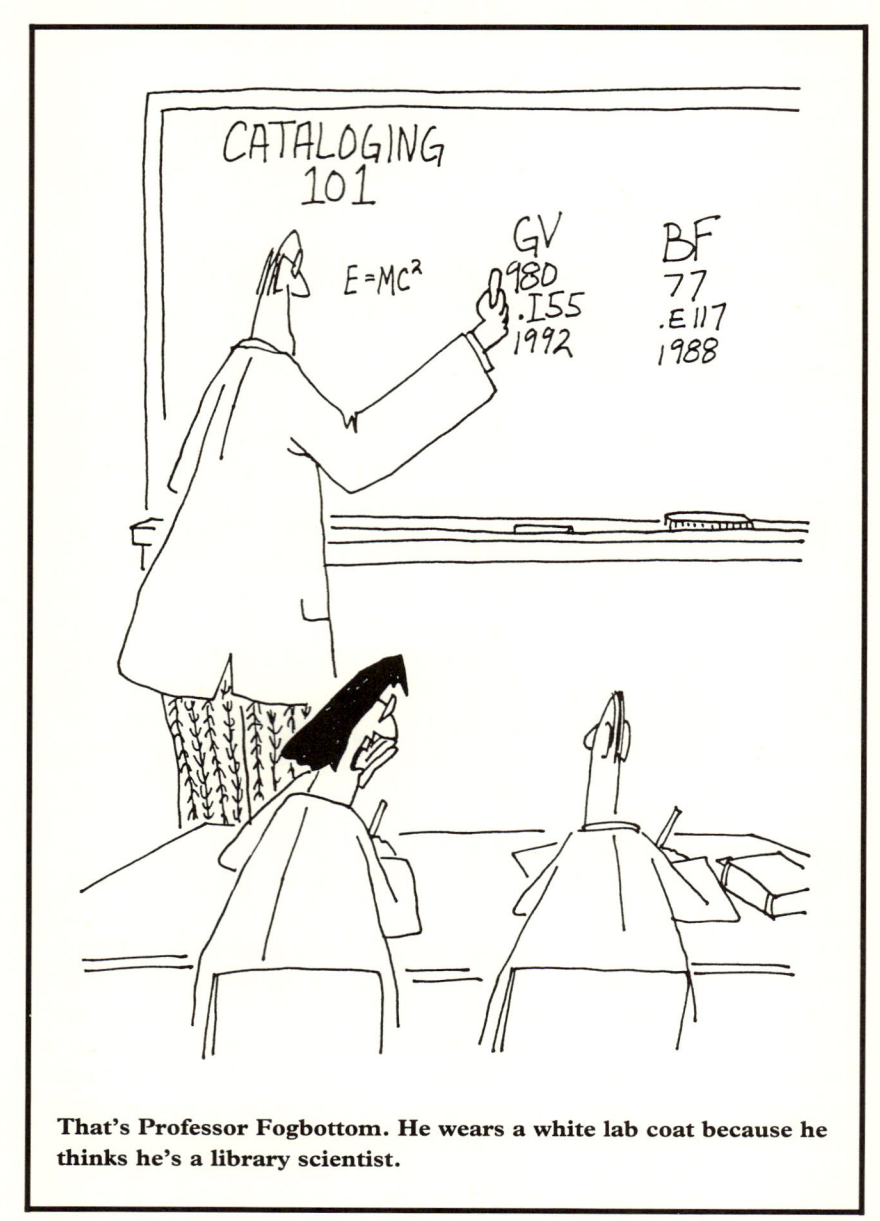

That's Professor Fogbottom. He wears a white lab coat because he thinks he's a library scientist.

other and begin building bridges. Too often when practitioners and theoreti-
★★★page 44★★★   cians get together the result is an exercise in finger

pointing and name calling. Practitioners accuse theoreticians of being too imperious, too arrogant and too distant from the real world. Not only are there insults thrown around about the quality and quantity of newly minted degreed librarians, but disparaging remarks are made about the capacity of the graduate schools to produce useful research. The professors on the other hand are quick to point out that of course the quality and quantity of their graduates are declining because what able-minded person wants to go into a profession that promotes poverty. It is not their fault that the practitioners braying at them persist in paying slave wages for entry level librarians.   **INSTEAD** of this mindless banter, the two sides should be, dare I say it, collaborating. Professors and doctoral candidates need to realize their research amounts to nothing more than self-absorbed drivel if it has no applications in the real world, and practitioners should stop complaining and start identifying practical problems where research is not only feasible but helpful. In this spirit I offer two current real world issues that desperately need research attention.   ***PROPOSAL #1*—The Town/Gown Issue**—Town/gown problems go back as far as the Middle Ages but rarely in the context of library issues. Anyone who works in a public library located in a college or university town, however, is faced with a problem that other public librarians are immune from. I can hear Councilman Hurley now, "Why in the name of common sense do we need a public library in this community when State University down the street has a large library with 3,000,000 volumes?"   **"YES**, that's true, Councilman Hurley, but the library at State is oriented for the use of students."   **"BUT** isn't it true, Mr. Manley, that as taxpayers of this state *all* of the residents of our community are entitled to free and open access to that library?"   **"YES**, Councilman Hurley, but the university library's collection is developed around the needs of a very select clientele—the students at the university."   **"ARE** you saying, Mr. Manley, that the average citizen of this community cannot find something to read in a collection of over three million books?"   **"YES**, that's correct, Councilman Hurley. There are public library constituencies for whom the university library is irrelevant."   **"SUCH** as?"   **"WELL**, the first group that comes to mind are the young people of this community. State U. has neither a juvenile collection nor a young adult collection."   **"OKAY**, Mr. Manley, wouldn't you agree to two points. First, that our elementary, junior high, and high school libraries cater to our young people, and second, that even if that weren't the case, it would be far cheaper for this Council to send a yearly grant of money to the university library to develop a youth reading collection than it would be to continue to support an unnecessary public library."   **THAT** is the kind of repartee that you get into as a public library director at budget time in a   ★★★page 45★★★

university community. I have labored in three different college towns and in each case I have been bedeviled with this kind of logic. The temptation is great to stand up and say, "Councilman Hurley, it's idiotic of you to think that the average citizen would want to use the library at State U. First of all, the parking there is horrendous; secondly, the staff is there to assist students in serious research and does not have the time to humor little old ladies who want contemporary works of fiction that **have no sex**, violence, or four letter words; third, have you ever tried to find anything in a library with three million volumes (I know airport parking garages that are easier to get around in); and fourth, where in the university library are you going to go to find the blue book price of an '82 Chevette hatchback without the hatch?"
BUT, of course, you can't say that and keep your job so you grit your teeth and start talking about "constituencies" in hope that Councilman Birdbrain will somehow make the linkage between public libraries and votes. Over time, however, you discover that Birdbrain simply doesn't possess the intellectual capacity to recognize the obvious distinctions between types of libraries and patterns of library usage. To him motor oil is motor oil and a library is a library.   **NOT** long ago while I was engaged in my perennial battle with Birdbrain, it occurred to me that the reason I was getting pushed around so badly was that Birdbrain had the advantage of always being on the offensive which put me in the position of having to constantly scramble around simply to stay on my feet. I needed an argument that would put him back on his heels, and then it hit me—the presence of a college or university actually *increases* the need for a public library for two reasons.   **FIRST**, there are a lot of college students, especially underclassmen, who prefer to patronize the public library because of its more user friendly size and its more tolerant reference staff (the average academic reference librarian assumes the patron knows how to use the library; the average public reference librarian assumes the patron knows how to get from the parking lot to the front door and sometimes this is even a push) and second, the university community has much higher education demographics, which is important because conventional wisdom would suggest that there is a direct relationship between public library usage and the educational level of the public that it serves.   **SO** what I wanted to say to Councilman Birdbrain was "Yes, Councilman, thank you for bringing up the point that State U. down the street has a library with three million books because recent research shows that the presence of a university actually increases the need for quality public library services." But alas I did not have any recent research to put into Birdbrain's brain because this kind of data hasn't been collected.
WOULDN'T it, however, make a neat and clean research project for some aspiring library scientist to pick a random

selection of communities with universities and without and compare public library usage patterns? Good heavens, it might even lead to research on the larger issue of correlating the myriad of other community characteristics (industrial levels, population levels, economic strata, etc.) with library usage. Not only would this information be helpful in the planning process but it would be absolutely invaluable in the political process of securing funds—"The latest research findings show that we are just the kind of community that *consumes* library services by the truckload!"   ***PROPOSAL #2—The "IF You Build It, They Will Come" Issue***—Here's the dilemma: You torture yourself for six years with a library building project. First there's the agony of getting the proposal on a bond referendum, then there's the ordeal of convincing people that they ought to get out and vote for a tax increase to support the new library, next there's the struggle to get the architect to actually design a library and not a stylized courtyard (yes, we do need a stack area!), and finally there's the pain of getting the building built (you mean to tell me that the fat guy who drives the dirty pick-up truck with the SHIT HAPPENS bumper sticker is in charge of my entire building project?).   **NOW**, after all that pain and frustration you are ready to move in and claim your new title of Library Building Expert. But there remains one last piece of business—you still have to staff the new building and increase your book budget for it. That is the most difficult challenge of all. Ask anyone who has been through the new building wars what the hardest part of the whole ordeal was and I guarantee you the answer will be, "Getting the building financed, designed, and built was nothing compared to getting it staffed. That was Hell!"   **ON** the face of it, of course, such a point would seem illogical. After all, how hard could it be to get your city council members to spend a quarter of a million dollars on new staff, after they have just spent ten million dollars on a new building? It's actually very hard, sometimes almost impossible. If you're a politician it's easy to spend the design and construction money because the results are tangible. You get your name engraved in stone on the building's dedication plaque, and you get to be there on grand opening day to make a speech and serve punch and cookies to your constituents. Plus, the construction cost is a one time expense covered by bonds that have been duly approved by the taxpayers.   **BY** contrast, the operating budget, of which staffing is by far the biggest expense, is a recurring cost that must be paid in ever-increasing amounts year after year. Politicians hate those kind of costs because they are usually covered by property taxes, and the easiest way to get booted out of office by the voters is to raise property taxes. But that still leaves the dilemma— you've built a new library building that is probably five times as big as your old one, and you know, you just know, that   ★★★page 47★★★

your circulation is going to at least double, and if you don't get some new personnel you yourself will end up spending 60 hours a week at the reference desk and even that will be the equivalent of putting your little finger into the leaking dike. It's not going to stop the flood that will engulf your library. **SO** you say to Councilman Hardhead, "In anticipation of the dramatic increase in library usage that will be stimulated by the opening of our new building, we feel that it is prudent to request that the city council increase our operating budget by $250,000 in order to accommodate the hiring of new public services staff." **TO** which Mr. Hardhead responds, "Yes, Mr. Manley, and what is your anticipation based upon? Do you have any data demonstrating your point?" **HARDHEAD**, as opposed to Birdbrain, has a valid point. Cost projections should be made on the basis of information, but when you turn to library literature and research the question of what happens when you open a new building you find two paltry studies that are of little or no help. This is frustrating because given the resources of most graduate library schools, this like the town/gown issue is ready-made for a neat and clean comparative study. **HOW** wonderful it would be to turn to Councilman Hardhead and say, "Yes, Mr. Councilman, the latest research shows that the opening of a new building results in an average of a 78% increase in circulation and a 134% increase in the number of reference questions asked."

Ahead of My Time

I'M not sure why at the age of forty I decided to start training for the A.L.A. Annual Fun Run, but I think it was more involved than the obvious explanation that I had just turned forty. **ACTUALLY** turning forty did have something to do with my decision but not for the standard reason that I was having a mid-life crisis and was making some desperate and demented attempt to reacquire my youthful figure through athletic training. Lord knows I had tried everything else from the watermelon diet to driving around in White Trash, my '82 Chevette, for three hours on a 112 degree day in August (we're talking standard Arizona weather here) with the windows closed and the air conditioner off (heck, the air conditioner hadn't worked for three years). And, oh yeah, I was dressed in one of those **rubber jogging suits** that make you look like an astronaut in orbit. **SO** no, this was not some sudden attempt to drop twenty or thirty pounds. Long ago (I think it was when I nearly passed out in the Chevette) I decided that in the battle of pounds versus Ben and Jerry's ice cream, Ben and Jerry were always going to win. So if you think I was having a mid-life crisis you're very wrong. The truth is I've rather enjoyed the aging process. It does after all have its advantages. **FIRST**, ★★★page 48★★★   the older you get the less people expect you to look like a fashion model. At age forty who really expects anything special out of you. The truth is nobody's even looking. Walk into a room filled with people in their twenties and thirties and you soon learn that you have achieved the trick of becoming invisible. It's a liberating experience to know that you can wear mismatched socks or a necktie spotted with pasta sauce and no one will notice, or if they do they'll dismiss it as the natural bi-product of being over the hill. **THE** point is the older you get the more you can be yourself and indulge your own eccentricities without worrying about how others will regard you. Chances are they won't even notice. The older you get the less you have to concern yourself with peer pressure. **ANOTHER** liberating aspect of the aging process is that the older you get the more you can actually enjoy your life because you no longer have to devote so much time and money to preparing for the future. Even if your career has not met the great expectations you might have set for it, you can at least wallow in the considerable comforts of mediocrity, which can be a lot more enjoyable than preparing for excellence. **THINK** about it. No more courses to attend, academic degrees to attain, entry level jobs to apply for, and promotional opportunities to claw for with thirty-seven other atavistic career opportunists. Okay, you didn't become the director of the New York Public Library, but look at the bright side—you don't have to deal with the stress of managing a library of unmanageable size or living in a city of unliveable conditions. **SO** what if you ended up running a nicely sized suburban public library? What's wrong with that? Sure, it's fashionable to ridicule suburban communities as culturally barren wastelands, but let's be honest—suburbs do have benefits like green grass, public schools where principals do not need to carry baseball bats down the hallways, spanking clean and spacious hospitals where the heart surgeons do not have arm tattoos, and wonderfully large supermarkets that sell everything from pipe cleaners to **gourmet pickles. PEOPLE** who live in cities always talk about how great the opera is. Let them have their opera. I prefer to sit on a lawn chair in my backyard with a glass of iced tea and listen to the soothing hum of my neighbor's electric mower. **SO** no, I was not having a midlife crisis. In fact I couldn't have been happier indulging in the mediocrity of my midlife years. Despite this bliss there was, however, one small thing missing in my life—games, official games, where people keep score and there are clear-cut winners and losers. Games are a very big part of growing up in America. From Little League and Pop Warner football through the end of our senior year in college we play games and experience the thrill of victory and the agony of defeat. And suddenly when we get out of college it ends. **SURE,** you might say that there are recreational softball and basketball leagues where

middle-aged men can keep their competitive fires burning, but to the serious athlete these activities are not the same—they are more of a social event that give mediocrities a good excuse to get out of the house and **tap a keg** after the game. The truth is that those leagues are more important to the guy who never made his high school team than to the more accomplished athlete who is used to a more challenging form of battle than hitting a softball **lobbed by a potbellied wannabe.**   **WHAT** I longed for was a tackle football league for men over forty. Flag, tag, or touch football just wouldn't do. The essence of the game is blocking and tackling, and once you play the real thing a less physical version is like drinking non-alcoholic beer. What's the point? Unfortunately every time I brought up the concept of a tackle football league to the recreation department in my community, I was looked at as someone who might be in immediate need of psychiatric care.   **THERE** was always golf and tennis but both of these sports, if you've never played them before, require too many lessons. I was too old for lessons. That left running, a sport that I did happen to have some experience and training in. For four years in high school I ran cross country even though my stocky build was not the classic physique for the distance runner, which at the time didn't deter me because I had fallen in love with a book called *The Loneliness of the Long Distance Runner.*   **UNFORTUNATELY** the most memorable race of my career was the district final where I broke out in front after the first half mile and five minutes later found myself completely distanced from the rest of the pack. There was no way I could lose. I was in what the sports psychologists now call a "zone."   **UNFORTUNATELY** the zone I was in was the lost zone. After about a mile I ran out of running lane and found myself all alone deep in the thick of a pine woods. I may have ended up finishing dead last in the district but I had at least finally achieved the loneliness of the long distance runner. My career was, therefore, not a complete flop.   **IT** was with some confidence then that I sent in my registration form for the A.L.A. Fun Run. This was an event I knew I could win even though I hadn't run distances for over twenty years. There were several reasons for my cockiness. First, librarians are not known for their athletic prowess, and second, competition was arranged by age brackets and so I only had to beat people who were in their forties. Since I had just turned forty I would probably be the youngest person in my competition. There was no way I could lose.   **FOR** that reason, I didn't train really hard. I mean it would be ridiculous to go on a rigorous work-out schedule. Imagine exercising at the local gym and having the guy standing next to you in line at the Nautilus machine saying, "Hey, I'm working out for the Olympic 4,000 meters. What's your event?"   **"WHO,**
★★★page 50★★★   me? I'm training for the A.L.A. Fun Run."   **SO**

I played it nonchalant. Every other night I jogged a couple of miles and then did some sit-ups in the privacy of my bedroom. By the time June 30th rolled around I wasn't a threat to break the world record in the marathon, but I wasn't a candidate for the John Candy lookalike contest either.   **THE** first hint, however, that I might have underestimated my competition came when I showed up at the starting line and found myself surrounded by very slim people dressed in serious track garb—expensive shoes, fancy sunglasses, tank tops bearing the names of local track clubs, and those chic little hats professional marathoners wear to keep their hair pushed back and the sun out of their eyes. Me? I was wearing cut-offs, hightops, and a Walkman.   **THAT** was my second hint. No one else was wearing a Walkman. I couldn't believe that. It was inconceivable to me that people were actually going to run two and a half miles without musical accompaniment. First you needed the hard driving beat from someone like Miles Davis to get you going and then you needed it to keep you from dying from boredom. "Why no Walkman?" I asked the young woman standing next to me.   **SHE** looked at me **like I was retarded** and then said, "It weighs you down and distracts you from the race." That's when I was quite certain that I was in competitive trouble. Ten pound weights on each foot might slow me down but a little thing like a Walkman on my head would never make a difference at my deliberate but steady pace.   **THINGS** got worse when someone in an official position handed me a flyer listing heat injury symptoms and giving first aid treatments for heat stroke, nausea, and convulsions. All of this for fun? I now knew that this was not a "fun" event and that the participants involved were not here to have a good time. They were here to humiliate amateurs like me. Where were all the wimpy librarians that everybody talks about when they call librarianship a "sissy" profession? Had I by mistake happened upon a race being staged for local competing athletic clubs? The people poised at the starting line couldn't be catalogers and serials specialists. They were hard, lean, and athletic. My only hope for not finishing last was to beat out some of the participants in the 50 and up age bracket.   **AS** the gun sounded I made the strategic decision to pace myself behind an old man (he had to be in the 62 to 65 range). I figured I would keep up with him for the first part of the race and then gradually begin to accelerate with the strategy of passing those overly ambitious runners who would inevitably run themselves into heat exhaustion on the hills that appeared to dominate the backstretch of the course.   **APPROXIMATELY** 500 yards into the race, however, I realized that I was the one who was going to have the stroke if I didn't slow down. **My sexagenarian pacer** simply ran me into the ground, which left me in the unenviable position of falling back to the ranks of female catalogers   ★★★page 51★★★

weighing over two hundred pounds. Things looked hopeless until I saw a donut shop with an OPEN sign blinking in the front window. This gave me the incentive to move ahead of the catalogers. I then ducked into the donut shop and had a chocolate eclair and a cup of coffee. With that fortification, I reentered the course and ran ahead to an ice cream shop where I stopped for a chocolate double dip with sprinkles, and from there it was on to a French bakery for a vanilla cruller, and finally my culinary tour ended with a Big Mac.   **YES**, I finished the race. Yes, no one was there to officially deem me last place, and yes, I had fun.   **FOUR** years later I was ecstatic to have the opportunity to vote for Bill Clinton, a man in my body fat category. Even though I didn't really care for his views on the economy and health care, I reasoned that any man who could so skillfully work a cup of coffee and a donut into a jog, could handle the job of president.   **IN** view of how Mr. Clinton has redefined the concept of exercise, I have to conclude that I didn't really finish in last place in Atlanta. Rather I was four years ahead of my time.

Five Days in June

THERE are few experiences more daunting to the graduate library school student than the A.L.A. Placement Center. Let's face it—why do people go to library school? Very simple—we go to get jobs.   **ALTHOUGH** library school can be an intellectually rewarding experience, most people don't attend for the inherent pleasures of learning the distinction between a dash and a hyphen in bibliographic records. Library school is not something you do out of fun or interest. When you get right down to it, library school is a place of vocational-technical training, nothing more and nothing less. The only reason any of us went to library school was to get a job.   **TO** the outsider, of course, it may sound slightly ridiculous that anyone would devote one or two years and spend twenty to thirty thousand dollars for the right to compete for jobs that have terrible working hours and low pay in a profession that is stereotyped as stuffy and boring. What most of these people don't understand, however, is that librarianship has the following advantages over many other types of work: 1. Librarians work with the entire realm of human knowledge. The endless diversity of materials that we work with—books, compact discs, videotapes, CD-Rom, computer software, ephemera, realia, and online databases—make our jobs interesting, exciting, and satisfying. 2. Librarians work with the entire realm of the human family. The endless diversity of patrons whom we work with—young and old; rich and poor; well educated and poorly educated—make our jobs interesting, exciting, and satisfying.   3. Librarians work in the entire realm of the post-industrial economy.
★★★page 52★★★   The endless diversity of institutions that have

libraries—businesses, hospitals, law firms, local governments, state governments, federal governments, and schools—make our jobs interesting, exciting, and satisfying. 4. Librarians work in the entire realm of geographical settings. The endless diversity of cities and towns that have libraries—from Honolulu, Hawaii, to Bar Harbor, Maine—make our jobs interesting, exciting, and satisfying. **YES**, when you really come down to it, there are very few jobs that can match librarianship for variety, interest, excitement, and satisfaction. How many other professions offer the kinds of career options that we librarians enjoy? It's mind boggling to contemplate what we have to choose from. We can get a cutting edge job as a computer services librarian in Silicon Valley, an information broker on Wall Street, or a job as a storyteller on Main and Oak. **WHEN** I got out of library school I decided that I wanted something in upper management in a public library in the San Diego area that would pay in the neighborhood of thirty to thirty-five thousand dollars a year. Sure my expectations were high but I felt confident. Unlike a lot of my classmates who had frittered away their spare change on frivolities like food, I saved my money for a trip to the annual conference of the American Library Association, where I would take full advantage of the A.L.A. Placement Service. Yes, participating in this service would give me the inside track to getting a head start into an interesting, exciting, and satisfying career. **ME** and 3,000 other job seekers. As soon as I saw the A.L.A. Placement Center **I knew I was in trouble**. It was not the intimate, club like environment that I had anticipated. Actually it looked more like a barn, a place where cows are sorted and housed—a stockyard. Here's how it went: **DAY 1:** The first thing they do is give you a number. You register and they give you a number. You then consult their job opportunity books and when you see a job you write down your number on an interest card and turn the card in to the person working at the desk. I was appalled by the impersonality of it all and frightened by the sheer numbers of people involved. Just to get an indentification number I had to stand in line for an hour and fifteen minutes during which time I discovered that everyone else was looking for the same job I was—big pay, lots of responsibility, loads of upward mobility, a warm climate, and a nearby ocean which probably explains why the page in the job notebook for a high paying management position in a San Diego area public library was tattered with the wear and tear of excessive use by the time I got to it. **SO** what if 500 other librarians were applying for this job? I still had confidence that I could talk my way into it. Forget the fact that I had no experience and that I was still three months away from getting my M.L.S. I just knew the folks from San Diego would recognize talent when they saw it. So, undaunted by the hopelessness of the whole situation   ★★★page 53★★★

and confident that some mysterious metaphysical force was just ready to go to work for me, I filled out an interest card with my hotel phone number, stuck it in the in-basket, and rushed back to my room to await the call.   *4:30 PM* I was back in my room and had hunkered myself down right next to the telephone. Not wanting to appear too eager, I made a solemn resolve to wait until the third or fourth ring to answer it.   *5:00 PM* No calls yet. I really wanted to take a shower but was petrified that I would miss my call.   *7:30 PM* I was now certain that the folks from San Diego had decided to take a break from their busy schedule and have dinner. No doubt over dinner they had begun the laborious process of discussing all the message cards and résumés that they had received at the Placement Center. That was obviously the reason why their dinner was lasting so long and why they were taking so long to call. By now, however, they were returning to their hotel rooms in order to call their top candidates. No doubt my phone would be ringing very soon.   *9:30 PM* Still no calls. I was now beginning to conclude that the San Diego people had gone off to Bookbinders to eat and had gotten held up in the inevitable long line of librarians waiting for a table. Bookbinders was a featured restaurant in *L.J.*'s convention guide.   *11:30 PM* This was getting frustrating. By now the San Diego people had finished their dinner and had concluded that I was their top candidate, but they probably thought it would be impolite to call me this late at night.   *11:35 PM* The phone rang. No doubt it was THEM, but I decided to play it cool and not answer it until the fourth ring. The idea was to make them think they had awakened me from a sound sleep. They'd feel guilty and offer me the job without even going through the time consuming formality of an interview. But a very unfunny thing happened. The phone stopped ringing after three rings.   **DAY 2:** *12:05 AM* They had not called back yet, which I decided was good because it gave me time to think about what I would say when they did call. I decided to hold out for $35,000, moving expenses, and a corner office with an ocean view. Actually the ocean view wasn't necessary, but it would give me some wiggle room to negotiate from.   *2:05 AM* They still had not called back. Sure, it was crazy for me to think that they would call this late but then again they had called at 11:35 and that was pretty late and, hey, this was 2:05 AM convention standard time not 2:05 eastern daylight time and there's a big difference.   *7:13 AM* I awakened fully dressed and ready to start the day. I knew it was going to be a good day because the first thing I noticed (other than the fact that I was fully dressed) was that the message light on my telephone was blinking merrily away. No doubt the folks from San Diego had dropped me a line at the main desk after they had failed to reach me last night.   *7:35 AM* "Yes I do have a message for you, Mr. Manley,"

★★★page 54★★★

said the desk clerk, "here it is." I ripped it open. "Will, where were you last night??? I called very late and you weren't in your room. **Hope you have a good explanation**—your wife."   *9:00 AM* Back at the A.L.A. Placement Center, the first thing I did was get in line to wait for the opportunity to ask the person at the desk if any messages have been left for number 1324.   *9:23 AM* No messages had been left for me.   *9:25 AM* Stunned that San Diego was not interested in me (they probably felt threatened by someone as talented as myself), I decided to get in line to wait for the opportunity of looking through the official A.L.A. job opportunity notebook.   *9:47 AM* Standing in line it dawned on me that if San Diego didn't want me I didn't want them, I then decided that I would be willing to take something up the coast in the Bay area. Sure, I'd be moving into a slightly cooler clime, but then San Francisco is everybody's favorite city. I could live with San Francisco.   *9:52 AM* Flipping through the job notebook, I alighted on the perfect job—assistant director of a public library in one of the high tech suburbs just down the peninsula from San Francisco. I couldn't have dreamed of a more ideal situation—a laid-back coastal lifestyle with easy access to the big city. Also this would be more administrative responsibility than the San Diego job had to offer. It would be a perfect way for me to start my library career. With no experience and no degree, a directorship would probably be too much to ask, but an assistantship—that was perfect. Now I knew why my guardian angel did not go to work for me yesterday. **It was God's intention** that I take this job. You can't believe the relief I felt that San Diego had not called. I was bound for the Bay area and couldn't be happier.   *10:03 AM* Dropped my résumé and message card into the Placement Center in-basket and hurried back to the hotel for the fateful call.   *12:30 PM* After watching "Guiding Light," I thought briefly about scooting out for a quick lunch. Nah, I decided, too risky. Best to stay put here by the phone.   *4:30 PM* I came to the difficult conclusion that of all the daytime soaps "As the World Turns" was the most absorbing. Unwed pregnancies, teenagers strung out on drugs, violent marriages, abused children and I'm worried about a phone that won't ring?   *7:30 PM* To eat or not to eat—that was the question. Decided not to eat. **Started fondling the phone** and sweet talking it. Still no rings.   *9:05 PM* In a rush of adrenaline I picked up the phone and very quickly called the main desk just to see if the phone worked. It worked.   *11:35 PM* The phone rang, and this time I picked it up in the middle of the first ring. What a disappointment—it was my wife. "Glad to see that you're in," she said curtly.   **"OH** Lorraine," I countered, "You wouldn't believe how busy I've been with this job search."   **"THEN** you've got some real prospects?" she asked hopefully.   **"WELL**, what's your pick—San Diego or   ★★★page 55★★★

> I don't have any recent administrative experience but in a past life I ran the Library of Congress.

San Francisco?" I replied. "**WILL**, that's fantastic. You've got job offers in San Diego and San Francisco?" "**NOT** exactly job offers. A few details still need to be hammered out—but I'm hopeful." "**THAT'S** great. What do these jobs pay?" "**MID** thirties." "**WHY**, Will, that's a wonderful starting salary for someone with no experience and no degree. I better get off the phone and let you get some sleep. All that interviewing must be grueling." "**THANKS** for being so understanding, Lorraine. I love you." "I love you too, Will. I can't believe it—San Diego or San Francisco and thirty-five thousand dollars to boot. You were right about becoming a librarian. The opportunities are much better than I thought they were. I'm sorry ★★★page 56★★★ I ever doubted you." **DAY 3:** *9:00 AM* I took my place in line on day three with a new resolve. Realizing that I could no longer put all my eggs in one basket, I decided that I had no other alternative but to broaden my search to include less desirable geographical locations. I was determined, however, not to compromise on pay and responsibilities. I still wanted thirty thousand dollars, an ocean view, and administrative duties, but I was now willing to sacrifice the warm climate, which is why I filled out interest cards for administrative positions in Portsmouth, New Hampshire; Portland, Maine; Portsmouth, Virginia; and Portland, Oregon.   **11:30 PM** For the first time in twenty-four hours my phone rang. Was it Portsmouth, Portsmouth, Portland, or Portland? No, of course not. It was Lorraine. "Will," she said, "I can't wait to hear. Are we San Diego or San Francisco bound?" **"RIGHT** now neither," I said.   **"WHAT** do you mean?"   **"WHILE** both situations are on the surface very attractive, I just don't feel good about the chemistry. I don't get the feeling that, you know, I'm really, really wanted, so I've decided to look into other opportunities where someone of my talents would be more deeply appreciated."   **"BUT** you haven't done anything rash like turn them down, have you?" **"NO**, Lorraine, I have most assuredly not turned them down. It's just that I feel it's important for me to consider all possible options and opportunities before I make a final decision. That's why I'm now in touch with people from Portland, Oregon; Portsmouth, New Hampshire; Portland, Maine; and Portsmouth, Virginia. Don't worry, I haven't lowered my standards. These are all administrative jobs paying in the mid-thirties."   **"OH**, Will, I couldn't agree with you more. This is one of the most important decisions you'll ever be faced with and you have to be absolutely certain that you're making the right choice. Plus all those cities sound wonderful. Good luck and get some sleep. You must be exhausted."   **"LORRAINE,** I love you and thanks for being so understanding."   **DAY 4: 9:00 AM** Standing in line after another phoneless and sleepless night and gripped by a vision of returning home jobless, the thought suddenly occurred to me that this was the next to last day that the Placement Center would be open. I won't say that I was overcome by panic, but I was infused by a new sense of urgency. Actually fear might be a more accurate term. I realized it was time to lower my standards again. Forget the ocean view, I told myself. Sun causes skin cancer, sand gets stuck between your toes, and salt water has a harsh and bitter taste. I decided that I would go anywhere in the country for good pay (which I now defined as $25,000 and up) and a reasonable amount of administrative responsibility. **9:13 AM** Thumbing through the Jobs Available notebook, it was immediately apparent to me that there were far fewer pages than there had been the previous three days and it became gradually apparent to me that the only job notices left were for low paying   ★★★page 57★★★

positions in weird places like Jacknife, South Dakota. At first I thought that maybe some greedy, backstabbing library school student had stolen all the good job notices. **"WHY** has the size of the Jobs Available notebook shrunk?" I asked the attendant at the Placement Service Desk. **"BECAUSE** many of those jobs have already been filled," she replied matter of factly and then added, "about the only ones left are the warm body jobs." **"WHAT'S a warm body job?"** I asked naïvely. **"A** job that is so bad that they're just happy to find a warm body to fill it." *9:30 AM* By now panic had definitely set in. I flipped frantically back and forth in the notebook between Jacknife, South Dakota (cataloging—$12,000), South Chicago Heights, Illinois (reference—$11,500), Wheatley, Nebraska (children's—$10,300), and Gravel Point, Texas (reference—$10,000). That was as low as I would go. There was no way that I would ever consider taking a job for less than a five figure salary—absolutely no way. Not only did I owe it to myself but I owed it to my profession not to succumb to slave wages. *9:45 AM* I had just finished filling out interest cards for Jacknife, South Chicago Heights, Wheatley, and Gravel Point when the desk attendant approached and took two more pages out of the notebook. **"WHICH** ones are those?" I asked her. **"JACKNIFE** and South Chicago Heights," she replied all too cheerfully. *1:00 PM* After hanging around my hotel room and waiting for the phone to ring for another two and a half hours, I decided that at this late stage of the game the best strategy might be to hang around the Placement Center and keep checking to see if any messages had been left for me there. *3:00 PM* "Are there any messages for number 1725?" I asked the desk attendant for the thirteenth time in an hour and forty-five minutes. **"NO**, sir, but if a message does come in for that number, I'll let you know immediately." *4:45 PM* Just as I was beginning to abandon all hope of ever becoming a working librarian, a slim and balding man approached me and said, "The desk attendant told me that you are number 1725." **"YES**," I responded eagerly, "I am number 1725. My name is Will Manley." **"I'M** very happy to meet you," he said. "My name is Harold Doaks and I am the director of the Wheatley Public Library in Wheatley, Nebraska." **"I** understand you're looking for a children's librarian," I said enthusiastically. **"YES**, I need a children's librarian," he said almost desperately. "Can you tolerate children eight hours a day?" **"I** love children!" I said. **"I** hate them!" he responded and then after an awkward pause added, "That's why I'm looking for a children's librarian. My library is really not big enough to support two professionals but since I will have nothing to do with children I need a children's librarian. You want the job?" **"WELL**, I'd have to talk it over with my wife, but yes, I'm definitely inter-

★★★page 58★★★   ested." **"THE** job is yours, but before you take

it you need to know a few things. Wheatley is a jerkwater 'do nothing' town; it's two hundred miles from the nearest city, Lincoln, which is a 'do nothing' city; the public school system is a joke; and the library building is eighty-seven years old. Most librarians don't last more than six months, but the last one stayed for eight, and oh yeah, the government did some atomic testing twenty miles west of Wheatley during the '50s. A lot of people in Wheatley have contracted leukemia. Still want to come?" "**WHAT'S** the salary?" "**Ten**-three." "**I'LL** take it." "**WHEN** can you start?" "**THE** fourth week of August." "**I** can't wait that long." "**BUT** I don't get my M.L.S. until August 21." "**LOOK**, I don't care if you have an M.L.S. or not." "**BUT** I do. I don't want my career to begin and end in Wheatley." "**SORRY**, but I need someone right away." "**BUT** you're not exactly in a position where you can be choosy." "**I** still have one other candidate from California. A woman with an M.L.S. and ten years of experience." "**WITH** those qualifications why would she take an entry level children's job?" "**BECAUSE** she just got out of prison." "**WHAT** was she in for?" "**MANSLAUGHTER**. She killed her husband." **DAY 5:** *3:00 AM* After taking a sleeping pill, counting sheep, and reading the Book of Deuteronomy and still finding myself wide awake, I grudgingly came to the conclusion that nothing was going to sedate me short of **a spinal anesthetic**, which actually seemed like not such a bad idea because in addition to putting me to sleep it would also ease the pain of being aced out of a fifth rate job in a jerkwater town by an ex-convict. How was I going to explain any of this to Lorraine? *9:00 AM* If you've never been to the final day of the A.L.A. Placement Service just reflect back to your high school days and think of all the people at the Saturday night post-football game dances whom no one would dance with. Put all those people in one room and you've got a good picture of the A.L.A. Placement Center on day five. It's a **study in wallflowers and geeks**—a kind of professional lonelyhearts club. **BELIEVE** me, it does a lot for your ego to be in such exalted company. Of course, as I looked around the room I instantly realized there were some definite advantages to this situation, not the least of which was that it was pretty obvious that the quality of my competition had greatly diminished from what it was on day one. **AFTER** standing in line for a few minutes and talking to my fellow sufferers, I came to the conclusion that day fivers were generally of five types—a) people with no degree and no experience (like me), b) people with some personal skeletons in their closets (like the woman who had been in prison for manslaughter), c) people with some professional skeletons in their closets (like the man standing in front of me who had been caught stealing books from his previous library), d) people with poor employment records (like the woman standing next to me who had been fired from three of her last four jobs), and e) people with dysfunctional personalities (like the "warm body" standing in back of me who seemed capable of speaking in only one word sentences).   *9:13 AM* Another observation about day five at the Placement Center that I made after leafing through the remains of the Jobs Available notebook was that the remaining employers at the Center were almost as undesirable as the remaining job candidates. They were offering low salaried (under ten grand) dead-end jobs (how does assistant original cataloger grab you) in awful places (mostly decayed urban jungles). Picking through these job opportunities was like trying to find a decent automobile at Richard Nixon's Used Car Lot.   *9:45 AM* I had come to the definite conclusion that I did not want to become a librarian if it meant working in any of the places left—Bronx, New York; Newark, New Jersey; or South Central Los Angeles. But wait a minute. There was one other possibility—Hammond, Indiana. The public library there was looking for a reference librarian at $7,600 a year, which had the distinction of being the lowest salary of all the jobs listed that year in the Placement Center—but really, what's money when you can live in paradise? Be honest, when you hear the word Indiana, what do you think of? Churches with tall steeples, barber shops on Main Street, corn fields, clapboard farm houses, and basketball hoops on every garage. It is the state where family values were invented. You ever wonder why Dan Quayle was so bent out of shape by Murphy Brown's baby? The answer is simple. Dan Quayle was born and raised in Indiana. Of course, Indiana is not for everyone, but for a young married man like me with a nine-month-old son, a better place was hard to imagine, especially when you thought about Newark and the Bronx.   *12:30 PM* The Placement Center officially closed at noon, but the director of the Hammond Public Library met with me in the little conference room adjacent to the center to talk about his job. He was a very nice man who was willing to let me finish my M.L.S. before starting work. The only thing he said that took me somewhat aback was "If you can't find anything suitable in the way of housing in Hammond there are some alternatives in the outlying areas."   **"I'M** sure that my wife and son and I will love Hammond," I responded.   *11:30 PM* My wife was at the airport gate to meet me with our little boy, David, in her arms. "So Will," she asked before even giving me a kiss, "where are we headed—San Diego, San Francisco, Portland, or Portsmouth?" **"HAMMOND,"** I answered enthusiastically.   **"WHERE'S** that?" **"IN** Indiana—a perfect place to raise David."   *11 Months Later* It was just as I was putting the last box into the U-Haul trailer when my wife said, "This is one move that I have no sad feelings about. In fact I feel like as soon as we ★★★page 60★★★   clear the Hammond city line my life will begin anew. No, it's even more basic than that—I feel like I'll be able to breathe again for the first time in eleven months." "OH, it hasn't been that bad here," I retorted.   "NO, not if you compare it to the tidal wave that killed 50,000 people in Bangladesh last week."   "SO our car got stolen. So our house got broken into. So our son's crib was taken. So one of our next door neighbors was a drug dealer and the other one was a pimp. So our roof caught on fire on the 4th of July when one of the kids in the neighborhood shot a Roman candle on it. So you were mugged on your way home from the corner drugstore. So our son's best friend has **a snake tatoo** on his back. I'm telling you, Lorraine, this year has been an education. We'll remember it for the rest of our lives."

Safe Sex the *L.J.* Way

ONE of the real treasures of our profession is *Library Journal*. Issue after issue since its inception back in 1876, it has formed a valuable record of librarianship. You're probably going to think I'm weird, but one of my favorite pastimes when I'm in my local university library is to head for the subterranean periodical room (two floors down), weave my way through the Byzantine rows of old steel shelves that sag wearily from the burden of supporting thousands of volumes of periodicals, and head for the big, black, bound volumes of *Library Journal*.   I like the room because it is a throwback to the pre-Rom days when we librarians spent a goodly amount of our book budgets on binding together a year's collection of each periodical title that we subscribed to. Redolent with the fragrance of dusty buckram book covers and stitched bindings, the ambience of the place is perfect for the kind of historical research that I like to do.   **THERE'S** a special feeling that you get from holding a vintage 1888 magazine in your hand that you do not get from scanning a cathode ray screen. The magazine is not just a source of information, it's an actual historical artifact. The typeface, the page lay-out, the quality of the paper, and the design of the cover give the kind of subtle clues about a time period that you cannot glean from a CD-Rom print-out.   **BUT** more than that, the accumulation of all those volumes of *L.J.* lined up side by side serve as an impressive and useful visual reminder of the deep historical roots of librarianship. It's an important lesson for us to learn today with our pessimistic proclivity to talk about our profession as a kind of bibliographic blacksmith trade soon to be automated out of existence.   **WHEN** you spend time browsing through those dusty but not dreary volumes you soon realize that the issues that we are so concerned about today—free vs. fee, quality vs. trash, and a.v. vs. print—have been kicked around and debated for years, decades, and even centuries. It's an   ★★★page 61★★★

important point that many of our professional pontificators ("we stand on the precipice of change") need to learn.   **THE** current editorial staff members of *L.J.* obviously believe that they have a responsibility to provide contemporary librarians with this historical perspective because in the past few years they have regularly reprinted a number of their older articles under the heading "L.J. Classics." While most of these articles deal with timeless issues of librarianship, lately the editors have been running the original *L.J.* reviews of books that were once obscure but are now classics.   **THIS** has been of great interest and value because it gives us a retrospective look at how well *L.J.*'s reviews hold up over time. Another important benefit is that these review reprints remind us that over the past century *L.J.* has created a comprehensive record of literary evaluation. You might say that's nice as a historical record, but what real value does it have for the practicing librarian of today?   **ACTUALLY** these reprints are useful for several reasons. First they show librarians the value of taking chances on the unknown writer or the first novelist. It's hard to believe now, for example, but in 1957 John Updike was a nobody. Why spend money on a nobody? The answer is obvious. Nobodies in the world of literature often become great authors, and it's always been to *L.J.*'s credit that its editorial staff has consistently given special attention to the nobodies. In fact *L.J.* often does feature articles on first novelists. It's a great service for librarians as well as authors.   **THE** other value of the reprints is that they remind us of the comprehensive literary record that *L.J.* has built over the past century. The important aspect of this record is that it is designed specifically with the librarian in mind. *L.J.* reviewers, in addition to evaluating the literary or informational merit of a book, also comment on the appropriateness of the book for libraries of varying sizes from a cost and community standards approach. Because *L.J.* is sensitive to the special concerns of librarians, the *L.J.* review often becomes the source of first referral with regards to books that have intellectual freedom implications. When the censors show up, the first thing that most librarians do is reach for the *L.J.* review because of the respect that *L.J.* has among library boards, school boards, and city councils.   **IT** is for all of these reasons that *L.J.*'s decision in November of 1992 not to review Madonna's *Sex* was both puzzling and disappointing. In explaining their decision the editorial staff wrote, "We got a chance to examine the book along with everyone else, after October 21. Had we reviewed it, our review would have come out weeks after the general media reviews and too late to be useful to acquisitions librarians. So we decided, like many libraries, **to abstain from *Sex*.**"   **THIS** rationalization, of course, was deceitful. It was as deceitful as the rationalizations that many librarians concocted to ★★★page 62★★★   either justify getting or not getting the book. Those who bought the book talked about its status as a bestseller and those who didn't get the book pointed to its impractical spiral binding, its sharp metal covers, its susceptibility to theft, and its high price. **NO** one talked about making the decision on the basis of what the book was about. No one talked about whether the book had anything important to offer the library or the patron in terms of content. No one talked about the way the book was written and illustrated in its attempt to explore the outer ranges of human sexuality. The dialog in the library profession over the book, therefore, was a bogus one because it politely skirted the main issue. I'm not sure what was more dominant in this sad chapter of librarianship—cowardice or hypocrisy, but I am certain that *Library Journal* abdicated its traditional role of leadership by refusing to take a stand one way or the other on one of the biggest controversies to hit the profession in some time. **THE** irony, of course, is that *L.J.*, by not taking a stand, did in fact take a very influential stand. One of the false excuses many librarians used in deciding not to make a decision one way or another on the book was that they were going to wait and see what *L.J.* had to say about the matter. *L.J.*'s ultimate decision to ignore the book, therefore simply served to validate the proclivity of many in the profession to procrastinate and let the book go out of stock and out of print thus relieving them of the responsibility of making a decision. **PERHAPS** the most appalling aspect to the article in which *L.J.* shamelessly **celebrated its celibacy** from *Sex* was the fact that in the article a number of librarians who had made decisions not to purchase it were quoted extensively. *L.J.*, in effect, seemed to be saying, "See, others have decided to abstain, so we're going to abstain also." *L.J.* the leader had officially become *L.J.* the follower. **APPARENTLY** a number of librarians complained about this journalistic cowardice because a few months later a very interesting editorial showed up in *School Library Journal*. The editorial was an impassioned attack on Warner, the company that had published Madonna's book. By criticizing Warner for not sending out advance copies of *Sex* to the standard reviewing journals, *S.L.J.* was in essence defending its sister publication for not reviewing the book. What was outrageous about this editorial was that *S.L.J.* had the nerve to brand Warner a censor and suggest that *L.J.* was the chief victim of this censorship! **BUT** the hypocrisy of the editorial did not end there. *S.L.J.* went on to criticize those librarians who bought the book and thereby rolled over "for a publisher's cynical precensorship selling campaign." Buying the book, therefore, according to the editorial was "not a celebration of the freedom to read. Quite the reverse. It supports the notion that censorship is O.K. when it's a marketing strategy." **SO** if you're keeping score, Warner is a censor, librarians who bought *Sex* are censors, and *L.J.* is a champion of intellectual

We didn't get Madonna's new book because she just wrote it to make money.

freedom. I don't think that I have ever seen or ever will see a more blatant bit of hypocrisy in a library periodical. **BUT** in all fairness, near the end of the editorial a solid point is made. Those of us who are responsible for selecting books for adult collections are condescendingly urged to "check the reviews" before we submit to a greedy publisher's media manipulation. I'm not sure if it ever occurred to the editorialist, but there are magazines and journals besides *L.J.*

and *S.L.J.* that publish reviews. And guess what? Somehow, many of these magazines (actually most of them) managed to run reviews of *Sex*. **HOW** does *L.J.* explain that?

Mom, Mozelle, and Me

I grew up in a brown clapboard house across the street from a red brick schoolhouse. We knew all our neighbors, their kids, their dogs, and their hamsters. People left their houses unlocked, their windows open, and their cars unattended. Milk was delivered to the back door and the newspaper was tucked neatly under the welcome mat of the front door. Everyone had a garden, and everyone bragged about their tomatoes. Boys played baseball, and girls jumped rope. Fathers went to work carrying briefcases, and mothers stayed home and baked cookies. It was a wonderful life. At least I thought it was a wonderful life until I met Mozelle. **EVERY** day at noon when I came home to the brown clapboard house for lunch, my mother would ask, "What happened today?" I would always reply, "Nothing." This, I think, reassured my mother. Although I am sure that she would have enjoyed a more descriptive account of my school activities, I'm equally sure that she was probably relieved to know that "nothing" had happened. Mothers like their children to lead **safe and boring lives.** **DAY** after day this lunchtime conversation was repeated for at least three years, and then Mozelle showed up one Wednesday morning to help my mother clean the brown clapboard house. She had come to us highly recommended by a woman down the street. How good was Mozelle with a broom and a mop? I really don't know—eight year old boys are not good judges of that sort of thing. **BUT** what I did know right from the start was that Mozelle was unlike anyone I had ever met. She ate lunch with us every Wednesday, and the treat was all ours because Mozelle's true vocation in life was obviously conversation. She was a non-stop talker with an opinion on everything and an observation for all occasions, but her best subject by far was her husband, Hubie. **HE** was a cook on a merchant marine ship and our Wednesday lunches quickly became a long running adventure series entitled "Hubie on the High Seas." One week we would be regaled with Hubie's adventures in Singapore and the next week we would hear of his adventures in Hong Kong. The cities and ports would change but the hero always remained the same, and it soon became clear to me that Hubie was **the key to America's power** around the world. **IN** time, though, I began to have mixed feelings about Mozelle. Sure, I loved her ability to take me to worlds far beyond my brown clapboard house and my red brick elementary school, but I now felt inadequate. My "nothing happened" conversations would no longer do, especially on Wednesdays when Mozelle was the one asking me the question about ★★★page 65★★★

what I had done that morning. Obviously dissatisfied with my "nothing" response, she would look at me with exasperation and exclaim, "Well, something must have happened!" I hated disappointing her, but the truth was "nothing ever happened"—at least nothing that would interest a woman whose husband was a modern day re-creation of Long John Silver.   I began to resent the snug security of my small-town life and all its simple pleasures and found myself waking up each morning hoping desperately for something dramatic to happen. Perhaps there would be a great fire at school or maybe Miss Francis, my fourth grade teacher, would have a heart attack during math class, or better yet Dogdirt Dorman would get into a bloody fistfight with Frankie D'Angelo on the playground. But alas, nothing would happen. **IT** was after several months of unfounded hopes, that I began to be tempted by the lure of exaggeration, which at the time I thought was a nice word for lying but which, ten years later in English Composition 101, I discovered was actually an art form dignified by a fancy name— "hyperbole." Looking back at my first crude attempts at hyperbole, I would have to admit that I was not much of an artist.   **MY** early exaggerations were far too heavy-handed and egocentric. They usually involved me in superhuman feats of athletic heroism. One week I would claim to have hit a softball six hundred feet in the air and the next week I would claim to have run the one-hundred-yard dash in eight seconds. Both feats, by the way, were world records—quite an accomplishment for an eight-year-old boy.   **THE** true significance of my athletic prowess, however, was completely lost upon my mother and Mozelle. To my great frustration I discovered that neither woman had sufficient enough knowledge of sports history to appreciate just how special my accomplishments were. In a word, they were unimpressed. My hyperbolizing had completely missed its mark.   **CONSEQUENTLY** I decided to shift into a disaster mode. By twisting a few facts and fabricating a few small details, I discovered that I could turn a damp and slippery school lavatory floor into a full scale flood replete with **bursting pipes and drowning kindergarteners.** This was more effective. While I unwound my tales of fires, floods, and rodent invasions (one week I claimed that two thousand white mice had taken over the school cafeteria), Mozelle would listen with complete fascination—at least she gave me the impression that she believed everything I said and hung on my every word with rapt curiosity.   **MY** mother, on the other hand, was more subdued. While I talked she would wander around the kitchen putting things away. Her indifferent disbelief, however, was not strong enough to damper my enthusiasm for hyperbole. Mozelle was all the audience I needed. Her alternating shrieks of delight and horror fueled my creative energies and turned me into the world's biggest hyperbolist. Even

Mozelle's Hubie stories paled in comparison with my own manufactured tales of wonder.   **ONE** of the unfortunate aspects of all of this youthful storytelling is that even now—thirty-five years later—my mother remains inherently skeptical whenever I open my mouth and start moving my lips. I would be quite surprised if she believes even half of what I have to tell her during our weekly telephone chats.   **IT** was with this acute sense of skepticism that she read *Unprofessional Behavior,* a book of mine that was published several years ago. "Will," she said, "I won't say that I didn't enjoy the book but really when you wrote the book did you think you were back in the fourth grade telling stories to Mozelle in our kitchen? Believe me, Will, she's the only person alive who will believe all those outrageous stories about what goes on in public libraries."   **"MOM,"** I replied, "librarians believe those stories because they've seen it all themselves. **Weird things happen** all the time in libraries. Our world is a real jungle. Everybody thinks that all we do is sit around and read, but nothing could be further from the truth."   **"DO** you mean to tell me that the story about the man who tried to get the horse that his daughter won in the summer reading program to sit down in the back seat of his car was true?"   **"SURE** it was true, Mom."   **"AND** Will, that story about the old woman who got hysterical every day because she thought your catalogers were staring into her bedroom was true?"   **"YES**, Mom, it was true."   **"WELL,** I say it's all very strange—very strange indeed."   **"MOM,** could you hold for a minute? There's a man at my office door."   **"WILL,** are you there?"   **"YES,** Mom."   **"WHAT** did the man want?"   **"HE** wanted to give me some papers. It seems that in my capacity of library director I'm being sued by somebody for two million dollars."   **"GOOD** heavens, Will, what did you do?"   **"ACCORDING** to the plaintiff, I prevented a library employee from testifying at the plaintiff's jaywalking trial."   **"WILL,** now stop putting me on! I'm your mother. Don't kid me about something like that!"   **"I'M** not kidding you, Mom. I've just been sued for two million dollars."   **"A** likely story, Will. A likely story."

Mr. Suspenders

THE most talked about statistic from my now infamous "Librarians and Sex" survey (the one that appeared in the June 1992 issue of *Wilson Library Bulletin* and which got me fired from my job as a regular columnist, a position which I had held for twelve delightful years) was the finding that 78% of the respondees reported that they at some point in their careers had been sexually harassed by a library patron. Although the 78% figure was much higher than I had imagined. I knew from my days as a reference librarian that sexual harassment by patrons is not an unusual phenomenon.   **IT'S**   ★★★page 67★★★

more like an epidemic that is raging out of control. There are several theories why this situation seems to be on the increase. The first has to do with the fact that the trend today is to **mainstream mental patients** into society rather than warehouse them in institutions. Where do mainstreamed mental patients often end up eight hours a day? That's right—in public libraries where they spend at least part of their time preying upon staff and patrons. **ANOTHER** theory is that our society has, for any number of reasons, turned nasty—too many guns, too many drugs, too much unemployment, and too few parents around. For whatever reasons, old-fashioned notions of politeness, civility, and manners have been replaced by a new "in your face, eat garbage and like it" attitude towards government workers. After twelve years of Republican presidents spreading the doctrine that government is the problem not the solution and that government workers are pigs at the public trough, it is no wonder that those of us who work in the public sector are routinely treated with contempt by angry taxpayers. A third theory pins the problem on the growing number of homeless people in America. We all know that the public library, more than any other agency of society, serves as home for the homeless. Because these people tend to be **unsightly and unpleasant** to be around, they are easy targets to blame all our social problems on. **WHILE** the homeless may serve as wonderful scapegoats for what is wrong in America today, I'm not sure that they deserve all the opprobrium that we heap upon them, and I say this as someone who is as guilty as the next guy for judging the homeless on the basis of their sight, smell, and sounds. My own consciousness raising happened last year shortly after I learned of the violent murder of a public librarian in a neighboring city. **THE** name of the woman who was murdered was Kay Blanton and the horror of her fate (she was stabbed thirty times with a paring knife by a patron who had allegedly harassed her in the past) forced me to think the unthinkable—that something as awful could possibly happen in my own library. My first thought was to institute a zero tolerance policy against sexual harassment by library patrons. "No one," I said to my employees at the next monthly staff meeting, "should have to endure the humiliation and fear of being sexually harassed by a library patron. From now on we need to wage war on those individuals who feel that they can verbally, visually, or physically abuse our staff. The first thing we need to do is identify all those individuals who harass employees on an ongoing basis." **NATURALLY** a task force was formed and a week later I was given a list of our local harassers. The first thing I noted about the list was that it was made up entirely of nicknames—Mr. Suspenders, Highpockets, Muscleman, Steel Buns, Jelly Belly, and Mr. Rodeo Drive. "We use nicknames," I was told by one of the committee members, "because we have no way of knowing what their real names are since they never check out books." I immediately assumed, therefore, that everyone on the list was homeless. "Look," I said to the committee, "the next time any of these

You say you were sexually harassed by a patron? What did you do to turn him on?

bums on this list bothers anyone, bring in the security guard and, if the security guard is not around, give me a call and I'll come right down and handle the situation."   **TWO** days later my phone rang. It was one of my reference librarians. "Will," she said, "Mr. Suspenders is cruising the library with a hand mirror, and he's using it to **look up women's dresses**."   "**I'LL** be right down," I said in an urgent voice. As I hurried down the stairs to the reference room I pictured myself picking this bum up by the scruff of his unshaven neck and pushing him and his sleeping bag and knapsack out the door with a dramatic flourish. The library would be rid of one more undesirable drifter. **BUT** when I bounded in to the reference department I saw no homeless people milling about. The librarian who had called me pointed in the direction of Mr. Suspenders. "He's over there," she said. **"WHERE?"** I responded very confused. **"RIGHT** over there. See him lurking behind the McGraw-Hill *Encyclopedia of Art?"* **"NO,** I don't." **"DON'T** you see that man kneeling on the floor pretending to look at the books on the bottom row of shelving?" **"YES,** I see him, but that can't be Mr. Suspenders," I said emphatically. **"WHY** not?" she asked with great confusion. **"BECAUSE** that man kneeling on the floor is wearing a nice, expensive business suit with an impressive Italian tie and he's even got a beeper attached to his belt. **Peepers don't wear beepers.** Now where is Mr. Suspenders?" **"THAT** *is* Mr. Suspenders. Don't you see the suspenders he's wearing?" **"BUT** this man can't possibly be homeless." **"WHOEVER** said he was homeless?" **"NOBODY,"** I said reflectively. "I guess I just assumed he was of that ilk." **"NONE** of the people on our pervert list are homeless," she countered. "You shouldn't jump to conclusions. Now are you going to go talk to him or not?" **"SURE,** sure," I said skeptically, "but first let me watch him for a while just to make sure that he really is harassing people. I really have to catch him in the act before I can warn him." I didn't think such a respectable looking person could be the deviate that my staff had made him out to be. I'd have to see it to believe it. **"FINE,"** said the reference librarian chuckling to herself. "It won't take you long. The only research Mr. Suspenders is doing is in the area of female anatomy." **TO** get a closer look at the supposed perpetrator, I walked down an adjacent aisle and all the while pretended that I was searching for a particular book. I now felt like a voyeur—cheap and vulgar. What was I doing spying on this perfectly respectable person? I hoped he didn't think that I was trying to pick him up. That was my fear—that he would report *me* to the police for harassing *him.* **BUT** then a shocking thing happened. I got close enough to Mr. Suspenders to get a good look at his face. Nothing could have surprised me more. Mr. Suspenders was actually Mr. Hubert Foxwoolley, leader of the choir at Our Lady of Perpetual Peace parish (where I attend church every week with my family) and a prominent member of the local Republican Party. **I** quickly walked back to my reference librarian and, with a big look of relief on my face, said, "No need to worry. Mr. Suspenders is actually Mr. Hubert Foxwoolley, a good Roman Catholic and Republican." **BUT** just as I was saying the word "Republican" the reference librarian who had been looking over my shoulder toward Mr. Suspenders suddenly interrupted me and said, "Quick, turn around and look at Mr. Suspenders now." I spun around and looked. There was Mr. ★★★page 70★★★ Hubert Foxwoolley looking up the dress of a middle-aged woman with the help of a shiny new hand mirror. I was mortified. **WORSE** yet, Mr. Foxwoolley looked at me looking at him looking up this woman's dress. The die was cast. I had to deal with the problem. Everyone on the reference staff expected it. Mr. Foxwoolley, of course, escaped into the jungle of the non-fiction collection. I followed him and found him looking quite innocently through a book on Japanese gardening. "**MR.** Foxwoolley," I said tentatively, "I think we know each other." "**LOOK**," said Mr. Foxwoolley, "you've got the wrong man. I saw you looking at me and I have to tell you that I am not gay." "**THAT'S** not why I was looking at you," I said. "Do you know that you have created the impression among the library staff that the sole reason that you come into the library is to, how should I say this, look at women?" "**WHAT** nonsense," retorted Mr. Foxwoolley. "You're just saying that because you're mad at me for not being gay like you." "**LOOK** Mr. Foxwoolley, we know what you're doing and we're watching you all the time. We are also going to make sure that our security staff monitors your every move in this library." With that, Mr. Foxwoolley got up and left and never came back. **ABOUT** the only time I see him now is when he sings with the church choir. He does a beautiful rendition of "Ave Maria."

The Most Controversial Book in Library History

THE biggest irony about my termination as a columnist from the *Wilson Library Bulletin* after twelve years of writing monthly articles was the unwritten assumption from Wilson management that my survey on the subject of sex and librarians was an inappropriate subject for a library trade journal. Haven't they ever heard of the censorship controversies centering around *Show Me, Where Do I Come From, The Joy of Sex, The New Joy of Sex, The Joy of Gay Sex, Playboy Magazine, Heather Has Two Mommies, Gloria Goes to Gay Pride,* and Madonna's *Sex*? Where have these people been living? What professional associations do they belong to? What conferences have they been attending? **THE** fact is, unless you eliminate such obvious candidates as moral theology, sex therapy, urology, or gynecology, there are very few professional disciplines that are forced to deal with sexual issues as much as librarianship. Not only are we librarians charged with the responsibility of providing a diverse array of information on sexual subjects to a diverse array of clients, but we are also constantly finding ourselves caught in the crossfire of the various religious and political factions who are waging war against each other in the arena of sexual politics. **YOU** name the issue—gay rights, reproductive rights, abortion rights, family values—and we've had to deal with it. You ★★★page 71★★★

name the group—Feminists Against Pornography, the Moral Majority, the National Organization for Women, Queer Nation, The Eagle Forum, Citizens for the American Way, Pro-Choice, Right to Life—and we've been challenged by them. Either we're doing too much or too little. It's a no win situation that is made even more difficult by the fact that our policies and decisions have to be forged and defended under the white hot light of media scrutiny.   **OF** all the sexual wars that have been fought in Libraryland, however, none has lasted as long or has been as hotly contested as the fracas over one simple twenty-nine page children's book—*Daddy's Roommate*. Produced by Alyson Publications in Boston, the book is directed toward children who have a homosexual parent, in this specific case a gay father. The text is simply written and startlingly straightforward. The entire book contains less than 100 words. The illustrations are so plain and modestly drawn that they seem almost primitive. At first glance it is the last book you would ever expect to trigger a major censorship controversy. Appearances, however, are often deceiving, and this book over the years has proven to pack ten times the punch of Madonna's X-rated pictorial celebration of eclectic erotic fantasies. Taxpayers have gotten so upset about *Daddy's Roommate* that they have organized campaigns to vote down funding referendums for libraries that keep the book in their collections.   **THE** story itself is a simple one that involves a boy whose parents get a divorce. Daddy moves out and sets up housekeeping with Frank, his gay roommate. Illustrations show Frank and Daddy working in the yard, eating dinner, going to the beach, watching television, and even arguing and making up. It's a typical conjugal relationship, one that is depicted as boring as your next-door neighbors' forty-year-old marriage. Even the picture of Frank and Daddy sleeping together is demure and wholesome (they're turned away from each other).   **THE** relationship seems so tame that if the book didn't come right out and say that "Daddy and Frank are gay" and that "Being gay is just one more kind of love," you would think that Daddy and Frank might be brothers, cousins, or maybe even college roommates. There are no depictions of sex acts and no descriptions of sexual feelings. The book goes out of its way to be almost puritanical. Talk about family values, this book is loaded with them. It's overflowing with love, warmth, understanding, and concern. We get the sense that the little boy in the story is safe, secure, and very, very loved.   **WHY** the controversy then? That's a good question—one that I haven't quite figured out. With its emphasis on love, affection, and caring, the book projects a message that is far more constructive than the messages portrayed by 99% of the cartoons that are presented on Saturday morning television. The problem, I guess, is that the love, affection, and caring in the book come from gay ★★★page 72★★★   people, and there is a fairly sizable portion of the

American population (remember Pat Buchanan's speech to the 1992 Republican National Convention) who feel that **gay people are the evil harbingers** of the decline of Western civilization. **WHAT** probably really rankles the homophobe community about the book is that the two gay men are not only nurturing and sensitive but that they also appear normal in every outward respect. They're simply too boring and average. If they had been depicted with shaved heads and wearing leather outfits highlighted by neckchains and body tattoos, that probably would have been acceptable. Gay people, after all, aren't supposed to look like everybody else, are they? They have to look sinister and perverted. **WHEN** all the flack about the book started reaching the library media, I dreaded the moment when my day would come. Surely someone in my conservative Arizona community would sooner or later come forward and accuse me of endangering the morals of our city's young people by having the book in our children's collection. I hate censorship squabbles in general, but absolutely detest them when they are based on the self-righteous hatred of an oppressed minority group. **SO** in anticipation of this dreaded day I began to marshall the arguments that I would use to defend the book's purchase. Fortunately this was not difficult. The book is very defensible on several fronts. First, it has received excellent reviews from the major library trade publications; second, it fills a real informational void in the youth library; and third, it is written and illustrated in a non-provocative way. I was ready to stand my ground, comfortable with the cogency of my defense. **SURE** enough, eight months after *Daddy's Roommate* first appeared on our children's room shelf, I got the proverbial knock on my door. "Will, there's someone here to see you about a book in the children's room," said my secretary ominously. **"SEND** her in, please." **"MR.** Manley, I have a concern." **"HOW** can I be of help?" I responded noticing that, yes indeed, this serious-looking, middle-aged woman was carrying the library's copy of *Daddy's Roommate*. I braced myself for a lecture on the decline and fall of Western civilization. **"MR.** Manley, I am not sure that you are aware of it, but you are carrying a book in your children's department that can be detrimental to the minds of young children." **"WHAT'S** the book?" I asked innocently. **"HERE** it is," she said placing the slim, little volume gingerly onto my desk like it was **a bomb ready to go off**. **"OH**, yes, *Daddy's Roommate*. I am familiar with this title." **"YOU'RE** familiar with this title," she said with indignation rising in her voice, "and you allow it to be on your children's shelves? I can't believe you would be so irresponsible." **"WHAT** is it you object to about the book?" **"REALLY**, do you have to ask? Don't you recognize the dangers of sexual stereotyping when you see it?" **"MAYBE** you're the one with the dangerous sexual stereotype," I said ★★★page 73★★★

deciding that the best defense is a good offense.   "**I** resent that, I really do. What are you? Some kind of sexist?"   "**I** resent that. What are you? Some kind of homophobe?"   **"HOMOPHOBE**? What could possibly prompt you to call me that?"   **"WELL**, what could possibly prompt you to call me a sexist?"   **"OPEN** the book to page 24," she instructed.   "**I** don't get it," I said turning to page 24.   **"WHAT'S** wrong with the picture on page 24?" she asked. I was sure that was the page showing Frank and Daddy in bed together.   **"YOU** must have the wrong page number," I said with confusion. Page 24 contained a simple illustration of the boy talking to his mother. They are in a kitchen setting and the mother is making a cake. "There is nothing in the least bit offensive about this picture," I said.   **"LOOK** closer," she persisted.   **"ARE** you sure this is the illustration you object to?" I asked incredulously.   **"YES**, can't you see it?"   **"SEE** what for goodness sakes?"   **"THE** sexual stereotyping!"   **"NO**, I don't see it."   **"LOOK closer.** I can't believe you're this insensitive."   "**I** still don't get it."   **"WHAT** is the mother doing? What is she wearing?"   **"SHE'S** making a cake and wearing an apron."   **"WHAT** does the apron say?"   **"WORLD'S** Best Mom."   **"BINGO!"**   **"OH**, I get it. You think that the woman in the story is being typecast as a happy homemaker whose natural habitat is the kitchen."   **"YES**, of course. Don't you think it's a bit ironic that a book that breaks new ground in the positive portrayal of gay men would resort to an old and negative stereotype of a woman?"   **"YOU** make a fascinating point," I said, "a fascinating point."

Librarians and Food

THREE years ago, shortly after I read an article in one of our library periodicals deploring the stereotype that many people have about librarians, the thought occurred to me that there is nothing that upsets us more than our image. It's our incurable obsession. We won't leave it alone. The irony, of course, is that the more we fight it, the more we reinforce it. **WHY** can't we just laugh off our stereotype in the same good-natured spirit that plumbers and blondes laugh off theirs? Is it because we really are overly stern and serious? That thought got me pondering the larger question of what we are really like. We complain about our image, but have we done the research we need to do to definitely disprove it?   **A** quick search of the literature revealed that precious little has been done in researching the private lives of librarians. That's when I decided to begin using my monthly column to run lifestyle questionnaires for librarians. A lot of people don't realize this but the first survey I ran was not on librarians and sex, it was on librarians and food. It appeared in the November 1991 issue of *Wilson Library Bulletin*. I got ★★★page 74★★★   over two thousand responses, and spent a great deal of time preparing a full report on the survey results for the September 1992 issue of the bulletin. Unfortunately I was fired in June of 1992 for running the infamous sex survey, and therefore never got an opportunity to report my food findings.   **SO** why did I start my library lifestyle research with a questionnaire about food? Food is simply one of the most talked about and written about subjects in the world today. When we talk about our rapidly changing world we usually make reference to high tech advancements in the areas of medicine, computers, and bioengineering, but the common person is more affected by the new discoveries about food. Thirty years ago if I had written that red meat and milk products were bad for you, I would have flunked my high school health and nutrition class. Now of course those of us who grew up eating steak and drinking milk are struggling to cultivate a new **taste for Belgian endive**. Some of us have made the transition and some of us haven't. The old expression "you are what you eat" has never been more valid.   **SO** what did my survey reveal? Among other things, if I edited a library trade journal I'd stock up on food critics, if I were responsible for planning programs at library conferences I'd go heavy on weight control workshops, and if I owned a company that produced dark chocolate I'd target the library profession as a major market.   **MORE** specifically, if there is anything you can say with complete accuracy about librarians it is that we do not suck yogurt through a straw. In fact a lot of librarians do not even like yogurt. Check that, a lot of librarians detest the stuff. There were over 120 unsolicited negative comments about yogurt, some of them completely unprintable. The fact of the matter is that none of the 2,058 librarians who filled out the questionnaire indicated that their preferred method of consuming yogurt, when and if they ever consumed it, was sucking it through a straw.   **WHEN** it comes to Thanksgiving we are for the most part very traditional. Only twenty-five percent of the respondents indicated that they do not always have turkey for Thanksgiving dinner, and various unsolicited comments revealed that some of the librarians who are not Thanksgiving turkey eaters are either staunch animal activists or devout vegetarians. One person responded, "**Burger King does not serve turkey**. Grilled chicken is as close as they come." A depressing thought, isn't it, that a librarian would be spending Thanksgiving in a Burger King.   **ANOTHER** area where respondents were largely in agreement with each other was in the section that dealt with the relative merits of sex, steak, and chocolate. Only 26% of the respondents preferred chocolate to sex, and only 20% preferred steak to sex. I could find no national data to compare these results against, but I found the responses reassuring. **LIBRARIANS** are much more divided on a number of the other food issues presented in the questionnaire. In my opinion,   ★★★page 75★★★

Participative management is fine but if you really want to improve morale feed your staff chocolate twice a day.

the most telling question in the survey was the one on fat and cholesterol. In light of all the research that has been done into the causes of heart disease, have librarians tilted their daily diets to foods low in fat and cholesterol? You would think that as information specialists we would be doing the right thing when it comes to food, but that's not always the case. **OUR** taste buds are often **stronger than our will to live**. Fifty-three percent of us continue to enjoy foods high in fat and cholesterol, and this may explain why 49% of us are overweight and why 55% of us have been on a diet at least once in the last five years. You can draw your own conclusions about all of this, but I think it points up the real need for more programs at A.L.A. conferences on the subject of "Cholesterol, Fat, and the Professional Librarian." If we really want to get serious about our image, we really need to get serious about weight control.   **TO** me the most surprising thing about the survey was that 47% of the respondents indicated that at library conferences they eat at restaurants recommended by library periodicals. We all know how important our trade journals are for book reviews, but restaurant reviews? Who could have guessed it? Now I know why I can never get into those places that have gotten the five star treatment in *American Libraries*. This points up the fact that we need more restaurants reviewed. Obviously there's an opportunity here for a librarian with a facile pen and an educated palate.   **WHEN** it comes to meals back home, however, librarians are much less discerning. Many of us microwave (44% of the respondents microwave five to fifteen meals a week), and most of us eat fast foods (59% of the respondents eat at least one meal a week at a fast food restaurant). Is this because we're poor or in a hurry? My guess is both.   **WHICH** meal do librarians think is most important? Dinner is the winner with breakfast a distant second. Doing lunch is obviously not a big practice in the library profession, and only 8% of us truly value the delights of a midnight snack. Many comments were inserted about how sleep is more important than food at that hour of the night. To me, it's a pity that more librarians don't understand the allure of eating a Dagwood sandwich while watching a "Gilligan's Island" rerun at 2:30 A.M. But then again my days of staffing the reference desk at 8:00 A.M. are over. **WHAT** the library profession does seem to appreciate, however, is the value of a fine piece of chocolate for snacks, for gifts, and even for an entire meal. Nothing unusual there, but take it from me if you want to talk about chocolate with a bunch of librarians you better know what you're talking about. Over a hundred respondents felt the need to lecture me on the difference between dark chocolate and milk chocolate. Dark chocolate, apparently, is the real thing, while milk chocolate is a sweetened imitation. If nothing else, my survey revealed that librarians are wild about dark chocolate. It is, apparently, **our professional drug of choice.**   **TO** end this little narrative, I throw out one of the more fascinating tidbits from the survey. For our last meal on earth, steak is the overwhelming selection. This in itself is not necessarily surprising. After all, your last meal on earth is no time to worry about fat and cholesterol. What is absolutely amazing, however, is that over thirty respondents indicated that they would prefer steak for their last meal, but they didn't think they could afford it!   **AND** we're upset about our image.

Art

"ART," my board president said. "We must have art. A new public library without art is like a birthday cake without icing. Art will be the crowning glory to this magnificent building— the pièce de résistance, the coup de grace, the cherry   ★★★page 77★★★

on top. **THESE** words were the precise words that I did not want to hear. I prayed that I would not hear these words, and I really thought that my prayers had been answered. After all I had gotten through my entire forty-five minute presentation to the board on the architectural plans for our new building without hearing them and I didn't expect to hear them now. **THE** board had never talked about art in relation to the new building, and in my presentation I had tried mightily to steer them away from any consideration of the subject. That's why I had spent so much time emphasizing the artistic nature of the design itself in an effort to convince them that a design so intricate and so unusual was an art work in itself, and that more art would be superfluous and would actually get in the way of the building and obscure its creative form and mass. **BUT** obviously my approach had backfired. With the enthusiasm that I had devoted to describing the "palette" of building materials, the double barreled arch, the interior atriums, the diversity of shapes, and the unity of function, I had obviously whetted the board's artistic juices. God forbid, had I actually inspired them to look at this project not just as a heap of bricks but as a creative expression? **THIS** is exactly what I didn't want. Mention the word "art" and I automatically think of a guy I knew in high school named Art—Art Fredericks—also known as Artie, Tee, Fred, Freddie, Rick, Rickie, Snaps, Shooter, Guzzler, Killer, and Snake. Yes, Art had many names and a mood to match each one. He could be alternately charming, ingratiating, deceitful, playful, devilish, elusive, incomprehensible, and even kind. The one constant with Art was that he was easily the best art student my high school ever had. He was adept at any medium and quite original in his style and subject matter. Whenever something artistic had to be done like designing posters or tee-shirts for class fund raisers, Art was always the one who got the job. Sometimes, however, we got more than we bargained for when we pressed Art into service. **THERE** was the time, for instance, when Art, who was in charge of designing and constructing the decorations and sets for the senior prom (which that year had a *Gone with the Wind* theme), wanted us to obtain some wrought iron yard furniture and statues from the yard of a certain prominent citizen. "These will be perfect for the prom set that I am building," he said to us with great enthusiasm. **"BUT** Art," we protested, "Old Man Prosch will never let us use his furniture. He's a **miserly old grump** who hates teenagers." **"WHO** said anything about asking Old Man Prosch for his furniture," Art replied, "I'm saying we should just, you know, borrow it for the prom." **"YOU** mean steal it?" said Stew Stiverson. **"IT'S** a matter of semantics," replied Art. "We'll return it all as soon as the prom is over." **SO** we "borrowed" the furniture. In the middle of a warm May night we snuck into Old Man Prosch's yard and lifted three ornately designed chairs and a ponderous old iron glider. For good measure we even unearthed a hitching post—one of those grotesquely designed yard ornaments topped off with a plantation **slave wearing a ring** through his nose. Everything went exactly according to Art's plan. We could even hear Old Man Prosch snoring through his bedroom window. Discreetly and quietly we piled the stuff into Frankie Angellini's pick-up and drove quickly away to the high school gym which Art was transforming into a South Jersey version of Tara. **WE** deposited all of this booty under the watchful eye of Miss Sarah Tomkins, our faculty prom advisor. "Bring those things over here, guys," Art said authoritatively and then added, "Miss Tomkins, what's your opinion, do you think we ought to repaint the hitching post or do you think it looks more realistic worn and beaten?" **"I** would definitely repaint it," responded Miss Tomkins who was the school's newest and youngest art teacher and therefore got stuck with undesirable jobs like overseeing the construction of the senior prom in the middle of the night. Like all the teachers in the art department, she revered Art. It was the conventional wisdom of the members of the faculty that Art was going to be the next Andy Warhol. Therefore they were always willing to forgive Art his questionable personality traits. What was considered a character flaw in anybody else (like lying, cheating, and stealing) was considered an eccentricity in Art—a creative, artistic eccentricity. All great artists are eccentrics. **"EVERYTHING** in your set looks so new and wonderful," responded Miss Tomkins. "The hitching post would stick out like a sore thumb without a fresh coat of paint. The same goes for the glider and the wrought iron chairs. They should be painted, but not black." **"I'VE** got it," said Art, "let's go with pastel colors. That will soften up the furniture, and make it look dreamier. That's what we're trying to achieve here—something dreamy, creamy, and fanciful. Let's go with yellow and beige. All the girls will love it, and remember, Miss Tomkins, the prom is for the girls. For some, this will be the highlight of their life. Let's give them some memories that they'll cherish all their lives." **"ART**, you're so brilliant and so sensitive," said Miss Tomkins. That's another thing that teachers liked about Art—his sensitivity. It's what set him apart from the rest of us **senior klutzes**. Art had feelings; we had brute instincts. **"BY** the way," added Miss Tomkins, "where did you boys get all of this wonderful furniture? It is so old and elegant. They just don't make lawn furniture like that anymore. Where did you come up with it?" she asked, looking directly at Frankie Angellini. **FRANKIE** looked up, startled. Quickly he scanned the room, looking for help from Art. Art had disappeared. Frankie looked back at Miss Tomkins and said, "Well, Miss Tomkins, if you can believe it, we were down at the city dump looking for some scraps of lumber and we happened upon this furniture." "**MY** goodness," said Miss Tomkins. "It's amazing the things that people throw away just because they get a little worn and tattered. Why these things are antiques. It's simply criminal to throw them away. I'm so glad that you young men were able to salvage them. I'll bet when the prom is over you can sell these pieces for a pretty penny. That will help pay for the cost of the prom." **IT'S** true what everybody said—our prom was the greatest ever. "I feel like Scarlet O'Hara," is what more than one wide-eyed petticoated girl was heard to say on that memorable evening, and Art, of course, was in his glory. Rarely do you hear the words "brilliant," "inventive," "original," and "creative" used to describe a high school artist, but that's what everyone was saying that night about Art Fredericks. **EVEN** our principal, Mr. Schwartz, a dour and unpleasant man who was convinced that there was an on-going school-wide conspiracy to make him look like an idiot, was moved to say nice things. "You've made us all proud to be educators, Art," is what more than one of my classmates heard him utter, and then near the end of the evening I saw him approach Art and say, "Art, this lawn furniture is quite attractive, what plans do you have for it?" **"You'd** have to talk to Frankie Angellini about it, sir. He and his procurement committee are the ones who are responsible for bringing it here." **SCHWARTZ** smiled at Art and then walked over toward Frankie who, I noticed, was working hard to rub up against Sandra Teasdale while dancing with his date Vickie Singleton. Sandra was wearing a strapless gown that revealed substantial cleavage by 1960's high school standards. Next to Art's *Gone with the Wind* set, Sandra was the big attraction of the night. **"MR.** Angellini," said Mr. Schwartz, "I'd like to see you for a moment." This startled Frankie and I'm sure he was thinking that the jig was up. **"YES,** sir, what can I do for you?" he asked nervously. **"IT'S** about the lawn furniture," said Schwartz. **"WELL,** yes, I can explain everything," Frankie stuttered, looking around desperately for help. **"ALL** I need to know is if I can take it off your hands after the prom. I'd be glad to pay for it. What do you consider a fair price?" "**WELL,** Mr. Schwartz, it's not really for sale." **"WHY** not? Miss Tomkins told me you pulled it out of the city dump." **"HERE.** Here's a check for a hundred dollars made out to the senior class and don't worry about transporting it to my house. I'll take care of all of that myself." **TWO** days later Mr. Schwartz was arrested for receiving stolen property, and three weeks later Frankie, Stew, and I were starting 120 hours of the community service work that we had been assigned by the juvenile court referee. Our first job was to strip the new paint off the furniture and repaint it black. Art Fredericks, of course, ★★★page 80★★★ got off scot-free. **EVER** since then I have equated art with trouble. But even before my relationship with Art Fredericks, I had my problems with art. From first grade on I was the kid whose artwork never got hung up at school art shows. At first this greatly bothered me, but later on I was relieved. That's how bad my paintings and drawings were. I was terribly embarrassed by them. It got so bad that I actually preferred math class to art class. About the kindest thing you could say about me as an art student was that I was doing abstract expressionism before it became fashionable. Unfortunately my abstractions were really intended as representational pictures of trees, houses, cars, and people.   **FOR** me, the best thing about graduating from the eighth grade was that I would never, ever, have to take another art class. The humiliation was finally over, but as much as I hated painting pictures, however, that's how much I respected people who did have real skills with the pen and brush. That's why to this day I have mixed feelings about Art Fredericks. Sure, he got me in trouble and sure, I'd never trust him again, but, boy, was he talented.   **SO** when I went to college I tinkered around with two or three different art history courses. These are courses where you don't have to do any art work yourself. Rather you sit in a large lecture hall where they show you slides of the great masterpieces and teach you how western art evolved from buffalo cave paintings to soup can silk screens. What fascinated me about these classes was the strongly stated premise that it's the artist not the scientist, not the inventor, not the statesman, and not the philosopher who senses the new and revolutionary and represents it in his or her work. If you want to understand the past, therefore, then you must study the art of the past and if you want to see into the future then you must examine the works of those artists who are struggling to develop new and different modes of visual expression. **THE** artist is always portrayed as having powers of perception that are different from the rest of us. That makes the artist a bit dangerous and sometimes difficult to understand. We react differently to people who are different. We usually look at them in one of two ways—either with mistrust or with admiration. It's either this artist is subverting the norms of society or this artist is a genius who is visualizing reality in radically new and brilliant ways. In one case the artist is a threat to society and in the other case the artist is a visionary. The interesting part of this dilemma is that in time most of the artists who were condemned either by the Church, the government, the art establishment, middle-class society, or even their own families came to **be seen as geniuses**. The list is almost endless. Name a great artist and if you do some research you will find that during his or her lifetime he or she was probably viciously attacked as a Godless, immoral, anarchistic, subversive malcontent. Brunelleschi, Michelangelo, Van Gogh, and Warhol are just a few names on the list of artists who have made the evolution from villain to visionary. **WHILE** not every artist working today is a Michelangelo or a Van Gogh, every artist is a potential threat to our sense of what's up and what's down. Recently I spent two entire days in the National Gallery of Art in Washington, D.C. My intent was not to look at art but to look at people looking at art. The National Gallery is a good place to do this because its collection very comprehensively covers all the major artistic movements from late medieval to post modern. In general I found that people, many of whom appeared to be ordinary citizens who had wandered into the museum to escape the crowds and heat of the nearby Museum of Aeronautics and Space, were a) bored by everything up to the French impressionists, b) thrilled by the impressionists and some of the Postimpressionists, or c) confused, amused, and even angered by the abstract expressionists and those who succeeded them. **MY** point is that when it comes to the appreciation of art there is about a 75-year gap between the art world and the ordinary person. Put another way, the art world is about 75 years ahead of the general public. Why? Simple. Most people (probably 80 to 90% of the American adult population) simply have not bought in to the premise of non-representational art—art that does not bear any resemblance to anything in the physical world. This does not mean that art has to be photographic. A tree, for instance, does not have to look exactly like a tree but it should look something like a tree. In fact I think that most people now prefer some stylization in art, and would therefore prefer a landscape by Van Gogh with all of its pulsing emotion over a more sedate and realistic rendering of trees and rivers by someone like Turner or Gainsborough. **BUT** the bottom line is that the vast majority of people in this country are very, very reluctant to accept a painting entitled "Tree" that consists of nothing but a random series of splatters, splashes, and slashes that bear absolutely no physical resemblance to a tree or any other object in the material world. The gut feeling about abstract art is that when you strip away all the fancy talk, it is nothing more than a swindle and the person who created it is nothing **more than a flim-flam man** with a fine arts degree. If rich people with social pretensions want to be swindled, that's fine, but the common man would rather spend his money on a fancy hood ornament for his car. **WHILE** Americans may be wary of being scammed, they can also easily be scammed. History bears this out. What is it that P.T. Barnum said about us? "There's a sucker born every minute." Actually, I think Barnum got it wrong—there's a thousand born every second. If you dispute this, consider this fact. Sixty percent of the American people believe most of the articles that they read in the *National Enquirer*. In other words 60% of the American people think that ★★★page 82★★★ Elvis is still alive. **WHEN** it comes to modern art, therefore, the average guy, although he will never admit it, is torn between two conflicting feelings. Although he is initially guided by his common sense, he doesn't always act or think logically. Sometimes he functions viscerally. When he looks at that series of paint drips he may see nonsense, but he also knows that this nonsense is worth 20 million dollars. So he thinks defensively to himself, "Why am I so stupid that I can't see why this painting is worth 20 million dollars?" That is the ultimate effect of the museum's Pollack painting. It makes people feel stupid, and how do people react when they are made to feel stupid? Yes, of course, they become angry.   **SO** when the average guy first sees that big canvas hanging there in the National Gallery he is amused because he thinks his first grader could have done better and then he's skeptical about the world art establishment because they've bought in to this scam and paid big money for the right to hang this in their fancy gallery and then as he starts to walk away he thinks, Wait a minute, 20 million dollars can't be wrong. People do not simply throw 20 million dollars away on nothing. He decides that there must be something in this painting that he's overlooked but the more he looks the angrier he feels because he can't see it. His emotions have run the gamut from amusement to anger, but what's most important is that the anger is the last emotion.   **AND** the anger increases as he progresses through the gallery and sees things that make the Pollack painting look conservative. There is, for instance, a series of paintings by Mark Rothko that are nothing more than black stripes on white canvases, but the coup de grace is the big blank white canvas. That's where all the anger culminates. The average viewer looks at this in utter confusion because it is a completely empty canvas. There is nothing there. There is nothing to look at, nothing to visualize. I saw one terribly upset person immediately seek out a museum docent after looking at the white canvas for two or three painful moments. "I'm almost afraid to ask this question," said the man, "but if I wanted to buy that all-white painting over there, how much would it cost me?"   **"SIR,"** said the guide with a blend of officiousness and condescension, "this is a museum, not a gallery. We don't sell paintings here."   "I realize that," said the man, "but I'm just curious. What do you think the value of that painting is?"   **"PROBABLY** close to 1.5 million dollars," replied the docent.   **"THAT'S** what I was afraid to hear," said the man who now seemed so angry that he was considering taking a knife to the painting. Actually, not everyone reacted with fury to the white canvas. I decided to hang around there for a while and listen in on more comments. While many people simply walked up to the painting and shook their heads in bemused confusion, others felt compelled to speak, sometimes to no one in particular. Here are the comments that I gleaned: **"I'LL** bet this is an unfinished work and that an artist will be

coming in every day to work on it. It's probably a way of getting repeat visitors in here—to see how the painting develops."   "**IS** that the color of the canvas or did someone actually paint the canvas white?" "**WHOEVER** painted this would make a good housepainter because he didn't miss a spot."   "I like this better than the painting with the angry purple slashes. At least this doesn't make me want to throw up." "I hope to God that they didn't spend my tax money on this."   "**THIS** is a put-on, right?"   "**IS** this the museum's way of making fun of modern art?"   "**THIS** must have been hung up by mistake."   "**THIS** is brilliantly conceived. It is the ultimate in minimalism."   "**THERE'S** a zen-like quality to this painting that informs it with an immediate sense of nothingness."   "**THIS** painting speaks to me in a very real way about the meaning of life in post-industrial America."   "**THIS** painting is the ultimate commentary on the current state of Western civilization."   **SOME** would say that ultimately a work of art should not be judged on form, line, mass, or color but on its ability to provoke thought and emotion. If this is true then the white canvas should be considered a masterpiece. It's hard to think of another painting that could engender a more diverse array of remarks. From my perspective as a public administrator and someone charged with a stewardship over public funds, however, the most interesting comment about the painting was made by the man who stated his hope that tax money had not been used to purchase the white canvas.   **THIS simple gut reaction** is an excellent commentary on the dangers inherent in public art. While it is true that most people's appreciation of modern art stops in 1910 with the Postimpressionists, it is also true that they do not begrudge anyone the right to spend 1.5 million dollars on a blank canvas. They may feel that such a person might benefit from psychiatric counseling, but they would definitely not be in favor of having Congress pass a law prohibiting anyone from spending his or her own money on bare canvases painted white. As hostile and confused as many people are toward modern art, they do not equate it with such banned products as crack cocaine or nuclear explosive devices. It is completely lawful for you to consume bare white canvases in excess in all fifty states.   **QUITE** another matter altogether, however, is the situation where Congress might want to spend 1.5 million tax dollars on a bare white canvas. Now the issue becomes inflammatory, and here is where the whole notion of public art becomes troublesome. It's important to note that the concept of public art is not inherently controversial. It only becomes so when tax money set aside for public art is spent on pieces that are incomprehensible to the masses of people. If Congress appropriates 1.5 million dollars for a statue of Abraham Lincoln, this is considered patriotic and good, but when it spends $60,000 on a cruci-
★★★page 84★★★   fix submerged in **a jar of urine**, as it did in 1987,

this is considered not only wasteful but idiotic. **DESPITE** the bad name that public art has received in the last ten years, the truth is that we Americans, whether we realize it or not, are quite proud of many public art projects. Think, for example, of the great urban landmarks in the United States—the Statue of Liberty, the Washington Monument, and the Gateway Arch in St. Louis—these are all public arts projects that were intended to impress and inspire the citizens whose

I love it. It has an eloquent sense of minimalism that borders on a stark portrayal of nihilism.

taxes made them possible. The problem then is not with the appropriateness of spending public money on art; it is with the appropriateness of the art itself. The problem is that most taxpayers are alienated by what passes for art today.   **GIVEN** this alienation, why do local, regional, state, and federal government officials accept the considerable political risks involved in funding public arts projects? To answer that we have to understand that there is a natural evolution to the development of most political jurisdictions. First and foremost is the physical infrastructure. In order to sustain urban life, governing bodies must, right from the start, provide clean water, an adequate drainage and storm sewer system, an efficient network of roads, the timely pick-up and disposal of trash, and an effective sewage treatment and disposal system.   **WHEN** all of that is done and the community begins to grow and prosper, a city council's attention then becomes more focused on protecting the lives and property of its taxpayers and so the new funding priority becomes police, fire and paramedic services. "We must defend what we have built" is the motto of the public policymaker in stage two of urban evolution.   **BUT** clean water and safe streets do not a city make, not completely anyway. People are important also and therefore stage three concentrates on "quality of life" services. While these programs are not absolutely necessary to sustain the life of the community they do make accessible those things that make life worth living. Schools, parks, and libraries are the first wave of "quality of life" facilities that are usually built, and they are often followed by museums, zoos, and botanical gardens.   **BUT** still there is something missing, something that distinguishes the average European metropolis from the average American metropolis—great works of public art. Great civilizations are distinguished by great artistic creations, and so Chicago hires Picasso to do a huge street sculpture and Dallas commissions Henry Moore to design massive statues on the front of its city hall.   **THE** result is instant culture and, while many people may look at the resulting creations with confusion and frustration, the names Picasso and Moore are widely admired and so the incomprehensibility of their work is offset by the celebrity of their names because if there is anything that Americans respect it is celebrity. All is forgiven.   **BUT** this poses a serious problem for many smaller cities who also want to be imbued with the sense of sophistication that only fine art can bring. They unfortunately cannot afford to engage in checkbook culture. They don't have the money to go out and hire a Pablo Picasso or a Henry Moore and so they end up hiring more obscure but affordable artists, and while many of their works are cleverly designed and well crafted, these artists do not enjoy the halo effect afforded by fame. A large abstract steel sculpture by Michael Anderson, for example, is looked upon with a great deal more skepticism than a similar structure by Picasso.   **IN** the communities where I have worked as a library director, any controversy that I might have had over any aspect of the operation of the library, paled in comparison to the tornado of criticism that was unleashed by the expenditures of large sums of money on art works that no one understood. Ironically enough, one of the most embittered book controversies that I have been embroiled in as a librarian had nothing to do with sex or violence, but with art.   **EARLY** one morning before I had even gotten a chance to get to the coffeepot, a woman walked quickly past my secretary and rushed up to my desk. She was brandishing a book with anger. At first I thought she was going to hit me with it or at least throw it at me but she proved to be more civil than that. She merely slammed it down on my desk and waited for me to react.   **"GOOD** morning," I said cheerfully, "may I be of assistance to you? Would you like a cup of coffee? I was just going to get myself one."   "I DON'T DRINK CAFFEINE," she said self-righteously and then looked disparagingly at me like **I was a drug addict.**   **"I** admire you," I said with a smile, "but myself, "I can't seem to do without it. It helps me wake up."   "LET THIS WAKE YOU UP!" she responded pointing to the book.   **"IS** there something in the book that you don't like?" I asked politely. I noticed it was a children's book, and I suspected she had found something objectionable in it with regards to sex or violence. Or maybe she had found some kind of an obscure demonic symbol hidden in one of the illustrations. A week earlier a man huffed and puffed his way into my office and claimed that if he held one of our library books, *The Three Little Pigs,* upside down in front of a mirror that he could see a "666" embedded in the illustration of the pig who had built his house out of straw. I showed the book upside down and in front of a mirror to twenty-seven other people and no one else could see the "666."   "JUST OPEN THE BOOK AND LOOK AT IT!" she snapped.   **"WELL,"** I said officiously, "are there any specific passages or illustrations that are particularly objectionable?"   "THE WHOLE BOOK!" she responded.   I picked up the book and flipped through the pages and was both surprised and relieved to find that there was no sex and violence in the book. There were also no four letter words. That meant that there had to be hidden signs of devil worship contained within the illustrations. The title of the book was *Roll Call,* and it was a whimsical account of all the animals that didn't quite make it on to Noah's Ark before the rains came. That had to be it. The woman probably thought the book was blasphemous because it was taking liberties with a traditional Bible story.   **"I'M** not sure I understand why you find the book so objectionable," I said to the woman. "It seems more fanciful than irreverent," I added with a polite smile. "IRREVERENT? WHO SAID THE BOOK WAS IRREVERENT!" she responded.   **"WELL,** I asked with confusion, "what exactly is it that bothers you so much?"   "THE FACT THAT IT IS COMPLETELY ABSURD!"   **"I'M** sorry," I replied, "but I still do not quite understand what the

problem is." "LOOK AT THE PICTURES!" SO I looked down at the illustrations. They were grotesque but funny. Pigs with noses shaped like milk bottles, camels top heavy with five humps, and birds weighted down with arms and hands were swimming furiously trying to catch the ark, which had just set sail into the waters of destruction. Sure the artistic style of the illustrations was very surreal in the manner of a Salvador Dali painting, but the message of the book was quite traditional: those who are **clumsy, unprepared, and morally deficient** will always miss the boat. "I like the book," I said to the woman. "It has a very constructive message for children. In fact, I have three children of my own and I wouldn't mind one bit if they checked this book out of the library and read it." "I DON'T CARE ABOUT THE MESSAGE. THE PICTURES ARE ABSURD AND YOU USED MY TAX MONEY TO BUY A BOOK WITH ABSURD PICTURES!" "WOULD you like to file a formal written complaint with the Library Board of Trustees regarding the book?" I asked. "NO," she responded, "I'D LIKE TO RUN OVER THE BOOK TWENTY TIMES WITH A CEMENT TRUCK AND THEN POUR GASOLINE OVER IT AND THEN LIGHT IT WITH A MATCH. ANYTHING LESS WOULD BE UNSATISFACTORY!" "THANK you," I responded politely. "I will give your request due consideration." AFTER the woman left I decided, after about two and a half seconds of consideration, not to run over the book with a cement truck and then ignite it with gasoline. It turned out, however, that my decision was irrelevant because two weeks later, not only was the book reported missing from the collection but it was also discovered that the catalog cards for the book had been ripped out of the card catalog. I have been through censorship battles with *Show Me*, *Sex*, *American Psycho*, *The Joy of Sex*, *Little Black Sambo*, *Where Do I Come From*, and even *The Total Woman*, Marabel Morgan's classic treatise of female subservience, but never before had I had a situation where a patron was so upset about a book that he or she decided to steal it and remove any bibliographic trace of it. This was real commitment, the kind of commitment that only an intense hatred of modern art can produce. IT was precisely this hatred that made me wish so desperately to avoid the whole issue of public art in my new library building all together. But I was not so lucky. Eventually the plea of my board president—"We must have art!"—became the mantra of the mayor, city council, and arts commission. THEY all wanted art too, which I thought was a bit strange in view of the fact that the city's first official public art project, a ceramic archway entitled "Temple," was a fiasco. Actually "Temple" was unveiled to great fanfare on a sunny Saturday morning, but on the following gloomy Monday morning this striking interactive park sculpture had a barbed wire fence around it after having been deemed unsafe by the city's safety inspec-
★★★page 88★★★   tor. The forbidding picture of this $70,000 artistic

creation being surrounded by chain link made the front pages of all the local newspapers and touched off a terrible outcry of protest from the citizenry. **EVENTUALLY** of course the situation was rectified—sort of. The artist was paid an additional stipend to modify the structure, which mitigated the safety issue but which also exacerbated the debate about the appropriateness of spending tax money on fine art. The backers of public art of course retreated back to their all purpose argument that not only were they not afraid of controversy, but they welcomed it since any art piece, if it is any good at all, should pique at least a little controversy. In fact, one art advocate was heard to say that there is a direct relationship between the controversy a work of art creates and the merit of the piece itself or in simpler terms—the bigger the controversy the better the art work. Using that formula, if you want to see the greatest thing since the Mona Lisa, come to my community and spend some time meditating at our "Temple." **PERSONALLY**, when it comes to my job as a public administrator there is nothing I hate more than a controversy and the impact that it can have on your job security. But when it was announced that the City had decided to invest $250,000 in an artistic fountain, that's exactly where I found myself—in the middle of a heated controversy with my sense of job security slipping away like an ice sculpture on a sunny day.
WITH the bitter taste of "Temple" in their mouths, a number of very vocal people were not pleased to read that the City had upped the ante in the high stakes public arts sweepstakes, and predictably, as the individual who was to administrate this project, I was being cast as a villain. Me! The guy who had tried to make the library an art-free zone in the first place. All of a sudden I felt just like I did in high school when I took the rap for stealing Old Man Prosch's lawn furniture and Art Fredericks got off scot-free. **NOT** only were the fiscal conservatives in a heat but they were joined by a most unlikely ally—the environmentalists, who felt that it was a bit hypocritical for the city to be building an expensive fountain at the very same time that it was embarking on a water conservation program. To break up this formidable collusion of liberals and conservatives a quick strategic decision was made to change the name of the project from the "Library Fountain" to the "Library Water Feature." Actually it became even more politically correct to refer to the project as the "Library Art Project Which Features a Minimalistic Use of Water in a Setting Appropriate to a Desert Community," but since this was a bit too laborious even for the most pompous public servant, the working project title was shortened to the more affectionate acronym "L.W.F." **ACTUALLY** a more accurate acronym might be "S.N.A.I.L." since the project is now in its fifth year of labor. My guess is that the full gestation period for the water feature will be in the neighborhood of six to   ★★★page 89★★★

seven years. This is what happens when you involve five different citizen boards in the development of a project and when you hire a Southern California artist whose biological clock must have been transplanted from a 300-pound land tortoise. If there was any advice that I would have to offer to other librarians embarking into the turbulent waters of public art, I would throw out three words, **take your time**.   1. $250,000 averaged over seven years is only $36,000 a year.   2. Some of the most vociferous critics of the water feature are now dead.   3. No one can accuse me of ramrodding the project through.   4. No one can accuse me of not soliciting citizen input.   5. As long as the project is still "in progress" no one can call it a fiasco, and consequently, I still have a job.   **OF** course a seven-year design/build cycle does have one serious potential drawback especially if the project turns out weird or mediocre. People are liable to look at the finished creation and say, "This thing took seven years? I know some plumbing contractors who could have done a better job in three months."   **DURING** this waiting period the city did decide to undertake a third, more modest sculptural project. Stung by criticism that "Temple" and the Library Water Feature were too abstract in design, the council voted to fund a representational sculpture—something that would surely be non-controversial. It would be something that everyone would recognize with affection and enthusiasm—a lifesize sculpture of Charles Trumball Hayden, the man who had founded the city.   **IT** was stated clearly in the competition guidelines that the city fathers wanted something realist, nothing abstract or stylized, and something classically traditional that would be befitting this dignified and heroic Victorian man. In assisting the Arts Commission in this project, the library staff did extensive research into the life and times of C.T. Hayden. Old photographs revealed him to be a very formal man who was dressed in white shirt and waistcoat even in the hottest summer months.   **IN** light of this research, what occurred at the final meeting of the jury was startlingly ironic. Three local artists had been selected based upon their experience and qualifications to submit a two-foot clay model of how they would depict Charles Hayden. The five-member jury would then vote upon these entries to determine a winner.   **THE** first two models were the kind of traditional and somewhat lifeless renditions you would expect to see in a local art contest. The third entry, however, was quite different. With a dramatic flourish, the final artist removed the plastic garbage bag that had been veiling her creation, and the jury couldn't have been more surprised if old man Hayden himself suddenly appeared in flesh and blood. Actually, shocked would be more accurate, for there standing proudly under that garbage bag was our city's founding father in **full frontal nudity**—a classical (think back to Michelangelo's David) and impressive (yes, he was very well endowed) portrayal. **"MY** God," the person standing next to me said, "I didn't know that Charles Trumbull Hayden had a penis." To which another wag added, "My God, what will the city council do if this one gets selected? The statue is supposed to stand right in front of city hall." **"WELL,"** said another, "They said they wanted realistic art and I can't imagine anything more realistic."

Shit Happens

I call it hula hoop management. I'm sure you know what I'm talking about. Every year some business guru comes up with a new management philosophy that promises to increase productivity, decrease costs, enhance customer satisfaction, and **make millions of dollars** for the guru.   **IT** all started back in the middle 1970s when we woke up one morning and discovered that the United States was getting its economic **brains bashed** in by Japan, Inc. The problem, according to the experts, was that we were using outmoded management styles. It was time for something new, and so the gurus got busy "reinventing" management. As a result, every year for about ten years, a new hula hoop rolled off the management assembly line. The Peter Principle, Theory Y, Searching for Excellence, Quality Circles, Empowerment, Reinventing Government, Total Quality Management, Downsizing, and Rightsizing are just a few of these hula hoops that have become everyday buzzwords. **YES**, the names change, but do the theories? Essentially not. Basically the theory behind all these theories is that if you are a manager you need to, surprise, surprise, treat people (employees and customers) like people and not like peons. This little analysis, although it probably wouldn't fly as an answer on an M.B.A. exam, is all you need to know when someone who looks and sounds halfway intelligent starts hurling buzzwords at you in hopes of impressing and/or intimidating you. **ALTHOUGH** treating people like people sounds easy, it's not. When you rise to the ranks of management, there's a great temptation to act like Genghis Khan for several reasons. First, there's a good chance that when you were a regular rank and file employee your boss acted like Genghis Khan and treated you like a peon. He was probably fond of saying something like, "Rules are rules," probably had a plaque on his desk that said, "What part of NO don't you understand?" probably had a coffee mug that said "Make My Day!" probably had a wall poster that said "Rule #1—The Boss Is Always Right and Rule #2—When the Boss Is Wrong, See Rule #1!" and probably had a pencil holder that said "I Don't Get Ulcers, I Give Them."   **SO** this boss was probably your role model and you thought that that's the way bosses are supposed to act. They're supposed to treat people like peons and they're supposed to rule through fear and intimidation. Anything less is considered weak and wimpy. So, when you first got into management you were eager to establish your strength and authority.

THEN just when you had your Gengis Khan impersonation down pat along came the hula hoops and you learned that managing autocratically in a democratic society does not work because it results in low productivity, low morale, and a dysfunctional organization. From this new research you discovered that excellent organizations are run by managers who listen to employees and customers, who stress creativity over conformity, and who transfer power downward and facilitate communication upward. The term "boss" was out. You were now a "facilitator."   **THIS** was a difficult transition to make. First you spent a good part of your career struggling up the organizational ladder with the objective of attaining a little power, and now that you had gotten to the top you suddenly found out that you were expected to give your power up. But the biggest challenge was finding the time and maintaining the patience to listen, encourage, nurture, facilitate, communicate, and coach your employees. It was far easier and more satisfying to the ego to **simply boss people around.**   **BUT** eventually and with training you began to become proficient at working each new hula hoop as it rolled off the line. You even began to take pride in your ability to change and adapt. But what was even more surprising was that you found that you were not just going through the motions of this new management style—you had actually bought into its effectiveness. You had become a convert, a disciple, and, as a result, you really were successful in energizing your staff, increasing productivity, and enhancing morale. You also discovered that this new collaborative style was effective in working with others like the architects you hired to design your new building and the consultants you contracted with to develop your new computer system.   **YOU** were quite confident, therefore, that this human relations approach could also be applied to your construction superintendent and his team of foremen. The first thing that eroded your confidence, however, was the bumper sticker on the superintendent's truck. In big black letters it said ***shit happens***. The other thing that bothered you was that the pick-up was parked diagonally across two handicapped spaces in your lot. When you inquired as to why he had done this, he replied simply, "Shit happens and you get in a hurry. Plus no one else will probably use them."
"**BUT** haven't you ever heard of the A.D.A.?" you responded with concern.   "**WHAT'S** the American Deer Hunters Association got to do with anything?" was his sensitive reply.   **EARLY** on into the project you began to realize that this man was not a nurturer. When he talked about preparing the site for excavation he said things like "We'll nuke those trees over here and we'll blitz those retaining walls over there. Yeah, we're really going to make

★★★page 92★★★

the dust fly around here in the next few days. This place is going to resemble a nuclear test site when we're done." "I hope you will take every precaution to mitigate the noise, dust, and chaos for the residents

> That's my construction foreman. He's very articulate. He can use shit as a noun, verb, adjective, and adverb all in the same sentence.

living in the adjacent neighborhood," you advised. "WE'LL try but, you know, shit happens and you can't make everybody ★★★page 93★★★

happy," he explained.   **THREE** days later after you had gotten thirteen calls from the neighbors and several accident reports had been filed from mishaps that occurred due to lapses in safety precautions, you realized that new age management had apparently not yet arrived in the construction industry. So you consulted with a colleague who had just built a building in a neighboring city, and learned from her that "If you want to be effective in the construction business you have to go back to being Genghis Khan because it's like going to war every day."   **THIRTEEN** months later, after hearing the phrase "shit happens" at least 553 more times, you have to admit that your colleague was right and you feel that you should share this insight with the rest of the library profession. Therefore the thought of a book entitled *Shit Happens* has some appeal to you. It will give other library directors a workable hula hoop to use in construction projects. As you envision it in your mind the book would have the following 7 chapters: **1.** "How to Speak to People in the Construction Industry"—Gives tips on swearing, including examples of how to use the p word, the s word, the f word, and the mf word as a noun, participle, verb, adjective, and adverb. **2.** "Getting Your Point Across"—Offers advice on how to use effective non-verbal body language techniques to emphasize your message, including chair throwing, flipping the bird, and slamming doors. **3.** "Constructive Criticism"—Provides help in critiquing slipshod work with a glossary of terms differentiating the fine distinctions between such evaluative ratings as "sucks," "screwed up," and "a piece of shit." **4.** "Shooting the Breeze"—Suggests pointers for discussing favorite leisure time activities with construction workers around the roach coach (food wagon) at lunchtime, with basic background information on country western music, beer bonging, tobacco spitting, and squirrel hunting. Also offers the latest insights into such favorite construction current affairs topics as David Koresh, Jeffrey Dahmer, Joey Buttafuoco, and John Bobbitt. **5.** "Conflict Management"—Provides helpful hints for judging construction worker fistfights, with proper attention given to recognizing when to call the ambulance and when to call the police. **6.** "Motivation"—Gives the ten magic words that never fail to motivate a construction superintendent: "Until you correct this problem, I'm withholding your weekly payment." **7.** "Negotiation Skills"—Gives the two eloquent words that every construction worker fully understands, "Shit happens."

Of John Bobbitt's Penis and the New Information Age

THE "information age" is a term that has been shoveled around with ★★★page 94★★★   a great deal of élan in our professional literature. The

information age theory is that in our post-industrial economy the real focus is on the production and transmission of information. A great electronic superhighway is envisioned that will facilitate the flow of data between producers and consumers. So complicated is this data and its means of transmission that there will be a vital role for librarians to play as intermediary information brokers. We will be the cyberwizards who will facilitate the electronic interactivity between producer and consumer.   **OKAY**, I guess in theory I can buy this brave new electronic universe theory. The world is getting very complex and just to survive we will need to access all kinds of highly sophisticated information. In practice, however, I'm a skeptic. If the information age is at hand and the electronic superhighway is under construction, why are our information needs becoming more and more primitive?   **UNLESS** you've been spending all of your time buried inside *AACR2*, you've no doubt noticed a big sea change in our culture's mainstream magazines, newspapers, and television networks. We have become **obsessed with sleaze**, scandals, and gossip. Subject matter—John Bobbitt's penis, Joey Buttafuoco's sex life, and Tonya Harding's marriage—that had traditionally been the journalistic table scraps that only the supermarket tabloids would stoop to nibble, have now become the main course meal that sustains our mainstream media.   **AS** I watch the steady stream of newspapers and magazines flow through our acquisitions office, it's difficult not to marvel at how far and how fast the journalism profession has fallen. It was just twenty years ago during the presidency of Richard Nixon that journalism rose to new heights of importance in the everyday life of our republic. It was the *New York Times* and its relentless pursuit of the truth that exposed the evil underside to our war in Vietnam, and it was the *Washington Post* and its courageous investigation into high level secrets that unraveled the Watergate coverup. By 1974 it seemed perfectly obvious to everyone that without an aggressive press corps our government officials could perpetrate as much deception, fraud and corruption as they desired. Journalists, therefore, were seen as essential to the effective functioning of democracy. Our new national heroes were Woodward and Bernstein, and our great father was Walter Cronkite.   **HOW** did things degenerate so quickly in twenty short years? How did the journalist go from being the protector of the people to being a bottom feeding, blood sucking parasite more interested in poking around into Bill Clinton's sexual shenanigans than in probing his policy toward the genocide being perpetrated in Bosnia? How did the journalistic food chain get reversed? Why is it that the mainstream media now feeds off of the table scraps left over by the tabloids? Why, to put it bluntly, did John Bobbitt's penis become a national issue? Here are my theories:
1. The Cold War is over, and the journalists have

nothing to write about. You have to remember that journalists thrive on dramas and disasters, and when the 45-year nuclear duel between *us* and *them* came to an end, the only big dramas left in the world were California earthquakes and fires and unfortunately that doesn't interest a lot of people because they think that California is the new Sodom and deserves everything it gets. The news industry hates good news. Good news does not sell, and since the end of the Cold War the news has mostly been good. So to fill the void left by the Cold War, journalists are now peddling sleaze.   2. With the advent of cable television and the proliferation of new viewing choices, the profit margins of the three major networks have shrunk. This has resulted in cost cutting, and T.V. news departments have been hit hard. With limited staff, it's a lot easier to cover the John Bobbitt penis trial in Virginia than the famine in East Africa.   3. In a society where S.A.T. scores are falling and illiteracy rates are soaring, **people are too stupid** to understand the historical complexities of the ethnic battles in Bosnia or the geopolitical nuances of the emerging countries in Eastern Europe. A severed penis, however, is something that everyone "gets."   4. Finally there is the chain reaction phenomenon to the news industry. When *U.S.A. Today* fine-tuned the format of the supermarket tabloids, major media giants had to get with the formula also or risk losing circulation. Did you ever think that you would read about John Bobbitt's penis on the front page of the *New York Times,* and did you ever think you'd read an opinion piece about it in the *Nation*?   **THE** new journalistic food chain goes like this: the tabloids break a story, the trash T.V. programs (*Hard Copy* and *A Current Affair*) develop it further, the newspapers report it, and the respectable journals of opinion tell us what it all means. Thus John Bobbitt's penis goes from being the wounded victim of a dysfunctional marriage to the symbolic manifestation of something amiss in the national psyche.   **ALL** of this is important to remember when one of your library colleagues starts pontificating about the new information age and what it means to librarians. The truth is that the means of transferring information may have gone high tech, but the information being transmitted is strictly low life.

The Theory and Practice of Managing People

"**LOOK**, Harold, I don't have time to deal with your little problem right now. I'm late for class."   "**BUT**, Will, it will only take a minute. Sit down and listen."   "**OKAY**, okay, but make it quick. Class starts in a half hour and it takes five minutes to drive to school, fifteen minutes to find a place to park, and ten minutes to walk to class. Harold, you've got five minutes."   "**WILL**, just out of curiosity, what's the class?"
★★★page 96★★★   "**ADMINISTRATING** Human Resources in the

Public Sector." "**SOUNDS** awful." "**I'M** keeping an open mind. This class is required for the Master's of Public Administration degree that I'm working on. I'm hoping that I'll be able to learn some new techniques to make me a better personnel manager. So what's your problem?" "**WELL, it's not my problem** exactly." "**HAROLD**, you're down to three minutes." "**OKAY**, okay, here's the problem in a nutshell: Maryjane in children's has moved all the furniture in her office and has replaced it with beanbag chairs." "**WHY'D** she do that?" "**BECAUSE** she thought it would break down the barriers to communication. She says that people—parents, staff members, even children—feel constrained by a formal office setting." "**SO**, what's the problem?" "**YOU** don't see a problem?" "**NOT** inherently." "**YOU** don't think Maryjane is making a mockery of the organizational structure?" "**NOT** necessarily." "**YOU** don't think that Maryjane is teetering on the brink of organizational anarchy?" "**NOT** really." "**WHO** ever heard of an office with nothing but beanbag chairs?" "**LOOK**, Harold, there's something you should understand about Maryjane. She's not **a yuppie in training** like you. She's a child of the '60s. Beanbag chairs are a sixties thing. So chill out. Look, I'm late for my class." "**WILL**, there's just one more thing." "**MAKE** it snappy, Harold. Better yet, why don't you walk me out to my car?" "**OKAY**, but you need to know that Tommie Dora Tompkins is very upset." "**WHO** is Tommie Dora Tompkins, Harold?" "**SHE'S** the new Aide II in the children's room. She's terribly creative with a paint brush and a finger puppet, but she must weigh about 250 pounds." "**WHAT'S** your point, Harold?" "**MY** point, Will, is that Tommie Dora Tompkins came to me privately and told me that she won't sit in a beanbag chair for fear that she won't be able to get back up. She's terribly worried about being called into Maryjane's office to discuss her three-month performance review. She's so upset and so embarrassed that she's thinking about quitting. What do you think we should do?" "**THIS** is a touchy one. Maybe I'll get some answers tonight at night school." **NIGHT** school—the very term conjures up in my mind images of classrooms crowded with submarginal students and incompetent teachers. It's a place for people whose pasts have been littered by mistakes, failures, and regrets and whose futures are clouded by false hopes, misconceptions, and impossible dreams. Night school, it always seemed to me, is education's backwater—an academic safety net for students who had fumbled badly their first time out. I had always imagined it as a glorified group tutorial filled with **underachievers and dropouts**. **IF** there was one thing I had done right in my life it was to manage to get through 18 consecutive years of schooling from kindergarten to graduate library school without flunking or taking a year

off for "personal reasons." I may not have been a model straight A student, but I did know how to play the game and I did get my ticket punched right on time at every stop along the way. As a reward, night school was one of life's unpleasantries that I had never had to bother myself with. I had my M.L.S. and would, therefore, never have to suffer through the grind of working a job and going to school at the same time. But now fifteen years after I had vowed never to step into a classroom again, I found myself sitting in a hard backed chair paying homage to a white-haired professor. **"WELCOME** to Managing Human Resources in the Public Sector," he intones in that pompous way that all professors have. This semester should be a productive one. Clearly, human resources managers who function in a public sector context are confronted with a diverse array of challenging issues in our post-industrial, post-historical, and post-economic world. All the old presuppositions that we could make about our organizations based upon the presumptions of the past are now inoperative. It's a new world that we are living in, one in which human beings will be called upon to play a role which in many respects has not yet been defined. **"SINCE** many of you are obviously already working, in one form or another in the area of human resources administration in the public sector, I'm sure that this class will have immediate value for you. One of the things, of course, that you have probably already noticed in your work environments is the revolution of change that is occurring in the organizational structuring of human beings. This has largely been caused by a diverse array of inherent pressures that are forcing a more synectic approach to the alignment of human resources." **AS** he comes up for air, I'm hoping this is where he's going to talk about what to do when your head of children's replaces her desk with a beanbag chair, but no, he drones on about "the exciting new morphological developments that are revolutionizing the whole practice of organizational development. **THE** first person I see in the morning is Harold. "So, Will," he says, "what did you learn in class last night?" **"WE** had an hour lecture on O.D." **"WHAT'S** that?" **"ORGANIZATIONAL** Development." **"WHAT'S** that?" **"ORGANIZATIONAL** Development is a designed and systematic process which applies the principles and practices of the behaviorally based sciences to an existing organization in order to effect morphological change and enhance organizational synergy. Want to hear more?" **"DOES** it have anything to say about supervisors who replace their office furniture with beanbag chairs?" **"NO**, but while I was driving home from class I remembered a situation where two of my kids, when they were little, had to share a room. One wanted the room furnished with Mickey Mouse furniture and the other wanted Star Wars furniture."
★★★page 98★★★   **"SO** what did you do?"   **"I** let the one buy

Mickey Mouse furniture and the other buy Star Wars furniture." "**SO** what's the point?" "**SO** go down to children's and congratulate Maryjane for her efforts to break down obstacles to communication and explain to her that some people, for whatever reason, don't feel comfortable sitting in beanbag chairs and then ask her to think about putting back some of her regular furniture so that people can choose the chairs they feel most comfortable with. Present it to her as a freedom of choice thing. Sixties people are into choices. She'll buy it."
THIS little vignette set the trend for the semester. I would work all day at managing my library staff of 65 employees and then at night I would go to night school to learn how to manage my library staff of 65 employees. The problem was that it was always the same, I would go from the ridiculous to the sublime and then back to the ridiculous. I would have been just as well off taking a course in chemical engineering. It would have had the same amount of practical value as my course in management science.   **WHEN** solving personnel problems I never, repeat never, was able to apply *anything* that I had learned in class to my job at the library. In fact I soon came to realize that what I had learned from parenting three children was much more useful than what I learned in graduate school. In fact, I became so disturbed by the gulf that exists between practice and theory of personnel management that I began to keep a log. Here are the relevant excerpts: **10/17**—Mary Beth Schenk, my reference head, reported to me that her staff was up in arms over a recent directive from city hall, that the city would no longer approve expenditures for bottled water services in staff workrooms and lounges. City management felt it was contradictory to be using taxpayers' money to pay for bottled water just because some employees didn't like the taste of city tap water. "What kind of a message," the directive asked, "does that send our citizens when city employees won't even drink the city's water?"   **10/26**—Professor Prudhomme's lecture today was about heuristics, which he explained as a "process that can be used by employees in discretionary positions to guide the examination and exploration of a work related problem in which possible solutions are developed by evaluating the evolutionary progress made toward the desired result." He went on to expound that "many theoreticians consider heuristics to be an anti-process because it represents a non-formulaic, pragmatic attempt to contain a multiplicity of complex variables which substituting the principles of maximization for the principles of optimization."   **10/27**—Three catalogers spoke to me for forty-five minutes about the difficulty of working with a mending and binding volunteer named Todd Hornbuckle. It seems that Todd, a very productive worker and a very nice man, has an incurable flatulence problem that is both noisy and noisome.   **10/29**—Francine Greasehopper is mad at Sally Ottoman because Sally has begun bringing

Will T.Q.M. tell me how to get Ralph the reference librarian to use a deodorant?

Monkeymeats, her pet white mouse, to work with her every day. "Is Monkeymeats caged?" I asked. "Yes," Francine replied, "but **he still gives me the creeps** and Sally talks to him all day like he's a human being." 11/2—Morphological Analysis was the topic of tonight's class. We had a special speaker—Dr. Ruth Frankington from the graduate mathematics department. A world renowned scholar in this area, Dr. ★★★page 100★★★ Frankington explained to us that morphological analysis is a "predictive technique that technically skilled employees should be encouraged to use to limit the range of futures resulting from a series of articulated decisions. The technique involves identifying variables involved in each decision, listing the irreducible values for each variable, and developing a series of strategies to control each variable."   11/3—Harold reported to me today that Bertha Boomersbach, a reference librarian, has been wearing biker clothes to work, and has gotten **a snake tattoo** on her left forearm. Harold feels that this does not represent an appropriate professional image.   11/8—Harold rushed into my office today and said, "What is our policy on nose rings?" "Oh no," I replied, "has Bertha gone out now and gotten her nose pierced?" "No," answered Harold, "Edwin in circulation has."   11/9—In class we went over the principles underlying the Markov Chain. According to Professor Prudhomme, "Markov chain theory is an amalgamation of operations research theory, systems theory, probability theory, chaos theory, and human needs theory." Fortunately he clarified this definition with this example: "Suppose a lizard is sitting on a particular stone in a Zen garden. Suppose there are a series of stones in the garden. Suppose that each of these stones is marked. By using the principles of the Markov chain theory we will be able to calculate the probability that the lizard will lie on any given stone after a finite period of time."   11/15—I found out today that morale in my children's department is at an all-time low. Apparently a birthday party was held for Susan Teegarden. Her children's room colleagues—Maryjane Marlowe, Roberta Ellen Stankey, Kristina Kelly, Gail Radmacher, and Tommie Dora Tompkins—gave her a chocolate marble cake and a Swatch watch with a paisley design. The next day Tommie Dora Tompkins noticed that Susan wasn't wearing the watch. Tommie Dora asked her why not, and Susan answered, "I returned it. Swatch just isn't me." Tommie Dora then went back to Maryjane, Roberta, Kristina, and Gail and announced, "Susan has taken her Swatch watch back to the store for a refund. She didn't like it. Kristina and I told you we shouldn't have given her a Swatch watch for her birthday." Now Tommie Dora and Kristina are mad at Maryjane and Roberta for not listening to them, and Maryjane and Roberta are mad at Susan for taking the watch back and even madder at Tommie Dora and Kristina for being right.   11/16—Tonight in class we learned about the practice of mathetics—that's mathetics not mathematics. Mathetics is the "utilization of reinforcement theory to analyze and reconstruct those behavioral components that are usually associated with the mastery of a knowledge base or a skill repertoire. It is a technique that is often used in developing training classes for employees who apply technical skills to task performance."   11/21—Reference librarian Herb Higgins stirred everybody up at our staff meeting today when he divulged the results of a recent study that supposedly "proved" that the emissions from a microwave oven can cause cancer. "What's particularly troubling about this issue," Herb said, "is that in our staff room we have not one, not two, but three, count them—three microwave ovens, all of which are often on simultaneously. This creates an unhealthy atmosphere, and I strongly urge the administration to have these ovens removed." What ensued, of course, was a verbal free-for-all fueled by personal attacks, medical misinformation, and complete confusion. **11/22**—Before I could even get into my office Harold confronted me with the crisis du jour. "Remember that Black & Decker Air Station that you allowed Buster to buy (Buster is our janitor) last week?" **"YES**, he said he needed it to keep up the air pressure on the bookmobile tires," I replied. **"WELL**, he kind of got carried away with it and overinflated all the tires. Now they're all flat. Do you want me to give him a formal written reprimand?" **"NO**," I replied, "I want you to **shoot him**." **11/23**—Professor Snoke from the psychology department lectured at class tonight on the value of Freudian psychology in arriving at a "better understanding of the significant impact that unconscious motives produce in employee behavior and the resultant effect that this may have on organizational operations." He explained that unconscious, psychological defensive signals transmitted between managers and subordinates can result in unproductive and ineffective interactions and that unique structural, sociotechnical, environmental, and cultural characteristics can contribute to the nature of these interactions. **11/26**—This morning Priscilla Ripley, circulation clerk, came bounding into my office with a formal written grievance. The nature of her complaint, although unusual, was fortunately not complicated. Priscilla believes that the library's medical insurance plan should cover the breast enhancement operation that she had done last month. **11/28**—This obviously was my week for formal written grievances because today Francine Greasehopper decided to escalate her complaint about Sally Ottoman's mouse, **Monkeymeats**. In her written diatribe about the situation she makes mention of the fact that it has gone beyond an annoyance to a health hazard and then makes reference to the latest theory that the deadly hantavirus that has claimed over fifty lives is probably being spread by mice and other rodents. **12/7**—Today we had our final exam in Administrating Human Resources in the Public Sector. It was a very weird exam—the weirdest exam that I have ever taken. We were given a copy of a *New Yorker* cartoon in which a mouse and a cat are standing in an art museum pondering a large painting of a Coke bottle. The caption is "People read too much into everything." We were supposed to write an essay on how that cartoon relates to human resource administration. For the

★★★page 102★★★   longest time I drew a blank, but when I looked at the mouse I thought about Francine Greasehopper's formal written complaint about Sally Ottoman's mouse, Monkeymeats. So that's what I wrote about. Apparently, however, that's not what the professor was looking for because I got a D on the exam. It turned out that the cartoon had something to do with morphological futures.   12/14—Monkeymeats died today. Sally Ottoman accused Francine Greasehopper of poisoning him. She requested that the library pay a veterinarian to **do an autopsy**. I declined and Sally is now filing a formal written grievance.

Stopping World Hunger

FOR me, becoming a librarian was a stop-gap thing. It was something that I would do to pay the bills while waiting for my writing career to take off. Ever since I read Carlos Baker's biography of Ernest Hemingway in my sophomore year of college I had believed that a writer's lifestyle would be hard to top.   **SIPPING** wine in Paris, running with the bulls in Pamplona, fishing for marlin in the Gulf Stream, hunting elephants in Kenya, swimming in the Mediterranean, and skiing in Sun Valley—this I decided was the life for me. I had checked the whole vocational thing out pretty thoroughly and could find nothing in the *Occupational Outlook Handbook* that even came close to the fame, money, and respect that accrue to a celebrated and serious author like Hemingway.   I was realistic enough, however, to realize that you don't simply wake up one morning and declare yourself a celebrated and serious author, and I was quite ready to struggle through an early apprenticeship and **endure the indignities** of poverty, insecurity, and rejection. I knew that it takes time and perseverance to hone one's writing skills.   **HEMINGWAY**, for instance, labored at his trade for ten years before producing his first great literary masterpiece, *The Sun Also Rises*. But I also knew that the early period of poverty and obscurity had given him the character he needed to infuse his books with a profound sense of humanity. Years later at the height of his fame, Hemingway would say that those early years of struggle constituted the happiest and most satisfying period of his life.   **SO** no, I wasn't exactly looking forward to an apprenticeship filled with hard times and humiliation, but like Hemingway, I knew that it would make me a better person and a better writer and that someday I would look back upon those years with a fond sense of longing. Naturally I had to do something to pay the rent and what better way for a writer to earn a living than to work in a library. This was a pursuit that almost guaranteed the poverty, obscurity, and social rejection that I was looking for to develop my own sense of humanity.   **AND** so after working reference every day for eight hours I would go home and hack away at my Smith Corona typewriter for at least four or five hours every night. The one thing you could say about me was that I was prolific. When I was twenty-three, for instance, I produced two and a half novels, and in 1977 I wrote thirty-one short stories.   **BUT** if I was prolific, I was also "overwrought, self-absorbed, and terrible," which is the way one editor described a novel I had written entitled *Who's Killing the Fat Men of Farmingdale?* He said he was sorry to be so blunt but he felt it was in my best interest to know that I had **no talent**. Obviously I was very disappointed because I thought the book had its moments. It was the story of an overly idealistic reference librarian who becomes disillusioned by the amount of money the library is spending on fad diet books in order to satiate the reading appetites of the steady stream of fat library patrons who are desperate to lose weight. When a goodly number of these **corpulent customers begin showing up dead** all over

I don't think it's such a bad rejection letter. Yes he says that your manuscript is "overwrought, tedious, and pretentious," but he never really says that he doesn't like it.

town, mass hysteria results.   I thought the book was a worthy successor to the works of Charles Brockden Brown and Edgar Allan Poe, but ★★★page 104★★★   I was the only one who drew that conclusion.

Eventually, of course, I tired of writing things that would never get published and began focusing more seriously on my day job—librarianship. While I never actually stopped writing, I did stop sending my stuff to publishers. All human beings have a certain capacity for humiliation and after receiving over 150 rejection letters I had certainly reached mine.   **SO** I abandoned the struggle to write the great American novel and began doing a three-hundred word library column in the local newspaper, a friendly little publication entitled *The Burlington Standard Press*. This paper came out twice a week and was read voraciously by almost everyone who lived in the picturesque little town of Burlington, Wisconsin (population 7,850). They would go through it quite methodically starting with the birth notices and proceeding through the police reports and marriage announcements and ending with the obituaries. My column, which poked fun at all the off-the-wall things that often occurred in the library, was entitled "Snowballs in the Bookdrop," and I think it provided a nice balance to the paper's more serious attempts at journalism—you know, reports on what the Fred Sterlings served at their backyard Hawaiian luau.   **WHILE** I didn't win any Pulitzers, I did amass enough material to create a manuscript entitled *Snowballs in the Bookdrop*, a manuscript that to my great surprise the friendly folks at the Shoestring Press graciously decided to publish. Now I had my break. I was a published author. Fame and fortune were just around the corner, and I began planning a two-month trip to Europe where I would sip wine in Paris, **run with the bulls** in Pamplona, and go swimming in the Mediterranean.   **BUT** first, of course, there were certain obligatory details that I needed to attend to. Phil, Oprah, Geraldo, and possibly Johnny would soon be calling me for appearances and the vast network of radio talk show hosts all across America and Canada would no doubt be begging for my services. Although these speaking engagements would be time consuming and physically exhausting, I realized that like any responsible author I would have to dutifully give the media their **pound of flesh**. This was just part of the ordeal of being an author in the 1980s. If you wanted to be successful you had to market yourself.   **AND** if I marketed myself effectively I was very confident that the creative communities in Hollywood and New York would be beating on my door and begging me to turn the book into a television sitcom, a Broadway play, or possibly even a full scale movie. I pictured someone like Woody Allen wanting to get together with me to discuss a possible collaboration. Yes, marketing would be the key.   **EVEN** Hemingway was being marketed in the '80s. Although dead for twenty-five years, **he was never hotter** than during the Reagan years of greed and avarice when everything from the Hemingway shotgun to the Hemingway fishing hat became all the rage. Even more astounding was the fact that a steady stream of new Hemingway titles kept appearing with grotesque regularity. While it was fun to think of Papa typing obstinately away **in his coffin**, the unseemly truth was that unscrupulous editors and executors were re-working old manuscript material that Hemingway had never intended for publication.   **THIS** grave robbing so alarmed me that shortly after the publication of *Snowballs* I decided to summarily throw away all my old manuscripts. Now that I was halfway to celebrity status I didn't want to run the posthumous risk of having my old "overwrought, self-absorbed, and terrible" working papers exhumed and published. You never know when death is going to come knocking at your door, and whenever he decided to appear at mine I wanted to be completely certain that my attic was empty.   **OF** course, as soon as I woke up the next morning I instantly regretted the rashness of my decision. Maybe the great American novel was lurking somewhere in those discarded thousands of pages of manuscript. Maybe that judgmental editor who had condemned them as "terrible" was in reality just some overprivileged Ivy League English major whose only sense of existential angst had occurred on the unfortunate afternoon when he opened his office refrigerator and discovered that he was out of French soda water. My books were about real people, people whom that sophomoric yuppie would have nothing but disdain for.   **I**, therefore, threw on some clothes and rushed down to the municipal trash dumpster by the back door of the library where I had deposited my manuscripts. The dumpster, of course, was now empty and my manuscripts were gone forever. I thought briefly about going down to the administrative offices of the city's solid waste disposal department to try to determine what landfill site my papers were deposited in but decided against it. A strong believer in fate, I reasoned that God had spoken and it was for the best. The world did not need *Who's Killing the Fat Men of Farmingdale?*   **IN** the long run **it didn't matter**. I was embarking on a new beginning and really didn't need to be weighted down by my literary past. With *Snowballs* I had developed a fresh new style (*Library Journal* said it had "the sparkle and spontaneity of a good conversation") and so there was no turning back. Besides, Oprah, Phil, Geraldo, and Johnny were waiting. **ACTUALLY** I was the one who waited and waited and waited. Oprah never called, Phil never called, Geraldo never called, and Johnny never called. No one from radioland called. No one from the *New York Review of Books* called. No one from Hollywood called. No one from Broadway called. No one from newspaperland called. And worst of all Woody Allen did not call.   **THERE** would be no sitcom, no talk show appearances, no nationally syndicated newspaper column, and no translations into fifty-three foreign languages. Despite the nice review ★★★page 106★★★   from *LJ*, the book didn't exactly take off. In fact, in its first year of publication its sales totaled 753. When you consider that my mother probably purchased half of that total you get an idea of how well the book riveted the attention of America's readers. Actually it occurred to me late one night that it was logistically possible to invite everyone who had purchased the book to a dinner party in my home, and several days later during a moment of extreme weakness I considered doing exactly that. If Johnny Carson didn't want to talk about my book maybe these people would. I was extremely desperate to bask in someone's adulation. I was now a bonafide writer for goodness sakes and I deserved some acclaim.   **MY** wife, however, was predictably practical. "That's a ridiculous idea. They'd track up the carpeting."   **SO** I dutifully put away the European travel brochures, stopped trying to figure out what I was going to do with all my money, and went back to being a nobody. **Being a nobody, I soon realized, had its advantages.** The pressure was off. I wouldn't have to worry about my sitcom ratings, I wouldn't have to hire an expensive tax attorney, and I wouldn't have to think up witty one-liners for the *Tonight Show*.   **SO** for ten years I was a nobody and basically enjoyed it. Whenever I got a hankering to be rich and famous all I had to do was go stand in line at the grocery store and peruse the tabloids to know that the worst thing that could happen to a person in America was to become rich and famous, and immediately I would offer a word of thanks to God that my book had been a flop.   **BUT** from time to time I would backslide and start thinking about those bulls in Pamplona and how I was getting too old to run with them. At times like that I would take out a cache of letters from my desk written by a publisher named Robbie Franklin and start dreaming again of being an author. Franklin wanted me to write a book for him (he owned a publishing company in North Carolina) and every couple of years or so he would remind me of his invitation. I always responded that with *Snowballs in the Bookdrop* I had received all the fame and fortune that a person could possibly handle in one lifetime and therefore I was not interested in doing another book ever again.   **THE** years, however, can have a way of dimming the disappointments of the past and renewing our hopes for the future. As time rolled by, *Snowballs* seemed less and less of a flop. It sold a few more copies each year and I figured that sometime in the next millennium its sales might hit the 10,000 mark, not exactly the kind of crowd that you could invite over for a dinner party. Some books obviously take more time to find an audience than others. *Moby-Dick,* for instance, was thought of as a complete failure for the first fifty years of its existence. I was confident, therefore, that like a fine wine, *Snowballs* would improve with age.   **I** was practical enough, however, to realize that the reemergence of *Snowballs* as a force on the literary marketplace would not occur   ★★★page 107★★★

unless I helped it along with the push of a second book. This, of course, was a strategy employed by John Grisham, whose slow-selling first novel, *A Time to Kill,* was brought back to life by the enormous popularity of his second novel, *The Firm.* I envisioned a similar scenario unfolding for myself.   **And** so in 1990, a full nine years after the publication of *Snowballs,* I accepted Mr. Franklin's invitation, and began writing a series of opinion pieces that came out a year later under the title, *Unintellectual Freedoms.* I was confident that this book was going to be a blockbuster bestseller because of Franklin's more aggressive approach to marketing, advertising, and public relations.   **AT** the core of his strategy was the idea that I break my nine-year **self-imposed exile** from A.L.A. annual conferences and sign books at his exhibit booth. An autograph party is just the thing we needed to give the book that extra push toward stardom. So enthusiastic was I about the idea that I decided to take my thirteen-year-old son Stephen with me and let him observe firsthand what a famous author I was.   **WHEN** we approached the exhibit booth I could see right away that my wildest expectations had been exceeded. There right in front of my signing table was a long line of people that stretched back into the next aisle. There were obviously at least fifty people just waiting for me to show up.   **"WOW,"** I said to one of the staffers at the booth, "if I had known that I was this popular I would have gotten here earlier." **"WHAT** do you mean?" he questioned with a very puzzled look on his face.   **"THIS** line of people," I replied, "it's enormous. I knew this was going to be an effective way to sell books, but I never dreamed how effective. Look at all those people."   **"WHAT** people?" he asked with confusion.   **"THIS** line of people standing right in front of the booth."   **"WILL,"** he said, "this line is not for you. This is the end of the line for Robert McCloskey, the children's author/illustrator. It wraps around two aisles and ends up right here in front of our booth." **"WELL,** then where is the line for my book?"   **"THERE** is no line."   **"OH."**   A half hour later there still was no line, and my son was beginning to feel sorry for me. "Dad," he said, "if the people aren't going to come to you then we need to go to the people," and with that pronouncement he proceeded to approach some of the people at the end of the McCloskey line and say, "Right now is a good time to go to the Will Manley booth. Currently the line there is very short." **ONE** of the women waiting in line looked up at Stephen and quickly said, "Who the hell is Will Manley?"   **THAT'S** pretty much how the next half hour went, although two people did approach my signing table, once to ask me if I knew where the bathroom was and once to ask me if I knew where the Robert McCloskey line was. There is nothing more embarrassing than sitting at an autograph table and having nothing to do but answer directional questions.

It was agony. "Don't worry, Dad, things will pick up," said Stephen. **AFTER** fifteen more minutes of overwhelming inactivity, Stephen began to employ strategy number two. He decided to divert traffic my way by lying down in the aisle in front of my booth. This unfortunately was ineffective. Stephen is very skinny, and librarians simply stepped over him as though he were a piece of scotch tape. Librarians are, after all, fairly used to having patrons lying on the carpet reading books. They're a tolerant lot.   **WHEN** it was obvious that the roadblock strategy was ineffective, Stephen did not despair. He simply hit upon another idea. This time he picked up a copy of my book, opened it to the middle, and began to laugh hysterically and proclaim in a loud voice, "This book is a riot. This is the funniest stuff I have ever read in my life. The part where the monkey gets loose in the biography stacks is simply a scream. This book is hilarious! I love this book. Will you please autograph it for me?" This approach did draw bemused attention to Stephen but when people noticed that the book he was holding was a library science title, the looks of amusement turned to looks of sympathy. The general consensus was obviously that Stephen was, clinically speaking, a nitwit.   **FINALLY**, with fifteen excruciating minutes to go, Stephen's creativity paid off. This time his scam had heart. In a moment of inspiration he grabbed the sign off my desk (the sign that said WILL MANLEY—NOON to 2 PM), turned it over, and wrote, STOP WORLD HUNGER—BUY THIS BOOK. He then taped this poster to a yardstick and began waving it high in the air.   **I'M** not sure how Stephen knew this, but when it comes to giving to charity and donating to good causes no one is more generous than the average librarian. I won't say that people now began to flock to my table but I did manage to sell thirteen books in the last fifteen minutes—nothing to make me rich, but at least something to **avert total humiliation**.   **IF** you're concerned about the professional ethics of all of this, don't be. Stephen had a perfectly honest answer to the cataloger from Nebraska who wanted to know exactly whose hunger the proceeds from this book were going to stop. "Mine," he said without hesitation, "all proceeds from this book will be used by my father to put food on our table." Proving that catalogers do have a heart, this woman plunked down her twenty dollars with a satisfied nod of the head.   **LATER** that day, I asked Stephen what he wanted to do. "If my recollection is correct," he said, "you owe me big time." **"HOW** so?" I said.   **"WELL**, whether you know it or not, you made a commitment to feed me today."   **"OKAY**, okay," I replied. "What will it be Burger King, McDonalds, Pizza Hut, or Wendy's?" **"WENDY'S** nothing. We're going to Nikolai's Roof!"   **"WHAT** is Nickolai's Roof?"   **"IT'S** Atlanta's only five-star restaurant, and don't forget your credit card. I hear the French food   ★★★page 109★★★

there is great."

See, I Told You So

IF you're a book-oriented librarian (a term that unfortunately is becoming more and more oxymoronic) you've got to wonder where your guardian angel has been hiding lately. First there are the constantly depressing financial indicators—annual inflation, chronically high unemployment, painfully slow economic growth, and the steady erosion of local tax bases. Then there is the shocking series of natural disasters that seem to be occurring with unnatural regularity. You name it and in the last five years we've had it—floods, earthquakes, tornadoes, and fires. It makes you wonder if maybe David Koresh wasn't onto something. And finally there is the growing pressure to invest our already scarce budgetary resources into non-book materials like videotapes, videogames, computer software, and electronic information sources. **THE** stormy weather in Libraryland today actually bears a strong resemblance to the chilly climate of the late 1970s when Jimmy Carter was president and the term "stagflation" (an unparalleled economic condition characterized by both high inflation and high unemployment) first entered our language. On top of all the bad economic news was the frightening specter that the passage of Proposition 13 in California would propel a grassroots tax revolt that would huff and puff across America and blow away all of our libraries. So morose was the prevailing mood at the time, that the lead essay in the 1979 *A.L.A. Yearbook* was a piece entitled "The Late Great Public Library—May It Rest in Peace?" **YOU** hear a lot of the same gloom and doom nonsense today. You hear that taxpayers can't afford to fund non-essential services. You hear that even if taxpayers could afford to support libraries, they wouldn't. And finally you hear that none of that makes any difference anyway because libraries will soon be obsolete for the simple reason that books are rapidly becoming obsolete. **IT'S** all very depressing, but the most depressing thing is that this time around so many librarians are joining in the funeral procession. That's right. We seem to be the ones writing our own obituary and orchestrating our own requiem. Sometimes when I attend a library conference I feel like I've just walked into a large **group session for the clinically depressed** where the main form of therapy is trying to top everyone else's tale of woe. "I'm more depressed than you are" is our new form of oneupmanship. It's always a relief for me, therefore, to return home and get back into the friendly confines of my library where at least the patrons still have a sense of the importance, value, and longevity of our services. **THE** prevailing mood of pessimism in the profession, although understandable, surprises me. By now you would think that most of us would have become hardened to the ways of the world. We librarians are a tough lot. We're used to doing our job without getting a lot of money or respect. When we got into this profession we knew we would never become rich or famous, but we went in anyway because we enjoy the creative process of bringing books and people together and because we take an idealistic sense of satisfaction out of enriching the people and communities whom we serve.   **AND** just as we knew that a life devoted to librarianship would consign us to a lifetime of personal financial uncertainty, we also harbored no illusions about the financial well being of the institutions where we would ply our trade. Libraries like all other publicly supported entities are subject to the unstable forces of politics and economics. There are good times and there are bad times, and no amount of complaining about the "idiots" who run our governments can change that simple, unpleasant fact.   **TRADITIONALLY** that has been one of our bulwarks—to have the strength and stoicism to weather the bad times and the enthusiasm and energy to capitalize on the good times. But even more importantly, at the core of the library profession, has been our rock-ribbed confidence that in the long term libraries will always transcend the vagaries of political trends and economic cycles. We have always had an enduring optimism that what we do and what we represent are so important to the individuals and communities that we serve that we will outlast depressions, recessions, floods, earthquakes, tax revolts, and even neo-conservative political movements.   **THERE** are signs, however, that our confidence is starting to crack and that we are beginning to lose faith in the power of our basic principles—that libraries exist to educate and enrich as well as inform and entertain and that book collection development is a long term investment based upon a holy trinity of values—quality, balance, and diversity. The first few fissures in the foundation appeared in 1979 with the publication of a much talked about article in *Publisher's Weekly* entitled "The Selling of the Library," which chronicled "the revolution taking place in the Baltimore County Library."   **WHAT** exactly was this revolution? By the third paragraph you got the sense that it wasn't a revolution at all, but rather the application of some rather simplistic retail bookstore principles to the operation of Baltimore County's many shopping mall branch libraries. The neon signage, the paperback display "dumps," the open-faced shelving and the decision to focus on bestsellers were hardly on the cutting edge of innovation. These "revolutionary" ideas were actually stolen just down the shopping mall hallway from retailers like Waldenbooks, B. Dalton, and Bookstar. Baltimore County was playing a slick game of copy cat and calling it a breakthrough of innovation and creativity.   **THE** article should have been re-titled "The Selling Out of the Public Library" not just because Baltimore County was dressing itself up in bookstore finery but because it was also sacrificing basic library principles. This self-styled "revolution" was, in reality, nothing more than a triumph of style over substance. Baltimore County had abandoned the traditional mission of the public library to inform and educate in favor of the more popular goal to amuse and entertain.   **IN** the article, a spokesperson for the library was even quoted as saying, "There are two things wrong with librarians. **They don't think** about where their money comes from so they don't spend enough on books and then they buy the wrong books. What are the wrong books? These are books that librarians have deemed as good, worthwhile, or important without ever considering whether the public will request them." Here are some other quotes: **"LIBRARIANS** can't bear to pass up that English poetry of the mid–19th century. Why? Because they're building a collection in that area or they liked poetry in school. And who gets cheated? The hundreds of taxpayers waiting to read *Chesapeake*."   **"THE** quality of the item is unimportant relative to its publicity and the number of people who ask for it."   **"WE** learned that the more books we eliminate, the higher our circulation goes. People want to be able to find the books that are new and interesting. They don't like crowded shelves."   **"ONE** of the questions we asked (in an interview for a librarian opening) was "If *The Odyssey* doesn't circulate what will you do with it?" If the applicant answered, 'But it's a classic, you must keep it in the collection,' we couldn't hire that person."   **WHAT'S** clear from these quotes is that the administrators at Baltimore County were not content to simply transform their libraries into publicly subsidized bookstores, they also felt the need to ridicule, burn, and slash the traditional principles of library management and book acquisitions. The rather obvious implication was that those of us who adhered to traditional principles of book selection based upon quality were old fashioned, stupid, and arrogant elitists who were stubbornly trying to force our patrons to read books that they simply did not want to read.   **BUT** there was also another, more cutting argument that Baltimore County Library administrators used to justify their decision to pander to popular tastes. Their way, they claimed, was more cost effective. If you buy nothing but bestsellers, they reasoned, you can cut down on the number of staff required to select books, and indeed, instead of involving a diversity of librarians throughout the system in the book acquisitions process, the Baltimore County director (in his own words) "imitated the chains and moved to central book selection." Under this new system, three people did all the selection for all of Baltimore County's twenty-one libraries.   **WHAT** was the impact of this change? The most obvious result was a drastic reduction in the number of titles purchased—from 15,000 titles per year to 7,000. "I suspect," added one B.C.P.L. spokes-

★★★page 112★★★   man, we could get that figure down to 3000." But that wasn't the only way that the number of titles was restricted. B.C.P.L. also went on a weeding frenzy. In one year alone, 19% of the collection was discarded. By drastically reducing the number of titles in the collection, the library was in essence practicing a subtle but very pernicious form of censorship. Balance and diversity—the twin values underpinning the whole concept of public library intellectual freedom—were ruthlessly abandoned. **THE** obvious point of all this activity was for the library to cater to the popular reader and turn its

We don't have the U.S. Code, but if you're interested in law we do have 100 copies of *The Firm*.

back on the serious student. So not only was Baltimore County abandoning traditional principles of librarianship, it was also turning its back on many of the library's traditional users with the objective of trying to circulate as many books as possible. Ten copies ★★★page 113★★★

of one Stephen King bestseller, the logic went, would circulate more often than single copies of ten lesser known works of literature. But not all of Baltimore County's patrons were enthralled. One woman, when she learned that many of her favorite poetry books had been discarded, was quoted as saying, "No one now risks stumbling across a book of poems that might unexpectedly hook him into the delights of literature.... Buy more Gothics, **buy more trash**. People like it. Especially if that's all they ever see." **THE** obvious stategy was to use spiraling circulation figures to demonstrate the need for increased funding. In other words short term gains were substituted for long term investment. It was, in my opinion, a desperate and shortsighted attempt to counteract the ill effects of a bad economy. The iconoclastic Baltimore County philosophy I predicted would enjoy its fifteen minutes of fame and then **fizzle like a fifty cent firecracker.** I was wrong by about ten years. Pretty much through the decade of the 1980s, B.C.P.L.'s "Give 'Em What They Want" strategy was not only taken seriously as a public library model but was also copied by impressionable library directors from East Coast to West. But then during the Bush recession things started to fall apart big time. When times got tough B.C.P.L.'s suburban public bookstore chain got cut by millions of dollars. And guess what the first thing to go was? You guessed it—the four mini branches that had been ballyhooed as "revolutionary" ten years earlier. They were the shopping mall storefronts that were stocked with paperbacks and staffed by volunteers. **WHEN** I read about Baltimore County's financial distress there was the greatest temptation for me to gloat and say, "I told you so," but ultimately, of course, such an attitude is self-defeating. None of us win when a library system loses, even a library system built upon the sands of a false philosophy. But while the B.C.P.L. budget cuts should not be cheered they should be held up as a case study of what happens when librarians abandon solid principles of service, balance, and diversity in favor of the illusory value of inflated circulation statistics.

Garbage In, Garbage Out

INPUT-OUTPUT, output-input. Now there's something called thruput, which is what happens, I guess, to input before it becomes output. **OF** the three—input, output, and thruput—input would on the face of it seem to be the most important factor in analyzing an organization. Consider the remarks of that wise old management professor Casey Stengel. Most baseball fans recognize Casey as one of the most successful major league managers of all times. His Yankee teams of the '50s and '60s dominated the big leagues like no other teams before or after. What a lot of people don't know about Casey, however, ★★★page 114★★★ is that he also amassed one of the worst won-loss records of all time during the years that he managed the Brooklyn Dodgers (1934–36), the Boston Braves (1938–43), and the New York Mets (1962–65). A sportswriter once asked Casey why he was such a good manager with the Yanks and such a poor one with the Dodgers, Braves, and Mets. Reportedly Casey replied, "You can't make **chicken salad out of chicken shit**." No one ever did a better job of explaining the value of input. Today of course in our computer age we put it a little differently—"garbage in, garbage out."   **KEEPING** all of this in mind, it's a bit astonishing to note that the role of input measures in evaluating a library has been largely abandoned. Today output measures are all the rage. In simple terms, the most important statistic a library now generates is the number of books checked out. What you put into the library—the number and diversity of titles—is of no inherent value. The only thing that matters is your annual circulation rate.   **THE** value of a book therefore, is directly related to how many times it circulates, and if it doesn't circulate you need to get rid of it to make room for one that will. Forget the fact that it might be a classic. That means if you have an old and tattered copy of *Moby Dick* you should discard it and buy a fifty-first copy of Rush Limbaugh's latest bestseller rather than going out and getting a new and attractive copy of Melville's masterpiece. Under this value system **the temptation is great**, therefore, to turn our libraries into recreational reading centers filled with beach books and blockbuster movies.   **THE** growing importance of output measures is due to the pressure library administrators are feeling to come up with an effective way to justify to city councils, county commissions, and state legislatures the need to spend more tax money on library development. The conventional wisdom is that politicians who hold the purse strings of public library budgets are swayed by one thing—votes. High circulation figures would seem to indicate that voters use and want libraries, and low circulation figures would seem to suggest that they are largely indifferent. So naturally the idea is to do everything possible to jack up your circulation, and buying nothing but trash is only one way to do this. Here is a list of other ways I have honestly witnessed in my twenty-three years of being a librarian: **1.** Multiply your total circulation by a factor of two or by three under the justification that "everybody else does it."   **2.** Pull up a pick-up truck to the back door of the library and fill it with books that you have checked out for the enjoyment of your family, friends, and neighbors.   **3.** Count every book that is left lying around the library at the end of the day as a circulated book.   **4.** Count every book on the shelf that is out of order or slightly askew as a circulation.   **5.** Give out free raffle tickets to patrons who check out more than ten books per week.   **6.** Distribute McDonald's coupons to children for every five books that they check out.   ★★★page 115★★★

7. Lower fine rates for people with more than 20 overdues. **8.** Multiply the number of magazine titles in the collection by a factor of 150 because that is the "estimated" average number of times a magazine title is read per month. **9.** Count each unfilled book request as a circulation because if the library had the book it would have circulated. **10.** Award a free toaster or canned ham to the patron who checks out the 1,000th book of the day. **THERE**, of course, is a huge irony in all of this. In trying to jack up circulation in order to get more money to support the library, you end up with a library that is not worth supporting.

Me and My Bookdrop

SOME people have chronic problems with their cars, others are always encountering difficulties with their plumbing, and still others have **persistent troubles** with leaky roofs. It seems curious to me that these types of problems are considered normal, and the people who have these problems are usually treated with sympathy rather than the scorn that I get whenever I start talking about my bookdrop troubles. **THE** truth is I've given very serious thought to getting out of the library profession all together because of bookdrops. But do you want to know what has carried me through this travail of frustration? Was it the support of my peers? No, of course not. In fact, my professional colleagues love to make fun of my bookdrop dilemmas. Was it the love and understanding of my family? Wrong again. My wife and kids are even more merciless in their ridicule of what they call my "obsession." No, it's been my total lack of ability to do anything else but librarianship that has steeled my resolve to cope with my bookdrop bedevilment. **THE** great joy I felt in learning that the citizens of my community had approved a 15 million dollar bond referendum had nothing to do with the fact that I would now have the opportunity to design and build a brand new 120,000 square foot state of the art public library and everything to do with the fact that I would now have the opportunity to design a brand new state of the art bookdrop. No longer would I have the bookdrop blues. My new bookdrop would be large and user friendly both for the staff and the public to use. It would be attached to the building and would empty right into the circulation workroom and would be designed so that patrons could drive right up to it. No longer would I have to listen to my **employees complain** about being made to wheel a grocery cart outside in **unseasonably hot** and inclement weather to empty our parking lot bookdrop, and no longer would I have to listen to my patrons complain about having to get out of their cars in **unseasonably hot** and inclement weather just to return their books to the bookdrop. **WITH** this new bookdrop, not only would I finally, once and for all, be liberating myself from a

maddening menace, but I would also be establishing myself as the industry wide expert on bookdrops. Librarians from all over the world would make it a point to visit my 21st century bookdrop, and I would be invited to speak at library conferences everywhere to talk about my great achievements in the area of bookdrop technology. I craved the recognition because I had always been behind the time when it came to computers, multimedia services, and on-line databases. But here was my own little niche, an opportunity to lead and get out on what everyone in the profession enjoys calling the cutting edge.   **THIS** is not to say that in the design and construction of my new building I didn't pay due attention to other aspects of library architecture like designing a youth services library, a reference center, and a special study room for students. In fact, I did give these lesser issues their due. But the truth is working on the building was a job, while working on the bookdrop was a passion, and I couldn't have been happier with the results—a large resplendent limestone structure replete with air conditioning, a spring loaded floor, immediate access to check-in computers, and a special depository box for fines equipped with a built-in safe. Also my bookdrop was big—big enough to house a family of three. And it had all the comforts of home—running water, locked doors, shuttered windows, everything but **a toilet**.   **AFTER** the bookdrop was completely designed and was in the process of being constructed I began my public relations campaign. Wherever I gave a speech at a library conference I always began by saying, "Thank you very much for inviting me here to speak on current issues in librarianship. I am very happy to be here because it gives me a wonderful opportunity to talk about the exciting things that I am doing back in my home library with bookdrop technology." Also, I wrote no fewer than three full-length articles for national library periodicals on my new bookdrop breakthrough. It wasn't long, of course, before my self-fulfilling prophecy took hold. I was rapidly becoming the **world's foremost bookdrop authority**. You name it and I was getting calls from there—Canada, New Zealand, Sweden, Illinois, Kentucky, and Virginia—all in a three-month period. Everybody wanted to know my advice on a particular bookdrop problem: **HOW** do you build secret cameras into a bookdrop to catch people who use the depository as a garbage pail? **HOW** do you keep people from putting snakes in the bookdrop? **WHAT** is the best way to design a bookdrop that would slide books down two floors to a basement workroom?   **HOW** big should a bookdrop be for a community of 10,000?   **HOW** many staff should you allocate for bookdrop duty in a library with a daily book circulation of 2,500?   **WHAT** is the optimum distance that a book should fall before hitting the floor of a bookdrop?   **WHAT** kind of a training program do you recommend for new employees   ★★★page 117★★★

who are assigned bookdrop responsibilities? **WHAT** percentage of the general public prefers to return its books to the bookdrop rather than directly to the circulation desk? **IS** it true that a cataloging professor in Denton, Texas, is very close to perfecting a mini-parachute that will minimize damage to books as they are deposited into bookdrops? **ARE** there any libraries that you know that have a provision in their bookdrop policies prohibiting the leashing of dogs? **MY** new identity as the world's foremost bookdrop expert was quite gratifying in two ways. First, it was wonderful to receive the acclaim that comes with being an internationally recognized authority, and second, it was very therapeutic to hear other people's bookdrop problems because for so many years I thought that I was the only librarian on the face of the earth who had these sorts of problems. **ALL** of this attention flattered me, and I began spending all my free time doing research into the art and science of bookdrops. I began surveying different types of libraries on the size adequacy of their drops and began working feverishly on a formula (you should have 1.2 cubic inches of bookdrop capacity for every 10 registered cardholders) and a training manual for library employees with bookdrop responsibilities ("always open the door to the bookdrop very slowly so that books will not come cascading down in a haphazard tumble"). **BUT** then something awful happened. The construction of my own bookdrop neared completion, and finally it was time for a trial run. The air conditioning worked, the spring driven floor worked, the fine depository worked, and the carefully angled chute worked. Everything worked perfectly. Well, almost everything. There was one slight problem. **You couldn't reach the bookdrop from your car.** Actually that's not quite true. You could reach it if you made like Gumby and stretched your upper body halfway out the window. **"OH** no!" I said to the architect. **"DON'T** worry," he replied nonchalantly. "Seven out of eight isn't bad." **"SEVEN** out of eight?" I responded with confusion. "What exactly does that mean?" **"WELL,"** he replied, "you asked for eight things to be incorporated into your bookdrop and seven of them work. That's not a bad percentage." **"BUT** the whole point of the bookdrop," I said with exasperation "was to relieve people of the need to get out of their cars to use it!" **"IT'S** a difficult angle, Will. Don't worry. We'll take another look at it. With a new building you can expect some bugs." I was devastated. One day I'm the Michelangelo of bookdrops and the next day I'm the guy who invented the Edsel. I couldn't sleep. I couldn't eat. I yelled at my kids. I yelled at my wife. I yelled at my mother. If I had a dog I would have yelled at him too. **"WILL,"** implored Arnold, a close professional colleague of mine from a neighboring community, "you need to take a vacation. You're losing ★★★page 118★★★ perspective. You've just managed a highly stressful building project and you're too close to it emotionally. You need some distance." **"YOU** just don't understand," I replied. **"WHAT** don't I understand?" **"YOU** see the bookdrop as an appendage to the building and I see the building as an appendage to the bookdrop." **"WILL**, that's crazy. You need to get a hold on life." **"YOU** think I need to get away?" **"ABSOLUTELY!"** **"WHERE?"** **"SOME-PLACE** more stressful than your building site." **"LIKE** where?" **"HOW** about a cruise through the Panama Canal? They're having

some civil unrest down there. Should be very helpful in putting your bookdrop problems into perspective." **SO** I went down to Panama, hung out on the beach, and took the Canal cruise. Nothing happened. It was sunny, bright, and calm. If there was no civil unrest to despair over, however, there was plenty of poverty to deplore. For a few days at least it put my bookdrop blues into perspective, but on the return home **the old knot in my stomach tightened**. As my plane approached the runway, most of the passengers focused on landmarks near and dear to their hearts—their houses, their schools, and their places of business—but I was intent on only one thing—my bookdrop. There it was, its resplendent limestone walls shining brightly in the shimmering afternoon sunlight. **THAT'S** the thing about vacations. They *are* effective in making you forget your troubles, but eventually they end, and you always have to return home and when you get home your problems are still there piled up like the **dirty mess of pots** and pans that you left in your kitchen sink with the faint hope that somehow they would magically get cleaned up and stacked away during your absence. **SO** yes, my bookdrop was still there and it was still stuck on the wrong angle, but to my great surprise there were no angry editorials in the local newspaper lambasting me for my fiasco, no angry mobs of library patrons waiting outside my office door, no stack of written complaints piled up on my desk, and no picture of me on the post office wall. **"HOW'S** everything going?" I asked one of my close colleagues at work on the day of my return. **"EVERYTHING'S** fine." **"ANY** problems with the new building?" **"NONE, everybody loves it."** **"HOW** about the height over the service counters? Has everyone adjusted to the change?" **"SURE,** everyone loves it." **"HOW** about the configuration of the non-fiction stacks? Do people think it's too confusing?" **"NOPE,** no complaints." **"HOW** about the bookdrop?" **"DITTO."** **STILL** possessing a stubborn streak of skepticism, I retreated to the privacy of my office which I had purposely located in perfect view of the bookdrop. Peering out the window, I noted with some surprise that there seemed to be some truth to what my colleague had said—people didn't seem to mind using my bookdrop. In fact they even appeared to appreciate the convenience of driving right up to it, and the fact that they had to step out of their car to use it didn't seem to bother them. Indeed, most of them had put their books in their trunks so they had to get out anyway. It really didn't matter, therefore, if the angle was right or not. While this didn't necessarily reestablish me as the Bookdrop King, at least I didn't have to worry about being exposed as **the Bookdrop Fool**. I could now get on with the rest of my life, and for the next six weeks I did just that. You don't know how wonderful it was to worry about normal things again—like getting hit by a falling satellite or getting my shoelace caught in the mall escalator. **AND** then, like an eccentric uncle who shows up unexpectedly at your front door with five pieces of luggage, my bookdrop problem reappeared on the front page of the local newspaper. "Since the new $12 million library opened in 1989," the newspaper reporter wrote, "I have raved about its beauty, design, and function. But I have been the library's harshest bookdrop critic." He then proceeded to say, "I watched a dozen drivers one morning return books. Eleven of them parked away from the building, got out, and carried the books to the bookdrop. Only the driver of a Chevy van stuffed books into the slot from her seat—but she opened the van door to make the reach easier." To highlight the story, the newspaper ran a large photograph of an elderly woman getting out of her car into the heat to return a big bag full of books. **IT** was my worst nightmare. **I was publicly exposed as a fraud.** I didn't want to leave my house. I wanted to take the phone off the hook and stay in bed for the next two or three years. But my wife, ever the practical one, rousted me out of the house with a reminder about thirty year mortgages, college tuitions, and car payments. I had to face the music. **BUT** oddly enough, nothing happened—no calls from the library board, no angry patrons, and no communications from the city council. No one cared any more about this reporter's bookdrop obsession than they cared about mine. It went that way all week. Not a murmur from anyone. In fact, the only comments I heard were from people who felt that this reporter needed "to get a life and write about something important." The prevailing attitude was that it was a complete waste of time and money for the newspaper to spill ink on a stupid bookdrop glitch when crime was going up and our streets were not safe. I did get one letter, a nice little note from a woman who advised me "to take heart because this too will pass." The trouble was, on the back of the note she added, "If it doesn't pass and you lose your job over the bookdrop mess, here is my business card." She was, you guessed it, a real estate broker. **HOW** heartening.

Bibliotherapy

I'M a big believer in the theory that physical health mirrors mental health, that the more you obsess about your health the worse it gets. That of course is easy to say. We would all like to go through life without worries or frowns. But these days that's getting harder and harder to do. It's getting to the point where you can't open a newspaper without finding a story about what you should or should not be doing to avoid an early death, which in our era of high tech medicine is around 78. **IT** used to be that 78 was a ripe old age and that if you reached 78 you could consider yourself lucky, but now the conventional wisdom is that life begins at 78. There is even a group, the Flame Foundation, that seriously believes that **immortality is possible** through a biochemical process called "cell regeneration." According to these people when your cells "reawaken" in this regenerative process, disease cannot take hold and life has no relationship with death. Their literature clearly states that "death is the result of genetic and cultural programming that can be reversed." **WHILE** these people may represent the extremist fringe of the health obsessed, the truth is it's hard to find a man today who, after a third drink, doesn't want to talk about the state of his prostate or a woman who, after a second cup of coffee, doesn't want to chit chat about the health of her ovaries. But an even trendier cocktail topic than internal body parts is the latest research on what causes everything from yeast infections to colorectal cancer. It used to be that reports on late breaking medical research were pretty much restricted to the trade journals serving the health industry. Ten years ago, innovations in gall bladder operations were not considered of interest to anyone but doctors and nurses.   **BUT** today that has all changed. Today you can open the average daily newspaper and read at least two or three articles of a fairly technical nature reporting on innovations in everything from testing for prostate cancer to treating groin injuries. Probably the biggest medical news bonanza, however, has to do with the linkage between food and physical well-being because that's an area that everyone can relate to. Never before has the old adage, "you are what you eat," been so widely accepted. The problem of course is that most of the data swirling around inside the funnel of this tornado of research is conflicting, contradictory, and confusing. One day **coffee is a killer**, the next day it's reported to ward off heart disease—the same with eggs, margarine, aspirin, turkey breast, and even oat bran.   **ONE** of the spinoffs from this information explosion is the increased business it has brought to reference librarians, many of whom are now as conversant about cholesterol and carcinogens as they are about crisscross directories and on-line catalogs. It's ironic that many Americans, obsessed as they are with living long and healthy lives, are still not entirely comfortable with physicians. While the average medical doctor is not held in the same contempt as the average lawyer, the medical profession is hardly seen as a paragon of service, selflessness, sacrifice, and trustworthiness.   **ODDLY** enough, many people feel more comfortable seeking the aid of a reference librarian in diagnosing that lump in their abdominal area than they do in going to the doctor. They probably feel that at least the librarian will not perform unnecessary and expensive surgery upon them.   **IN** my years as a reference librarian I dispensed all kinds of medical information to my patrons from how to stop the hiccups to what to do if a child swallows **half a bottle of Pine Sol**. While I was always careful to give information and not advice, there were times when I wanted to say to my patients, especially those who complained of stress related ailments like upset stomachs, hives, and nervous tension, that the best medicine is laughter. To me a book by Dave Barry or Lewis Grizzard would have been far more effective for these sufferers than tranquilizers or transcendental meditation.   **YES**, I was always intrigued with the concept of bibliotherapy and was always surprised that it was not an area that was given more attention by the library profession. After all, in this era of shrinking budgets and recessed economies, we've been going through a huge identity crisis. Are libraries really as important to our taxpayers as we let on and will our communities suffer greatly if libraries are eliminated all together? We've always convinced ourselves, if not our citizens, that libraries are an indispensible component of the democratic way of life, but is that really the case?   **MY** point here is that the medical profession has never had that identity crisis. No one has ever doubted the importance of doctors, nurses, and hospitals to the lives of the people and communities that support them. Why? Because doctors and **nurses deal in the deadly** serious business of keeping people alive in a state of minimal physical pain.   **BUT** what is it that we librarians say to justify our existence? We say something like "If we are not exactly needed to sustain life, we are needed to make accessible those things that make life worth living." It's a nice little saying but one that doesn't exactly **grab anybody by the jugular** and make them cry "uncle." We base our appeal on enhancing the quality of life rather than extending the quantity of life, and that is precisely where we are misguided. To be truly persuasive we should be bragging that libraries can make people live longer and more enjoyably.   **THE** current climate of confusion about what makes a man or woman healthy actually makes this the perfect time to reconsider the concept of bibliotherapy. You name it—crystals, step aerobics, carrot juice—these have all been identified as being the key to insuring good health and happiness, and next to them the concept of bibliotherapy actually looks plausible. First of all, books bring happiness, and secondly, the very act of reading is healthy. I have this from a source no less impressive than a medical doctor—that's right, a bonafide physician with not one, not two, but three diplomas on his wall. Yes, it is the highest irony that one day I would end up in a doctor's office and **become a victim** of my own medicine.   **THE** fact that I was **in the doctor's office** in the first place was highly ironic. I had started a jogging program to, among other things, lose weight, lower my heart rate, and improve my chances of living past 78, and on the third day of training had done something severe to something (muscle, cartilage, tendon?) in the back of my left leg making it excruciatingly painful to walk and completely impossible to climb stairs.   **THE** agony aside, my injury did have its advantages. It gave me a good excuse not to cut the lawn, trim the pyracantha bushes, mop the floor, wash the windows, clean out the rain gutters, and fix the chimney. While at first my wife tried hard to be sympathetic and supportive ("I don't expect you to mow the lawn, but there's no reason why you can't make the beds and do the dishes") she eventually began to grow a bit testy about having to do all the heavy work around the house ("I hope you appreciate me!"). Finally after a week of these chore wars, her frustration grew to the point where she insisted that I see a doctor.   **"BUT**   ★★★page 123★★★

Lorraine," I protested, "what's a doctor going to do? What I need is time to heal, not a doctor. Just be patient. In a few days I'm sure that I'll be just fine." **"WHAT** harm can a doctor do?" she countered. **"MISDIAGNOSIS**, unnecessary surgery, malpractice—take your pick. These days when you go to a doctor you don't know what to expect." **"WILL**, you're going to the doctor!" **"YOU** want me to be crippled for life because some incompetent doctor slipped with a surgical knife?" **"WELL**, it couldn't be any worse than your present condition. Look at it this way—you have nothing to lose." **"LORRAINE**, that's precisely what's wrong with the health care mess in America today. Every time anyone stubs a toe, they feel they have to go to a doctor and have a cat scan done. It's wasteful and expensive and I don't want to contribute to this societal problem." **"BUT** you haven't stubbed a toe. You could mow the lawn with a stubbed toe." "I have nothing more than a slight muscle tear. I consulted three different medical books in the library's reference section yesterday and each one indicates that my symptoms suggest a slight muscle tear and the only thing that can fix a slight muscle tear is time. There are no magic ointments, pills, or surgical procedures that a doctor can provide that will do me any good at all." **"WILL**, you're a librarian, not a doctor." **"THIS** may surprise you, Lorraine, but back in the days when I worked reference full time, I had a quasi-medical practice going. People with all sorts of physical problems flocked to me for information and advice. My reputation was impeccable." **"HOW** did you help them?" "I usually recommended a good book." **AS** with most debates in my household, Lorraine won this one. Actually we decided on a compromise. We decided that if my leg still hurt in two days I would go to the doctor, which is exactly what happened. The leg kept aching and I ended up going to the doctor. **THE** doctor was a nice man who looked a little bit like Wilford Brimley, the fat old guy who does the Quaker Oats commercials. This was reassuring because I like Wilford Brimley. "What seems to be the problem?" he asked with just the right balance of warmth and professionalism. **"IT'S** my leg. I hurt it jogging." **"WELL**, let's just take a look at it," he said and then started holding and squeezing the back of my leg as if it were a piece of fruit he was examining in the produce section of the grocery store. From time to time he would pinch me and ask, "Does this hurt?" or "How does this feel?" After two or three short minutes of this he looked at me and said authoritatively, "You have a minor tear in your calf muscle." **"THAT'S** all?" I said, amused that my own diagnosis had been confirmed by someone who had spent five years in medical school. **"THAT'S** all. Just stay off it for a couple more weeks and you'll be fine." **AS** I got up to leave, the attending nurse, one of those older, no-nonsense women

who seem permanently attached to a clipboard, looked at me and said, "Wait a minute. I need to take your blood pressure and weigh you before you leave. It's standard procedure for every visit. We must keep our charts current."   **"THAT'S** fine," I said as she began to strap the blood pressure monitor around my arm. "I'm in no hurry."
"THERE must be something wrong," she said as she looked at my reading. "Let me try it again."   **"FINE,"** I said, getting just a bit impatient.   **"OH** my," she said as she wrote down the second reading. "It's even worse than the first time."   **"HOW** bad is it?" I asked with surprise.   **"VERY** bad. Let me try it on your other arm."   **"OKAY,"** I said, shrugging my shoulders.   **"GOODNESS,"** she said when she wrote down the third reading. "It's even worse. Your blood pressure just keeps getting higher and higher. Right now it's 160 over 123."   **"IS** that too high?"   **"DANGEROUSLY** high," she replied with authority. Then she said, "Lie down while I get the doctor."   **AS** I lay there on that awkward office bed my mind raced through the bits of medical data that had been stored in my brain during my reference desk days. "High blood pressure," I remembered reading in the *Family Circle Medical Dictionary*, "can result in a paralyzing stroke."   **"GOOD** God," I told myself, "that doctor better get in here right away." While waiting, I listened to two nurses chit-chatting in the hallway. "It's **a wonder he's alive**," one of the nurses seemed to be saying. I hoped desperately that she wasn't referring to me.   **AFTER** what seemed like twenty minutes but which was actually two, the doctor appeared before me. "Why don't you take off your shirt?" he said, "Maybe that has something to do with these abnormally high blood pressure readings."   I took my shirt off and took a deep breath as he wrapped the monitor around my arm. "168 over 128," he said, shaking his head. Then he added, "There's no point in taking it again. This is obviously no fluke," he said, looking down at my chart. "I need to ask you some questions."   **"WHAT** kind of questions?" I asked cautiously.   **"LIFESTYLE** questions," he replied.   **"FINE.** Go ahead." I said, even though I hate lifestyle questions.   **"HAVE** you ever been diagnosed with high blood pressure before?"   **"NO."**   **"DO** you have a history of high blood pressure in your family?"   **"NO."**   **"DO** you drink alcoholic beverages?"   **"YES."**   **"EXCESSIVELY?"**   **"SOMETIMES."**   **"DO** you smoke?"   **"YES."**   **"EXCESSIVELY?"**   **"SOMETIMES."**   **"DO** you eat foods high in cholesterol and fat?"   **"YES."**   **"EXCESSIVELY?"**   **"SOMETIMES."**   **"DO** you eat salty foods?"   **"YES,** I love salty foods and often eat them excessively, especially pretzels and potato chips which I can eat by the bag full while drinking beer and watching football games on television."   **"HOW** about recreational drugs?" asked the doctor gingerly. "Do

you ever take recreational drugs?" "**DO** you consider Reeses Pieces to be a recreational drug?" I said with a chuckle. **THE** doctor wasn't amused. "No, I mean cocaine, crack, hashish, marijuana, heroin—drugs like that." "**NO**," I said with as much righteous indignation as I could muster. "**YOUR** weight. I don't see your weight on the chart. Nurse Greenaway, could you weigh our patient?" "**PLEASE** get on the scale over here," she commanded and when I started taking off my shoes, she added, "You don't need to do that. We always weigh our patients with their shoes on." "**BUT** these are heavy shoes," I said and continued to untie the laces. "**YOU** don't understand. We always weigh our patients with their shoes on. It's our policy." "**BUT** you don't understand. These are substantial shoes. They're Allen Edmonds wing-tipped Oxfords and I swear each one weighs at least three pounds." "**WE** take that into consideration when we evaluate your weight." "**ACTUALLY** they feel more like five pounds apiece," I said, while continuing to loosen the laces. "**PLEASE** get on the scales now with your shoes on." "NO! I'M TAKING THE SHOES OFF!" **JUST** as Nurse Hitler and I were ready to lock into **mortal battle**, Doc Brimley interceded. "Nurse Greenaway, go ahead and weigh him with his shoes off, and Mr. Manley, I'd like to see you in my office down the hall as soon as you're done with Nurse Greenaway." **THE** doctor's private office was not what I expected. It was a mess, a disturbing mess. His desk was strewn with papers, there were medical trade journals piled up haphazardly on the floor, the walls were covered with droopy watercolors signed by "Brandy," the computer terminal was turned off and on top of it was perched a coffee cup that probably hadn't been washed during the Clinton administration, the credenza was adorned with a silly wooden sign that proclaimed "Pobody's Nerfect," and the windowsills were cluttered with an eclectic grouping of plants that were in **various stages of death**—not exactly the image that a doctor would want his office to project. **FRANKLY**, the disarray made me nervous. Normally clutter doesn't bother me too much, but I tend to get skittish when I see it around doctors, airplane pilots, and accountants. These are people whom I expect to project an image of being precise, orderly, and in control, and since Doc Brimley was obviously not in control of his office I got a little nervous, so nervous that I began to compulsively straighten up some of the papers on his desk. "**MR**. Manley," he said, watching me straighten the papers, "I am going to give you some obvious lifestyle recommendations." "**YES**, doctor, I know what you're going to say. No smoking, no drinking, and no recreational drugs." "**ACTUALLY**," Mr. Manley, "that's not quite correct. Certainly smoking and recreational drugs are completely out, but drinking is not inherently bad unless it's abused.

A drink or two per day is not necessarily harmful." "CAN these drinks be stored up?" I asked. "WHAT do you mean by that?" "LET'S say I go five days without a drink. Does that mean I can have ten drinks on the night of that fifth day? It's what I call the SDF—Stored Drink Formula." "ABSOLUTELY not. The very idea of the lifestyle changes I'm prescribing is that you pace yourself more and avoid episodes of excess." "OKAY, I think I can handle all of that," I said quickly and got up to leave. "JUST a minute, Mr. Manley, I'm not finished yet. You also need to change your eating habits. Although I haven't seen the results of your weigh-in, my educated eye tells me that you're twenty to thirty pounds overweight. You're eating the wrong types of food. No more fat, cholesterol, and salt. Nurse Greenaway will give you a list of recommended foods on your way out." THIS was getting depressing, and once more I got up to leave. I didn't need any more recommendations. I had to get out of there. "I'll try my best, Doc," I said grimly. "Thanks for your help." "PLEASE, Mr. Manley, sit down. I'm not finished yet. Please just try to relax. Since your blood pressure is so high, I also need to put you on medication. Here's a prescription." "THANK you, Doctor. Is there anything else?" "JUST one thing." "WHAT is it?" "DO you have any hobbies?" "WHAT?" "HOBBIES, Mr. Manley, do you have any hobbies?" "YOU mean like model railroading or needlepoint?" "YES, that kind of thing—something that you do for pure enjoyment or relaxation." "I like to read. I'm a librarian." "GOOD, very good. Perfect. What kinds of things do you like to read?" "EVERYTHING," I replied. "I'm actually pretty compulsive about it. I read everything—airplane safety instructions, cereal boxes, arena football box scores, the fine print on a Budweiser can, and Shakespeare." "HOW about Henry James? Do you read Henry James?" "NO, Doctor, you've got me there. I don't read Henry James." "HAVE you ever read Henry James?" "ONLY in college. My freshman year we were assigned *Portrait of a Lady* and it was the only time in my life that I used *Cliff Notes*. I hated myself for it, but I hated Henry James even more." "WHAT exactly did you find so disagreeable about James?" "NOTHING happens in his books and it takes forever for nothing to happen." "THAT'S precisely why I'm prescribing a steady diet of Henry James for you, Mr. Manley." "DOC, I don't get it. The smoking, the drinking, the food, the medication—I can understand all of those things and their connection to my high blood pressure, but what's Henry James got to do with it?" "MR. Manley, we've got to slow you down. We've got to get you to learn how to relax. High blood pressure can be caused by a variety of factors—age, heredity, weight, diet, lifestyle, and stress. While you certainly have not been living the healthiest of lifestyles, it is obvious to me in the short time I have been around you that your biggest problem is that you are an extremely tense person. Your spat with Nurse Greenaway, the way your blood pressure kept rising every time we checked it, your compulsion to straighten up

Nurse, another unit of Henry James please.

the papers on my desk, and your impatience to get out of here—all these things are indications to me that you're obviously

★★★page 128★★★

a very nervous person. We've got to slow you down." "FINE, but what's Henry James got to do with it?" "NOBODY can read Henry James without slowing down." "NO kidding," I replied morosely. "Reading Henry James is like walking through very deep mud while you're wearing shower slippers." "PRECISELY," said the Doctor smiling. "You can't read James in a hurry. It won't make any sense to you. You have to plod through his work very slowly and methodically. Eventually you'll acquire a taste for him." "THAT'S what my mother told me about asparagus, and I still hate asparagus." "HERE'S what I want you to do," said the doctor, ignoring my last comment, "find a quiet, solitary place where you can retreat every day for one hour—exactly one hour. Go there, take some deep breaths, and very slowly begin to read James. Start with *Washington Square*. It's my favorite and I think you'll like it too." "THAT'S it?" "YES, that's all. See me again in a month." IT was not hard to find a quiet, solitary spot in my house because at the time my two oldest kids were away at college and my youngest son was constantly squirreled away in his room mainlining Nintendo. My wife, however, was a bit of a problem. "Let me get this straight," she said with a frown, "you go to the doctor for a muscle pull in your leg and you come back with a prescription from a doctor to spend one hour every day in solitary confinement reading Henry James novels?" "YEAH, Lorraine, that's pretty much it." "ARE you sure that the doctor you went to see didn't have his degree in American literature and not medicine?" "LORRAINE, how many times do I have to tell you that he had three medical degrees hanging on his wall?" "A likely story. I can't help but think this is one more ploy to get out of doing yard work." "LORRAINE, this has nothing to do with the muscle pull. I've got high blood pressure, for God's sake. Do you want me to have a stroke? The doctor says he has to slow me down." "SLOW you down!" she exclaimed. "This quack obviously hasn't seen you cut the grass!"

The Death of the Book—A Case Study

THERE'S been so much talk lately about the role of the library as an electronic fueling station on the cybernetic superhighway of the 21st century that any day now I half expect to pick up the newspaper and read an article about how OCLC has become an integral part of NASA's computerized navigational system. ALL of the **futuristic technobabble** about the inevitability of the virtual library in a post-print society has as its premise the startling assumption that the book, like a dismembered reptile, is writhing around desperately in its last days of existence. If you're a book lover like me, however, don't despair and even if you're not, don't succumb to the temptation of betting against the ★★★page 129★★★

book the next time you're vacationing in Vegas. It's beaten the point spread every single time.   **THE** fact is that the prophets of doom have a terrible track record with the book. They've had it dead, buried, and forgotten too many times to count over the past 125 years and, like a stubborn cockroach, it keeps reappearing stronger and healthier than ever in the face of new and more powerful technologies.

THOMAS Edison of all people began the funeral obsequies for the book in 1878 when, shortly after unveiling his first fragile phonograph, he boldly predicted that his new talking machine would supplant the printing press as a transmitter of culture. Picking up on this theme, *Scribner's Magazine* published an article in 1894 entitled "The End of Books" which envisioned a day in the not too distant future when libraries would be transformed into "phonographotecks." Reading was portrayed as an exercise that wearied the eyes and distracted them from their natural function, the contemplation of the beauties of nature.   **BUT** even that rhetoric seemed muted compared to the

Today's shuttle mission had to be aborted when the on board navigational computer failed to link up with the OCLC computer.

prediction of Professor Guido Biagi, the librarian of the Royal Library of Florence, who at the World's Fair in St. Louis in 1904 recklessly declared, **"The librarian who reads is lost."** Biagi went on to ex-
★★★page 130★★★   cite his audience by singing the praises of that most

miraculous invention, the phonograph. When you read his rhetoric now you think immediately of the rhetoric flowing from Silicon Valley. **DESPITE** the loftiness of Biagi's promises on that autumn St. Louis afternoon in 1904, very little was done concerning the phonograph in the public library until 1913 when the Milwaukee Public Library recognized that it could be a useful instrument in telling stories to children. It was the St. Paul (MN) Public Library, however, that first began to collect phonograph records on a wide scale. This service was inaugurated in 1914, and by 1919 the collection of records, which was oriented around classical music, numbered 600. By 1925 record collections were fairly common in both public and academic libraries, and predictably the main professional concern regarding this new medium now centered on the area of cataloging and classification.   **JUST** as these issues were being settled, however, something very interesting happened. The sound waves of radio broadcasts began to reverberate on an international level and cause a tremendous sweep of public interest. In comparison to the radio, the phonograph was now looked down upon as a forgotten mechanism of bygone years. Prior to the advent of the radio, phonograph manufacturers had experienced a steady year to year growth in their business. Not only was this expansion halted but most phonograph companies suffered a rather substantial loss in business. Early radio broadcasting, despite its **scratches and screeches**, had captured the imagination of America. For all its inadequacies it gave a quality of sound reproduction that was far superior to the phonograph.   **BY** the middle of the 1920s more than three million radio sets were in use, 600 commercial broadcasting stations were in business, 3,000 manufacturers were turning out parts for radio sets, and 20,000,000 Americans were listening faithfully to their favorite radio programs. The phonograph, that miraculous device that would supplant the book and transform the world, was as outdated as last year's almanac. America had a new darling, one that social commentators now predicted would become the nation's dominant educational resource, a catalyst for the development of an international language, and a major tool for insuring world peace by bringing foreign peoples closer together.   **CONFRONTED** with this kind of commercial success and popular opinion, the phonograph could not wage an effective campaign against the radio. The only way that phonograph manufacturers could save their industry was by jumping onto the radio bandwagon and building combination phonograph-radio consoles. This new partnership seemed to be symbolized by the merger of Victor with the Radio Corporation of America, but events soon demonstrated a different reality. Within one year of the merger the main Victor production plant in Camden, New Jersey, was remodeled for radio production. Despite the talk of the phonograph and radio joining together on an equal basis, it turned out that R.C.A. had little interest in the record player. Rather R.C.A. was most interested in Victor's large plant and well-organized system of distribution. **THUS** only a couple of decades after it had been declared the conqueror of the book, the phonograph had seemingly been dealt a lethal blow. Edison closed his phonograph works, and lesser manufacturers succumbed to bankruptcy or struck hastily made surrenders to radio companies. In 1932 a writer for the *American Mercury Magazine,* rang the death knell: "The story of the phonograph as a self-contained independent industry is done." **DESPITE** this and other obituaries, news of the phonograph's demise was about fifty years premature. It would cling to life and even prosper before its final burial in the mid 1980s. The upswing began in the late 1930s when R.C.A. started to reevaluate the potential profitability of its long dormant record business. At that time R.C.A. engineers undertook experimentation with electrical transcription and reproduction. By means of new recording and amplifying devices the phonograph record could, for the first time, render a close approximation of actual sound. **AT** the same time that R.C.A. was experimenting with new acoustical techniques, a brand new company, Decca, entered the phonograph field with a fresh set of ideas. Its president, Jack Kapp, and co-director, Edward R. Lewis, contended that good phonograph records did not need to be expensive. Ever since 1918 the phonograph firms had been charging from seventy-five cents to two dollars for one record. But Decca began to market its products at thirty-five cents. Also Kapp began to sign exclusive contracts with big names in popular music such as Bing Crosby, the Dorsey Brothers, and Guy Lombardo. By 1940, with Crosby as its major attraction, Decca achieved an annual gross profit of four million dollars. **WHILE** Decca was capitalizing on the market for popular music, R.C.A. Victor was gaining eminence in the field of recording serious symphonic productions. Exclusive contracts were made with the Boston Symphony and the New York Philharmonic, and to publicize this relationship R.C.A. Victor bought time on the NBC radio network and broadcast part of an actual recording session in Symphony Hall, Boston. By 1940 R.C.A. was selling 300,000 symphonic records in a six month period. **THE** renaissance of the phonograph in the public library mirrored its rebirth in the private sector. In the 1940s library trade journals were filled with articles about the cataloging and circulation of phonograph records. There was also much debate about the appropriateness of including pop music (as produced by Decca) in library record collections. The trash vs. quality debate had taken on a new form. **BY** the end of World War II, librarians had established a definite place for the phonograph in their institution. Although the "talking machine" had not reached, nor would it ever reach, the heights set for it by Professor Biagi in his speech to librarians in 1904, it had survived the vagaries of time and had opened up a new frame of reference for the public library. If librarians had not burned their books and filled their storage space with cylinders and discs, they were at least willing to open their shelves to new media of communication.   **BUT** forty years later in the mid 1980s the phonograph record died a very certain death at the hands of a superior sound technology, the compact disc. In reality the importance of the phonograph had diminished progressively throughout the '50s, '60s, and '70s with the development of reel to reel tape, eight track tape, cassette tape, and digital tape. Its final demise in the 1980s was, therefore, not unexpected.   **BUT** the case study of the phonograph represents more than just the birth, struggles, growth, and death of a new communications medium, it also serves as an excellent illustration of the significant differences that exist and will continue to exist between the book and electronic media. The book is essentially the same now as it was a thousand years ago. Sure, its means of production has changed from hand, to press, to computer, but a book is still a book. It has two covers and a clump of printed pages in between. Its form has endured because of its utter convenience.   **AS** endurable as the book is, that is how mutable other communication media have proven to be. Look at the evolution of the phonograph—from cylinders to records to tapes to discs. Consider the history of film—from 16mm to 8mm to super 8mm to ¾ inch videotape to ½ inch beta tape to ½ inch v.h.s. tape to videodiscs. The ongoing revolution in computer technology can probably best be expressed by pointing out that most of the records documenting the Vietnam War are now inaccessible because they are contained on computer tapes that cannot be read by current working computers.   **IN** this whirlwind of technological change, it is very easy to get swept up in the rhetoric about the obsolescence of the book. The irony of course is that the book will survive precisely because it does not change. It is not dependent upon accompanying hardware. The only microprocessor you will ever need to access the book is your own brain.   **SO** here's my prediction: When the brain becomes obsolete, the book will become obsolete.

A.L.A. not Allah

NOTHING gets kicked around more in Libraryland than the American Library Association. It's the one thing that we librarians love to hate and hate to love, but love it we do and hate it we must. Why do we love it—because it's big and sprawling and uncontrollable. Why must we hate it—because it's big and sprawling and uncontrollable.   **THE** good thing about a big, sprawling, and uncontrollable organization is that everyone can find something in it to nibble. The American Library Association has so many task forces, boards, councils, divisions, departments, round tables, and caucuses that they had to form the mother of all committees (something called the Committee on Committees) in order to keep track of them all. Are you a left-handed, bi-sexual, tri-lingual, non-smoking, pro-choice, anti-gun, Slavic cataloger? I'm not sure, but I'd be willing to bet you **lunch money for a week** that if you are, A.L.A. has a committee tailored just for your needs.   **THAT'S** probably what we love best about A.L.A. It provides us a gathering place to get in touch with other left-handed, bi-sexual, tri-lingual, non-smoking, pro-choice, anti-gun, Slavic catalogers. It's a tough world out there, and life is not an easy proposition. Just as in the song, it helps to have someplace where everyone calls you by name and is happy that you came. In that respect A.L.A. is a lot like Cheers, and it's not coincidence, by the way, that a lot of A.L.A. business gets talked over in bars, taverns, saloons, and cocktail lounges.   **MYSELF**, I like to hang out with other library directors, **sip a brew or two**, and listen to my colleagues tell horror stories about their employees ("can you believe I have a reference librarian named Ralph who hasn't washed his hair in two years because he's afraid it will fall out") and their trustees ("you won't believe this, but I have a new trustee who thinks that *The Emperor's New Clothes* is a dirty book because it glorifies nudity). At the end of every A.L.A. conference, I always return home feeling a lot better about my employees and trustees.   **IN** fact I think that we librarians have a greater need than other professionals to get together and **smooze and booze** because we are more misunderstood and underappreciated than they are by the outside world. There is great comfort in socializing with our own, and A.L.A. provides us that opportunity and usually in sparkling settings like San Francisco, New Orleans, Chicago, and New York.   **THE** other great thing about A.L.A. is that it produces a diverse array of interesting paraphernalia, and I'm not talking about those dreadful audit reports or those dreary self-study reports that get so much attention from the library periodical editorialists. No, those ponderous pieces of pomposity are more than balanced off by things like the official A.L.A. necktie, key chain, squeeze bottle, coach cap, luggage tag, and iron-on transfer. But even better than those great gift items are the official A.L.A. READ posters. My support for A.L.A. will be forever unwavering because of the READ posters. They are sharp, simple, and direct.   **SHARP**, simple, and direct, of course, are three qualities that A.L.A. needs more of. Too often the association seems bloated, bureaucratic, and Byzantine, and those are the organizational shortcomings that we members love to attack and ridicule. We rue the times that the association moves with the slowness of a glacier in acting on major issues like library funding and library education while it moves with the quickness of an avalanche in addressing general political issues like the Persian Gulf War, Martin Luther King's birthday, and Middle Eastern censorship. **IS** it the purpose of A.L.A. to save the world or to see that libraries grow, develop, and prosper? That is the question that rankles many librarians who struggle daily with low salaries and substandard funding. It does not seem fair to them that their considerable dues are being wasted on attacking global controversies that have little relevance to their own local professional plight. **BUT** perhaps an even greater source of frustration to many members is the amount of time, money, and attention that is devoted to the petty and pointless internicene bickering that goes on incessantly between A.L.A.'s myriad of organizational entities. What is the relationship between the association and its divisions? Where does the authority of the Council end and the Executive Board begin? What rights of freedom of organizational expression accrue to the round tables and caucuses? **WHAT** difference does it all make and who really cares? It seems to many, that when the association is not pontificating on global issues, it is sniveling about the most insignificant of organizational issues. In the minds of many members the American Library Association is either preoccupied with the sublime or the ridiculous but nothing in between. **THESE** perceptions will, however, probably never change. With size comes unwieldiness. No matter how many times A.L.A. studies itself and tries to reinvent itself, the same problems will inevitably resurface. Any professional organization with 60,000 members that tries to run itself as a democracy simply cannot avoid a certain amount of operational irony, and it's pointless and naïve of librarians to keep harping about it. We should simply accept it and move on to more important points like the hypocrisy that the American Library Association constantly displays with regards to intellectual freedom. **DON'T** get me wrong. **A.L.A. is a great and courageous defender of intellectual freedom.** It is constantly defending librarians, trustees, and school boards who are under attack from censors. No organization with the possible exception of the American Civil Liberties Union has done as much as A.L.A. to extend the bounds of freedom of expression. That's why it's so incongruous that A.L.A. programming as it relates to intellectual freedom and social responsibility issues is completely one sided. **THINK** hard, when A.L.A. brings in big name speakers to make keynote addresses or to pontificate on key issues, who do we get? It's always a lineup of liberal all stars, people like Pat Schroeder, Gloria Steinem, Jesse Jackson, Al Gore, Barbara Jordan, Jimmy Carter, Major Owens, Nat Hentoff, and Mitch Snyder. **AGAIN**, don't get me wrong. I have a great deal of admiration for all of these people, but I would much rather have my convictions challenged than validated. If nothing else, it gets boring hearing the same liberal platitudes conference after conference. Think of how much more enlightening and fun it would be to invite a Dan Quayle, a Phyllis Schlafly, a William Safire, or even a Rush Limbaugh to talk about libraries, intellectual freedom, and social responsibility. I may be wrong, but I always thought that the principles of balance, diversity, toleration, and open-mindedness were the underpinnings of the concept of intellectual freedom. It would be nice if the A.L.A. would recognize that too. **OTHERS** may want to try to radically reform the American Library Association through self-study reports and consultant analyses, but I pretty much like the organization the way it is. I just wish it would practice what it preaches when it comes to intellectual freedom.

Soft Pretzels with Mustard

REMEMBER when the Annual Conference of the American Library Association was held in the City of Brotherly Love? I know it was long ago and faraway, but think hard. Who was the most popular guy in town? Was it Senator Bill Bradley, actor Paul Newman, commentator Charles Osgood, or librarian Will Manley?   **WELL**, I'm sure that Bill and Paul and Charles had their moments in the sunshine of librarian adulation, but let's face it, I had almost a whole week of the limelight. Count them—five full days of praise and adulation. It got so thick that I almost became tired of hearing my name connected with adjectives like "challenging," "innovative," and "exciting." Almost.   **ACTUALLY** the secret of my popularity had nothing to do with my "winning personality" (although a lot of people told me I had one) or my "rugged good looks" (although a lot of people told me I had them too) or the fact that I knew where all the good vendor parties were (I did but I didn't tell anyone). No, the truth is I had arrived in the City of Brotherly Love on Saturday morning with three jobs to fill. These were well-paid entry level children's services positions. At that time it was my lofty goal in life to put together the finest public library children's department in the country, and I was going to start by hiring three brand new children's librarians—the best three children's librarians that libraryland had to offer. That's why my popularity index was so high.   **THE** exciting thing about these openings is that they were all newly created by my governing board. These were positions without a history. Candidates did not have to worry about measuring up to their predecessors or treading upon the sacred ground of history and tradition. Even more exciting was the fact that the people who got the jobs would be given the charge of creating a children's services division from scratch. **UP** until 1982, the library's children's department was for all intents and purposes non-existent. I suppose that some people on my board thought that maybe I was going overboard putting these three new positions in children's, and I suppose that I could have put at least one of them in reference but the truth is there is nothing I value more than children's services. To me, children are the absolute foundation of the public library. **THIS**, of course, is **no earth-shattering thought**. For one thing, throughout history the leaders of every major religious, social and political movement from the Roman Catholic Church to the Chinese Communist Party to the Branch Davidian Church of Waco have been smart enough to recognize that their long-term success depends upon the inculcation of the movement's ideals and purposes into the hearts and minds of children. It's axiomatic that children who are instilled with a love and appreciation for library services will support library funding when they grow up and become taxpaying voters. **THERE** is also the rather compelling argument that we public librarians have an ethical obligation to help make the world a better place, and what better way to help the world than to lure young people away from *Brady Bunch* reruns and introduce them to the rich treasures of children's literature. Give me the child who grew up on a steady fare of A.A. Milne and Kenneth Graehme any day over the child who had the Disney channel as a constant companion. If the human race is ever going to mature and evolve into something beyond its present state it will do so with people who know how to read, think, dream, and analyze, and you don't develop those skills by **sitting moronically** in front of an electronic tube. **ALSO** there's the illiteracy issue. In the past ten years educators and sociologists have exposed our great, dark national secret—that many of the people who live in this the wealthiest country in the history of the world, cannot read or write. This of course is not only a cause for shame but also a source of waste. How do you eliminate illiteracy? You certainly don't do it by **cobbling together a crazy quilt** of adult literacy programs. You do it the same way you eliminate all diseases. You inoculate people when they are young, and what better place to run an illiteracy inoculation program than in the public library. **BUT** I'll be honest with you. None of that really mattered to me at the time. When you make a decision it's nice to have a lot of high-minded reasons to back you up, but the truth is, very few of us make decisions based upon a sense of idealism. I certainly don't. The truth is I generally make decisions based upon self interest. **AND** in this case self interest meant survival. It shouldn't have been, but at that time I was still young enough and naïve enough to believe that you could take risks in public sector administration and live to tell the tale. Actually A.L.A. couldn't have been located in a better place for me simply because it was 2,500 miles away from my library where I had been on the job as director for only two short months, and had managed to annoy, antagonize, and alienate a goodly number of patrons, employees, and board members. The community needed a break from me and I needed a break from it. **THINGS** had gotten very heated in those eight weeks and it had nothing to do with the weather. I was in a frightful hurry to implement what I considered to be a grand new experiment in public librarianship. While the rest of the profession seemed to be just dying to sell its collective soul to either the recreational model (give 'em what they want and make 'em pay for it with user fees) or the informational model (give 'em electronic databases and make 'em pay for it with user fees), I was headed in a different direction. **MY** vision was an educational model—the public library as a catalyst for erudition, enlightenment, and evolution. Properly structured, the public library could become the social instrument that would change lives and transform society. Operationally there would be three priorities: 1) developing a book collection that emphasized diversity, balance, and quality and deemphasized popular demand and commercial success, 2) making all programs and services free and accessible to all irrespective of socioeconomic levels, and 3) reallocating money and staff away from adult services and into children's services. **WHAT** was it that impelled me to be so contrarian? Did I really think that I was going to change lives and transform society. Well, yes, but that honestly wasn't my first priority. Did I simply enjoy being a non-conformist? No, **getting hate mail** really isn't all that gratifying an experience. Well, then, what was my real motivation? The truth is as librarian I wanted to survive, and I looked upon the recreational and information models as leading to eventual institutional death. I reasoned that in tough economic times local politicians would find it much easier to cut and eliminate recreational and informational services than educational ones. **DESPITE** the fact that everyone likes to criticize the American educational system, the reality remains that "education" is still a sacred word in our national vocabulary. In our multicultural, polyracial democracy, we see education as the great equalizer. It's the tool that allows the have-nots to become haves. We have come to believe that education is as important to our democratic way of life as free elections and a free press. **AND** so I set out to be what the management gurus were calling a "change agent." My strategy was a simple one. On day one of my new directorship, before the nameplate for my office door had even arrived, I would begin turning the library upside down. The way I saw it I'd never have a better opportunity because just that morning when I opened up the local newspaper I saw that the library board had (after conducting an "exhausting national search") pronounced me the most qualified librarian in America for the job. Then they went on to say how fortunate the city was to have someone of my caliber. **AFTER** reading this I quickly ★★★page 138★★★ made two conclusions: 1) I should have asked them for a lot more money and 2) I could do just about anything my first six months on the job short of coming to work with purple hair and plum lip gloss. No way were they going to can me after saying all those nice things about me. Nothing would make them look more incompetent. I had my window of opportunity—my honeymoon—and I intended to drive through it with a Sherman tank.   **AND** it's not like I didn't tell them what I was going to do. In the interview I laid out my blueprint in great detail: 1) transform the library from a recreational reading center to an educational resource center, 2) emphasize children's services, and 3) guarantee free and open access to all citizens. At the time I sensed that they were impressed with my boldness and that they were sincerely interested in taking on the difficult challenge of bringing radical change to a public sector institution that had been drifting for years without a serious focus.   I soon discovered, however, that talking about change and actually doing it are two entirely different things. People like the concept of change much more than change itself. To put it simply, people do not like change in their lives. No, that's not quite right. People do not like change and they do not like the people who try to bring about change. No, that's not quite right either. People hate change and they hate the people who try to bring about change. **THAT'S** right—people hate change even when change is desperately and immediately needed, even when the change is for the better. Nothing illustrated this phenomenon better in my library than the leaky roof. The very first day on the job while I was walking around the library meeting with my new staff I noticed that there were twenty or thirty wastebaskets placed haphazardly around the building. Some were located on the tops of study tables, some were on the floor, and some were even perched high atop our book stacks.   **THIS** interested me. Why were our patrons generating so much trash and why was it being generated in such improbable locations? "Oh," said one of the reference librarians, "those trash cans are not meant for trash, they're meant for rain. Our roof has more holes than **a piece of Swiss cheese**."   **"WELL,"** I replied, "we're just going to have to get building maintenance over here to get it fixed."   **"OH**, you can't do that," she said matter of factly.   **"OH**, I can't?" I said quizzically, "Why in heaven's name not?"   **"BECAUSE** if you get the roof fixed," she said calmly and logically, "you'll end up putting Jason out of a job."   **"WHO** is Jason?"   **"HE'S** Tucker's assistant."   **"WHO** is Tucker?"   **"TUCKER** is the janitor."   **"TUCKER** has an assistant?"   **"YES**, that would be Jason."   **"WHAT** does Jason do?" **"HE'S** in charge of making sure all the roof leaks drain into a trash can."   **"OH."**   SO when the roof finally gets fixed, am I a hero? No, of course not. I'm a jerk because I've put Jason out of a job. **BUT** getting the roof fixed was just one of many

changes that I forced during my first two months on the job. Here were some of the others: **1.** Made the secretary begin answering the telephone. **2.** Cleaned out the staff room refrigerator by throwing away all pieces of food that had at least a three-day mold build-up and all cans of pop that had already been opened and had lost all fizz.
3. Had the peep holes in the men's bathroom partitions filled in.
4. Threw out all dead or dying plant materials from both the public and private areas of the library. **5.** Decided that patrons could no longer chain their dogs to the bike rack. **6.** Made Tucker the janitor take down his gallery of pin-ups from the boiler room walls. **7.** Asked Margaret at reference to start using an antiperspirant. **8.** Asked Fred in cataloging to keep his pet mouse Freddie in a cage and not perched precariously on his shoulder like a four-legged parrot. **9.** Transferred $100,000 from the adult book budget to the children's book budget.
10. Decided that the three new professional positions funded by the library board should all be children's librarians. **NOW** be honest, with the exception of #9 and #10 (and I'll explain those in a minute), you have to agree that there's not a change that I've listed above that does not sound reasonable, logical, and much needed. They all make perfect common sense, right? You'll never guess, therefore, what happened when I set them all in motion. **FIRST**, the secretary quit. She said that she was not hired to answer the telephone. Then Tucker quit. He said, "If **I can't have my pin-ups** to relieve my intense job stress then I don't want to work here." Then I got accused by many people of being a thief—"You probably took all that old food from the refrigerator home with you to feed your family." Then I got accused of violating animal rights—"Freddie is not bothering anyone on my shoulder. You just hate him." Then I got accused of being an animal rights extremist. "If you don't let patrons chain their dogs to the bike rack, then the dogs will run all over the library grounds and we can't give dogs that much freedom." Then I got accused of being naïve about perverts—"If you plug up their peepholes in the bathroom, you're going to force them out into the library and that's the worst thing that could happen." Then I was accused of being a sexist by Margaret who said, "You would never tell a man to use a deodorant, would you?" It was, to say the least, not a pleasant time in my life.
WHATEVER I did, it was wrong. I got the feeling that if I had simply holed up in my office and drank coffee and read the newspaper that everyone on staff would say that I was doing a great job. The point is people don't like changes. The hubbub over the little things, however, was nothing compared to the fury over the reallocation of resources from adult services to children's. **HERE** the reaction was not so much "You're a jerk"; it was more like **"You're a jerk and you're out of your freaking mind."** No doubt about it, if you

If you get the roof fixed Jason will lose his job.

had polled everyone on my staff and board in June of 1982 you probably would have found a strong consensus of opinion that there was nothing wrong with me that couldn't be fixed by twenty intensive years of professional psychotherapy. **THE** whole concept of dumping money into children's services was so utterly unconventional in 1982 (actually it still is) that everyone simply assumed that the board had made a terrible mistake in hiring me. In fact I overheard one of my top supervisors gossiping to one of her colleagues: "The ★★★page 141★★★

board made a gross miscalculation with Manley. He's a nut case. They'd have been better off hiring PeeWee Herman. Cleaning out **the refrigerator was weird** and making Fred put his mouse in a cage was cruel and making Sylvia answer the phone was unfair and making Margaret use a deodorant was insensitive even if she does stink but putting all that money into children's services—that is simply insane. There's no other word for it. The board must feel terrible about hiring him." **ACTUALLY** she was quite right. The board did sort of freak out when I explained my blueprint for revitalizing the library. "Let me get this straight," said one of the trustees, "you want to use the three new positions that we fought so hard for in children's services and you want to reallocate $100,000 from adult books to children's?" **"YES,"** I answered. **"DON'T** you think that's quite extreme?" **"YES."** **"DON'T** you think you should moderate your position just a little?" **"NO."** **"WHY** not?" **"IT'S** all quite simple. This library is dead. Most days you could shoot a cannon through it and only kill half a dozen people. With the demographics of our community, this library should be doing two or three times the business that it is now doing. Did you or didn't you bring me in here to shake things up and make this place come alive?" **"BUT** wait a minute. The demographics of the city are overwhelmingly adult. Sure we have thousands of children but they make up less than 10% of the population." **"THAT'S** right," I responded, "but the money I'm putting into children's services is not for the children." **"SAY** what?" **"THE** fact is that by emphasizing children's services we will be targeting adult users." **"YOU** can't be serious. Stop the doubletalk." **"THAT'S** not doubletalk. It's common sense. Investments in children's services pay their biggest dividends in adult usage of the library." **"YOU'VE** lost me." **"IT'S** simple. Kids bring adults to the library. If you want to get the whole community involved in the library, you need to exploit children. They are the catalysts. They bring their mothers, fathers, aunts, uncles, grandparents, brothers, sisters, and babysitters to the library. There is no salesman in the world who is as persuasive as a three year old who wants to go to the library to attend story hour or check out a book. The bottom line is that in today's world kids bring adults to the library; adults don't bring kids. They don't have the time or the dedication." **UNFORTUNATELY,** my logic was not all that compelling. The board members looked at me with confusion as though they weren't sure whether to pity me or despise me. Their reactions, of course, were tempered by the knowledge that I was their responsibility. They had hired me. It was their job to keep me in line. One by one they spoke: "I think you're wrong." "I think you're wrong too." **"ME** too." **"YOUR** thinking doesn't make sense." **"THE** numbers don't add up." **"YOUR** formula sounds good, but it doesn't compute." **"YOUR** theory won't work in the real world." **"GOOD** intentions, bad plan." **"THE** road to Hell is paved with good intentions." **THIS** was not exactly the solid consensus that I was looking for, but I was not willing to surrender. In the back of my mind was the hope that now, only two months after calling me the finest librarian that America had to offer, the board would give me some rope—I mean slack. **"YOUR** skepticism," I said, "is quite understandable. If I were you, I'd be skeptical too. Changes, especially radical changes, are always difficult to accept, but you must trust me that this plan will work, and to make it easier for you to trust me, let me make you a deal. Allow me to implement my plan, and if adult circulation does not increase by at least 30% by next June, I will resign my position here. That's how confident I am that this plan will work." **THE** consensus, surprisingly, was to let me have my way. At first, I was overjoyed with this vote of confidence. But later on—maybe five minutes later on—I, like everyone else in town, began to doubt my own sanity. "What have you done?" I said to myself on the drive home from the board meeting. "You have given no thought to the security of your wife and three children. You have moved your family 2,500 miles across the country and now you have wagered their future. On top of that the ink on your brand new thirty-year mortgage is barely dry. Are you nuts?" I didn't have to wait long for an answer to my question. **"Yes, you are nuts!"** exclaimed my wife as soon as I told her what I had done. "You're totally nuts! Don't you care about the security and well being of your family? You move us 2,500 miles across the country and then gamble with our future. And to think that last week we signed a thirty-year mortgage. This is crazy. You are crazy!" **THE** next week, of course, I was in Philadelphia, happily distanced from my problems. To not have people looking at me like I was a madman was wonderfully refreshing, but to have them gazing at me with real kindness and genuine respect was absolutely heavenly. To put this into perspective, let me point out that this conference was taking place right in the middle of the Reagan recession when both interest rates and unemployment rates were sky high. **Librarians were desperate** for work. They seemed to be willing to say anything to get a job. **DESPITE** the temptation of succumbing to the most eloquent flatterers of the 138 A.L.A. attendees who had applied for my openings, I decided to stay objective and hire the best qualified applicants. I had no choice. Whoever filled these jobs would determine my fate. It was imperative, therefore, to find three dynamic, live-wired, creative librarians. No résumé would go unread, no applicant would go uninterviewed, no phone message would go unreturned. The rest of the library profession may have ★★★page 143★★★

gone to Philadelphia to make merry and celebrate A.L.A.'s 100th anniversary, but I had gone to fulfill a mission.   **ANOTHER** good thing about being in Philadelphia in this most stressful of times was that's where my mother was. My father was too. But when you're hip deep in controversy and everyone's calling you a moron, it's your mother you want to tell you how great you are.   **ACTUALLY** my parents lived about twenty miles east of Philadelphia in the sleepy little town of Pitman, New Jersey. It's the place where I was born and raised. But I knew all about Philadelphia. It was the big, dark, dirty city where you went to get fitted for braces, to have your tonsils removed, and to sit through the torture of a symphonic concert.   **PHILLY** did, however, have one attractive feature—the many street vendors who sold soft pretzels with mustard. To this day whenever I am in Philadelphia my mouth begins to water for those pretzels. There are many imitations of Philadelphia street pretzels but none taste anything like the real thing.   A Philadelphia cab driver once told me that the **secret ingredient was the water.** "It's the Philadelphia water that gives them that special taste," he said with authority. This was quite a revelation because Philly water never particularly struck me as one of life's great gourmet treats and because my mother had always told me that the special ingredient was dirt.   **"REMEMBER**, please remember," she would always say to me as we drove across the Walt Whitman Bridge into the City of Brotherly Love, "to stay away from those awful men who sell pretzels on the street corners. Their hands are filthy and you'll get some dreadful disease if you eat one of their pretzels."   **THAT** of course was the most counterproductive approach that my mother could have taken, but she was in good company because even God made the same mistake in the Garden of Eden. Never, ever expressly forbid someone to eat something. The lure of forbidden fruit is simply too tempting for the average mortal to resist. For me those pretzels were fruit from the tree of knowledge. They held all the sinful secrets of big city life and whenever my mother had her back turned, I headed right for those mysterious little men with the dirty hands and the doughy treats, and I never got sick. It was my first lesson in the futility of censorship.   **IT** was not surprising then that almost three decades later when I was leaving my parents' house (I decided to stay there rather than in one of the conference hotels) to go to the first day of the A.L.A. convention, my mother after telling me to drive safely (yes, I was borrowing their '67 Toronado), added the rejoinder "to stay away from those awful **street vendors with the dirty hands.**"   **IT** made no difference to her that I was now a grown and aging man with three boys of my own. In her mind, and maybe with good reason, I will always be somewhere around eleven or twelve years ★★★page 144★★★   old. Now, thirteen years later, as I settle comfortably into my middle forties I am resigned to this fact, but at the time I was a tad exasperated at being treated like a pre-adolescent.   "**MOM**," I groaned, "look at me. At this point in my life, do I strike you as someone who wants to get a social disease from a soft pretzel?" As I was halfway out the door, fortunately I remembered to ask her to be sure and take full and accurate messages from any job candidates who might be trying to get in touch with me while I was out. With a twinkle in her eye she said she'd be delighted to.   **NATURALLY** the first thing I did after parking my car at the Philadelphia Convention Center was seek out the cluster of pretzel vendors who were hunkered down by the front entrance. I picked out the one with **the dirtiest hands** (by now I was convinced that my mother and not the cab driver was right—it's the dirt, not the water, that make Philly pretzels unique), bought three pretzels strung together, smeared mustard on them, and headed for the Placement Center where there were 96 résumés waiting for me in my designated message box.   **AT** first, I dutifully began to read each one in its entirety but soon decided that my masochism had limits. Why did everyone have to be so wordy? Did they think that I was born yesterday? Did they really believe that I didn't know that a patron services coordinator is a simple reference librarian and that a youth services specialist is a children's librarian and that a community cultural programming facilitator is a person who does absolutely nothing but drink coffee and set up art exhibits?   **I** soon tired of reading résumés that made even Proust seem succinct. What kind of people were the library schools churning out? I didn't mind these people portraying themselves as the second coming of Jesus Christ, but couldn't anyone pad their résumé anymore with brevity and wit? Since when had the word résumé become synonymous with the word autobiography.   **DECIDING** that I didn't want anyone working for me who couldn't fit their job qualifications on one simple sheet of paper (imagine what their inter-office memos would look like!) I quickly eliminated about 75% of the candidates. That still left a couple dozen prospects, whom I dutifully called. Most of them were not in so I left messages instructing them to contact me at my parents' house. Then I went about the business of pursuing quality conference activities—the exhibits, wine and cheese reception, the C.L.S.I. cocktail party, and the A.L.A. President's reception.   **THAT** night when I got home, there was Mom waiting up for me. "Where in heavens have you been?" she demanded. "Do you know what time it is?"   "**MOM**, it's about three minutes past midnight."   "**WHAT** did your father tell you about getting in past midnight?"   "**MOM**, are you in a time warp? The midnight curfew ended 15 years ago when I turned 18."   "**WELL**, where were you? Your father and I were worried sick."   "**MOM**, Dad is upstairs sound asleep."   "**SO**   ★★★page 145★★★

where were you?" "I was at a special reception for the Librarian of Congress, two United States senators, and three members of the House of Representatives. Is that respectable enough for you, Mom?" "**CONGRESSMEN** and senators, oh no," she said, "that means hookers. Were there hookers there?" "**NO**, Mom. It was all very boring." "**YOU'RE** sure you haven't been hanging around with your old friend, Frankie Angellini? He used to get you in some real pickles." "**MOM**, that was back in high school. Look at me. I'm a grown man. I have three sons. I haven't seen Frankie Angellini in almost twenty years! How about some milk and cookies, Mom? Just like the old days." "**YES**, I think that would be nice, but is that a speck of mustard I see in the corner of your mouth. You haven't been eating those awful pretzels, have you?" "**MOM**," I said, trying to change the subject, "did you get any calls from job candidates?" "**OH** my, yes," she said with a sudden twinkle in her eye. "The phone was ringing off the hook while you were gone." "**WELL**, did you get names and phone numbers?" "**OH** yes, and I wrote down pertinent information about each candidate." "**MOM**, what kind of pertinent information?" "**MY** impressions." "**MOM**, what did you do? Interview each one?" "**NOT** interview exactly, but I did ask each one a few questions." "**QUESTIONS**, Mom, what kind of questions?" "**YOU** know—the little things that you wouldn't think to ask, like hobbies and grandparents and recipes and pets and tomatoes and water softeners." "**MOM**, tell me you didn't." "**I** found out so much. For instance, Will, did you know that Harold Feasley's grandmother just died and that Saran Birdsong is seven months pregnant but that child care won't be a problem because her husband, Fred, runs his insurance company out of his house and that Dorothy Pettigout's mother just died and so she's free to relocate and that Frieda Belisle makes her own draperies and that Malcolm Goode just had gall bladder surgery and that Hannah Redder's banana nut bread recipe was published in her church cookbook? I asked her to send me a copy of it and then she asked me if I had a fax? What's a fax, Will?"
"**DON'T** worry about it, Mom. It's librarian talk. I'm suddenly feeling very sleepy. I think I'll go to bed. Thanks for the cookies, Mom."
THE entire conference was like that. I would spend my days in Philly asking librarians about children's literature, finger puppets, and felt boards, and Mom would hang out at home by the telephone asking librarians about vegetable gardens, carpeting, and needlepoint.
AFTER much hard work I finally found three qualified people, and though I never really consulted Mom's notes, she enthusiastically endorsed all three. The only snag I hit was when I called my third selection and she began to waver. I did the best I could to sell her on my library and community but she wasn't totally

convinced. "Let me think about it," she said. "Can I call you back tomorrow?" **THE** next day at noon the phone rang. It was the third candidate. "I've decided to take the job," she said enthusiastically. "**WHAT** was the determining factor that swayed your decision?" I asked. "**IT** was your mother," she replied. "I figured anyone who had such a nice mother would be a good person to work for." "**WHAT** exactly did my mother say to you?" "**SHE** was so sweet and concerned about me. She warned me not to eat the soft pretzels from the street vendors."

History

WAS I having a good day? Actually I wasn't particularly conscious of having a good day, nor was I particularly conscious of having a bad one. Most of the time when I get home from work and my wife and kids pop the perfunctory "How was your day?" question at me I have no idea what to answer, and this panics me because it's an important question—one that I should be able to answer with some accuracy. **AFTER** all, life is a time span continuum made up of minutes, hours, days, weeks, months, years, decades. Our lives are historical. The present builds upon the past and the future is founded upon the present. A periodic accounting of how we're doing and where we're going is not a bad idea if we're at all interested in getting in control of things and pointing our lives in some preconsidered direction. Was it **Plato or Peewee Herman** who said that the unexamined life is not worth living? **THE** problem is that the substance of our daily lives leaves little time for the kind of introspection needed to determine exactly how our day was, which of course presupposes that we have even determined what distinguishes a good one from a bad one. Is a good day one in which Ralph the reference librarian has remembered to use a mouthwash and has thus relieved us of the burden of having to raise this uncomfortable issue with him one more time? Or is a good day one in which we have caught onto the fringes of some eternal truth by experiencing some small epiphany that allows us a **short, frightened glimpse** of something—dare I say it—transcendental? The final determination, I suppose, about whether a day is good or bad depends upon the historical view. In twenty years I might be able to make a definitive determination of how good a day this was, but right now I knew that nothing particularly sublime or ridiculous has happened, but then again the day wasn't over and the phone suddenly rang. "**HI**, this is Will." "**IT** better be!" "**WHO** am I talking to, please?" "**HAROLD** Salter. Commissioner Harold Salter—just in case you forgot." "**YES**, Commissioner, what can I do for you today?" "**YOU** can throw away every single one of those bleepetybleep history books that you were in charge of." "**COMMISSIONER**, I'm ★★★page 147★★★

not sure I know which books you are referring to." "**THE** community history book. Remember you were chair of the committee to oversee the writing and publication of a history of our fair town." "**OH**, that book. Yes, I understand that several advance copies were due to arrive at Town Hall sometime today. I haven't seen the finished product." "**WELL**, I have seen it and I am not happy!" "**OH** no. Was there something wrong with the printing?" "**NO!**" "**THEN** it must have been the binding. I was worried about the company that we contracted with to do the binding." "THE BINDING IS FINE!" "**THEN**, sir, what exactly is the problem with the book?" "**THE** problem, young man, is that my name is nowhere to be found in the book!" "**IT'S** not?" "**NO**, it's not." "**IS** this a problem for you?" "YES, OF COURSE THIS IS A PROBLEM FOR ME AND IT'S GOING TO BE A BIG PROBLEM FOR YOU TOO!" "**YOU'RE** sure you're not mentioned?" "YES, OF COURSE I'M SURE!" "**NOT** even in a footnote?" "**NO**, not even in a bleepetybleep footnote." "**ARE** the other commissioners mentioned?" "**THE** mayor is mentioned." "**BUT** are the other commissioners mentioned." "NO, NONE OF THE OTHER COMMISSIONERS IS MENTIONED BUT I'M NOT JUST ANOTHER COMMISSIONER, YOUNG MAN. I HAVE BEEN ON THE TOWN COMMISSION FOR SIXTEEN YEARS. I HAVE WON FOUR, COUNT THEM, FOUR ELECTIONS. I WAS ON THE COMMISSION WHEN YOU WERE IN JUNIOR HIGH SCHOOL!" "**YES**, sir, I know that, sir, but you must remember I did not write the book." "**YES**, I realize that, but you were the one who chaired the committee that hired that pencilnecked egghead, Dr. Freegard, to write the book. I knew when you hired Freegard that this thing was going to end up in a fiasco." "**THE** committee felt that Professor Freegard was the logical choice. He has lived in this area all of his life and is widely recognized as being the foremost expert around on local history. He's a walking encyclopedia of historical facts." "**BUT** he obviously forgot one fact." "**WHAT'S** that?" "**THAT** very few people have had more of an impact on the history of this community than me." "**COMMISSIONER** Salter, I can understand your frustrations and I can sympathize with your sense of disappointment, but you and the rest of the Commission were advised that this was not to be a political history, but rather a community history." "BUT THE HISTORY OF THE COMMISSION *IS* THE HISTORY OF THE TOWN. POLITICS IS THE DRIVING FORCE BEHIND DEMOCRACY." "**I'M** sorry, Mr. Commissioner sir, but there's really not much that can be done now. The history has been written, and the book has been printed." "**THAT'S** what you think. Those books can still be recalled. They should not be distributed as they now stand. I will do everything in my power to keep them from seeing the light of day. Otherwise you'll be history!" "**THIS** expe-
★★★page 148★★★   rience, of course, shed a whole new light on the

word "history" for me. I had always thought of history in terms of a geological bedrock with strata consisting of names, dates, and events, and to a certain extent, that is true. It is a matter of history that the Declaration of Independence was signed on July 4, 1776, and that John F. Kennedy was assassinated on November 22, 1963. All of these events are easily verifiable from written documents and eyewitness reports.   **BUT** behind the hard and crystalline facts, look what we have—**murky and convoluted controversies**. Nothing has been as productive for historians, publishers, and movie producers as the Kennedy assassination. As an economic stimulus, it's been unparalleled. It has produced over three hundred books, thousands of magazine articles, and scores of movies. And what does all that material tell us? Well, it's pretty definite, isn't it? The list of suspects has been narrowed down to Lyndon Johnson, Fidel Castro, Nikita Khrushchev, Sam Giancana, Jimmy Hoffa, Clay Shaw, the Mafia, the C.I.A., the American Communist Party, the F.B.I., organized labor, organized crime, disorganized labor, disorganized crime, scores of irate husbands, the Diem family, the John Birch Society, and the Ku Klux Klan, just to name a few. Actually it's probably easier to name the people and groups that have been eliminated from the suspect list: Peewee Herman, the Daughters of the Confederacy, the faculty of the library science department at Texas Christian Women's College, and Lee Harvey Oswald.   **I** know, I know. It is a documented fact that Oswald fired four shots at John F. Kennedy. But very few people believe that he was the one who killed Kennedy. There had to have been a second gunman, and even if one of Oswald's bullets did shatter the president's head, **Oswald was not the killer**. He was simply doing the bidding of a mysterious but powerful person. Someone big, someone mysterious, someone who will eventually emerge chillingly out of the mists of history. It is the greatest irony in the world that Oswald, who at the time of the Kennedy assassination, was considered the very personification of villainy is now, over thirty years later, seen as one of the victims of the assassination. This poor, misunderstood man was enticed and exploited by some powerful cabal of manipulative schemers to kill the president and take the rap. Not only did he pay the ultimate price (a Jack Ruby bullet to the brain), but his name now lives on in infamy alongside dastardly characters like Benedict Arnold, John Wilkes Booth, and Alger Hiss in America's pantheon of villains. How unfair.   **AND** if Oswald is now the victim, what does that make Kennedy? That's right, he's the villain—an arrogantly wealthy womanizer who treated his enemies ruthlessly and bought votes and elections with remorseless regularity. In 1963 at the time of the assassination, if you mentioned Kennedy's name people would automatically think of Martin Luther King, Jr., civil rights, the peace corps,   ★★★**page 149**★★★

and a new found sense of idealism. Mention the same name today and people think of Marilyn Monroe, the Mafia, and Vietnam. **THIS** irony proves another point about history. History is fickle. I used to think of history like I used to think of God. History was this white-haired old man with a long flowing white beard. He was infinitely wise, fair, and unbending. After a thorough consideration of all the facts, History would make his judgment about someone or some event, and this decision would stand rock solid for all time. Washington and Jefferson were good guys and Hitler and Mussolini were bad guys. But if you still believe that, you haven't read the latest in revisionist history. Washington and Jefferson were self-aggrandizing slaveholders, and Hitler and Mussolini were charismatic leaders who brought their countries back from financial ruin, and if you're worried about the way they treated the Jews, don't be, because the Holocaust never really took place. So now I am beginning to think that History is less like God and more like an adolescent girl who keeps changing her mind about who she wants to go to the prom with. She's fickle and superficial.
TO prove this point, consider the curious case of Christopher Columbus. No historical personage has been revered as long as Columbus in American history. Everyone from five to a hundred and five knows how the poem goes—"In 1492 Columbus sailed the ocean blue." For hundreds of years before George Washington was born and hundreds of years after, Christopher Columbus was celebrated as the intrepid adventurer who discovered America and opened up its shores to our ancestors. "We wouldn't be here today if it weren't for Columbus" has always been our collective view of the man, and "brilliant," "bold," "strong," "clever," and "resourceful" are the adjectives that we have always used to describe our first and foremost national hero. **BUT** recently History has changed its mind about Columbus. Now the words "cruel," "intolerant," "exploitive," "deceitful," and "murderous" are what you must say about Columbus in order to be politically correct. He has suddenly taken Hitler's place as the worst villain in the history of the world. Today Columbus is seen as the man who rapaciously invaded a whole hemisphere and either killed or enslaved all of its inhabitants not only in the years of his voyages from 1492 to 1503 but also in all the centuries following his death. He is **the villain who keeps on killing** because it was his bloodthirsty and intolerant Eurocentric view of the world which succeeding generations of American missionaries, adventurers, businessmen, and politicians adopted and revered. Columbus is the eternal villain because his self-righteous zeal to make a whole continent safe for Christianity has served as the justification for 500 succeeding years of raping the land and killing its native peoples. **NOTHING** illustrates the shifting sands of history
★★★page 150★★★   more effectively than Columbus' rapid descent

into disgrace. History, contrary to the common misconception that it is dry, dusty, and about the past, is actually quite lively, controversial, and immediate. In fact, a history book often tells us more about the time when it was written than it does about the time period it was written about. A biography of Columbus written in the 1990s will deal with a radically different set of issues than a biography of Columbus written in the 1890s.   **LOOK** at the history courses that are listed in a recent catalog of any university or college. These listings tell us more about the present than they do about the past. Black history did not become important in this country until the civil rights movement of the '60s, women's history did not interest anyone until the feminist movement of the '70s, and environmental history wasn't even an articulated concept until the environmental crisis of the '80s. The past becomes important to us only when we need it to interpret the present, and as George Orwell said, "He who controls the present controls the past." Just ask Commissioner Salter.

Mr. Big

IT'S a Friday afternoon in Arizona in August, which means that nothing is happening. Survival is the mode. You go to work, pack a lunch so you don't have to go outside, and keep a low profile. It's a good month to lay low. Don't go looking for a fight, and be sure and keep the blood pressure down. It's 115 degrees Fahrenheit—day after day. Don't leave your dog locked up in the car even if you're just running into Safeway to pick up a sixpack unless you like to **eat fried dogmeat** while you drink your beer. In short, avoid aggravation.   **THE** phone rings. "Mr. Big is going to be in town next month," says the caller. My blood pressure is beginning to rise. This is not good, but I can't help myself. First of all, I don't like the woman on the other end of the phone. She's too much of a true believer. I don't like true believers. I like murky people. The world is a murky place. Reality is murky, therefore **murky people are real**. True believers are hollow. That's why I tend to be skeptical of vegetarians, nudists, Rush Limbaugh Republicans, and anyone who worships another human being, be it Michael Jordan, John F. Kennedy, Madonna, or Mr. Big.   **THIS** woman (let's call her Ms. Little) worships Mr. Big, but she is not alone. A lot of librarians seem to be convinced that Mr. Big has all the answers. Mr. Big, after all, is a very "important" public library pontificator who runs a big public library system and who has held some big A.L.A. offices. Mr. Big, in other words, is a big political poohbah in the profession.   **I** do not like Mr. Big. In my mind he is a big pompous know-it-all. Still sharp in my memory is my first encounter with Mr. Big which happened over ten years ago. It was at an A.L.A. reception and several people in the group I was with mentioned that they had seen me on the *CBS Morning Show* where I had been asked to debate the merits of public libraries lending videogames.   "**YOU** were good," said one of the people in the group. "**YOU** were funny," said another.   "**YOU** were terrible," said Mr. Big, who then proceeded to explain for a full ten minutes how much better he would have handled the situation. In that ten-minute period my emotions ranged from hurt and embarrassment to bitterness and rage. I had done nothing to offend Mr. Big, and I did not, therefore, deserve to be humiliated by him in front of my professional peers. Even if my television debut had been a disastrous one (actually the 90 seconds that I was on was far too short a time to achieve a true disaster) it was not socially correct of him to inject his personal venom into the polite chitchat of our late afternoon conference cocktail party. **MY** resentment was tempered somewhat, however, when a few minutes later a woman who had obviously noticed my embarrassment took me aside and said, "Don't let Mr. Big get you down. He's obnoxious with everybody."   **THIS** was good to know and not so much because I now know that Mr. Big was not picking on me but rather because it confirmed my suspicion that Mr. Big is always obnoxious and so should be avoided at all costs and at all times. In my book, consistently obnoxious people have no redeeming characteristics. Life is **too short to expose yourself** unnecessarily to personal unpleasantness even if there is a thin stratum of truth under the unpleasantness. **SO** for years I simply stayed away from Mr. Big and outside of a few unpleasant conference encounters with him, I managed quite successfully to avoid his venom. But that all ended with the phone call from Ms. Little.   "**MR.** Big is coming to town two weeks from today. When will you be available to give him a tour of your library?"   I felt like saying, "Why don't you take him on a tour of the Chernobyl Generating plant instead," but being the new sensitive male of the nineties I decided that I didn't want to counterbalance Mr. Big's obnoxiousness with some of my own. So I said, "Anytime after lunch." While I could possibly survive spending an hour or so with Mr. Big, I knew that I would have an upset stomach if that hour also included lunch. I, therefore, wanted to make it clear that my tour did not include food.   **IMMEDIATELY** after I hung up the phone, I regretted my commitment to meet with Big. I really didn't have to do that. I could have told Mr. Big's flunky to take a leap or better yet I could have started laughing hysterically at her until she hung up. I'm not sure, however, that this woman would have gotten the message. True believers tend not to have a sense of irony.   **WHEN** would I ever learn to be more assertive, to refuse to do things that are inherently unpleasant? Why didn't I just say, "I'd rather have heart bypass surgery ★★★page 152★★★   without an anesthetic than meet with Mr. Big"?

How could I be so stupidly masochistic as to agree to show Mr. Big my library?   **THE** worst part of agreeing to meet with Mr. Big, of course, is not just having to interact with him face to face but in dealing with the nausea I would experience during the two weeks of waiting for the dreaded event to take place. And that's exactly what would happen. I would wake up in the morning and think, "Oh no, nine more days to Mr. Big." Then during my working hours at the library I would look at all aspects of the new building and cringe at how Mr. Big would carp at and criticize every little thing. My previous experiences with Mr. Big had taught me that humiliating people seemed to be his favorite hobby.   **AND** of course I wouldn't have been so fearful of Mr. Big if he wasn't so good at his hobby. His tongue was not only sharp and bitter but also quick and cutting. Mr. Big is not an unintelligent man. That much I admired about him. His ability to shape words into bullets is simply unparalleled in the library profession.   **THIS** is what I feared most—Mr. Big's critical mind and sharp tongue being turned loose in my building. Why had I ever consented to give Mr. Big a personally guided tour? I already knew what he would think of my building. He would hate it. I am a traditionalist who loves 17th-century English poetry and 19th-century French novels—the very things that Mr. Big would banish for lack of public interest. Even more antithetical to Mr. Big are my tastes in architecture. Where he favors shopping mall libraries with neon signs and openfaced metal shelving, I favor Greek columns, granite walls, high ceilings, and rich oaken shelving. Mr. Big's philosophy is that public libraries should mirror public tastes; my philosophy is that public libraries should stretch them. For me, the purpose of the public library is not to satisfy the public but to challenge it. To Mr. Big, of course, I am an elitist who would arrogate the public library to the level of an academic institution.   **BUT** knowing that someone dislikes your work is different than having him tell you directly to your face that he dislikes it. This, I suppose, is one of the rules of the civilized world. If someone asks for your honest opinion then, yes, by all means, put forth your honest opinion, but if it's not asked for, then don't say anything that is not positive. In this case I was not asking Mr. Big for his opinion. But this, of course, would make no difference to Mr. Big who seems to have a fetish for unsolicited honesty.   **IN** defense of Mr. Big, you might say honesty is certainly preferable to dishonesty, that you show someone the greatest respect by saying what you really believe rather than by saying what you think that person wants to hear. If I lie to you and tell you what you want to hear, aren't I simply manipulating your emotions in order to curry your favor, and isn't there something essentially deceitful and diabolical about this? Ordinarily I would say yes, but in the case of someone who has just built a new building,   ★★★page 153★★★

honesty is by no means the right policy.   **OUTSIDE** of raising teenagers, the hardest thing that most of us will ever be called upon to do will be to build a library building. While building a building has its highly technical aspects like devising floor plans, calculating space allocations, picking out colors, approving exterior elevations, planning circulation patterns, and laying out parking areas, there is also a more visceral part to the whole process.   **BASICALLY**, building a library building is like taking a three- or four-year roller coaster ride. Anyone who intends to direct a library building project should be given an emotional fitness test. Building a building is not something you should do if you're already dealing with some major psychological issues. A word from the wise to schizophrenics, manic depressives, nailbiters, **bedwetters, and the criminally insane:** DON'T UNDERTAKE A LIBRARY BUILDING PROJECT UNLESS YOUR MEDICAL INSURANCE PREMIUMS ARE UP TO DATE AND YOUR POLICY INCLUDES COMPLETE MENTAL HEALTH COVERAGE.   **IF** you're already nuts, building a building is only going to make you more nuts and if you're not already nuts, building a building will make you nuts. Why? Easy. There's a lot of money involved. There is a direct relationship between stress and money. The more money involved, the more stress there is.   **THINK** about it. When you order a book and the book turns out to be a dog, it's no big deal. You've wasted maybe twenty or thirty dollars, but when you build a building and it turns out to be a dog, it is a very big deal because you've wasted maybe twenty to thirty million dollars. This is a very big deal to librarians because more than most professions we are not used to dealing with money. We are used to dealing with poverty.   **SO** what do we do when we are in charge of a building project? We obsess. We worry and fret and go over every little detail at least two dozen times a day. Why do we micromanage? Because above all we want to avoid a fiasco. Mediocrity we don't mind as much. Mediocrity, although it can be quite mediocre, will not expose us as a laughingstock. The best situation, of course, is to produce an attractive building that is functional, but in the final analysis functional is what we're really after. If ugly is the price we have to pay to get functional, we'll take ugly. Ugly, after all, is subjective. With the right words ugly can be made to sound beautiful—"It's supposed to look grim and taut. Anything else would be irrelevant for our times."   **BEAUTY** can be faked but you can't fake functionality, and if the building we create is not functional, we will never hear the end of it from our fellow librarians, and these are the people we are really trying to impress. The average citizen's opinion is not as important because it can be dismissed as unprofessional and uninformed, but we would hate to be made fun of by our fellow professionals. It is hard to think of a greater force at work in the library profession than peer pressure. **THAT** is why we bring in professional librarian consultants—to make sure that we have all our professional bases covered. This of course insures both ugliness and functionality. There simply are not very many library building consultants to choose from.

Portrait of a library director in the middle of a building project.

Outside of three or four time tested firms you might as well stop looking. **THE** problem with most of the library consultants in business today is that after you pay them their forty or fifty thousand dollars they give you their standard building boilerplate. ★★★page 155★★★

Sometimes they don't even change the wording in their reports. Consequently their buildings all look the same—functional and ugly. What you see is what you get.   **UNFORTUNATELY** most librarians are satisfied with this approach because it protects them from being involved in a fiasco. The advantage of hiring one of the profession's standard consultants is safety. The consultant manages to stay in business because he has developed a product that is fiasco proof. What he lacks in imagination he makes up for in reliability. What you get is a Lego box and a set of instructions—nothing new, nothing different, no radical statements, and no risks.   **THE** upside, of course, is that you don't have to worry about being censured or even criticized by your colleagues. In fact, you'll probably get praises because your building will look just like their building, and imitation is the sincerest form of flattery. The single number one trait of the library profession is conformity. If you want the respect of your colleagues simply conform to their set of professional norms and principles. Stray from the norm and you risk opprobrium.   **AND** that oddly enough is the one thing I actually liked about Mr. Big. In a profession of sheep, he dared to be different. He was willing to take risks and stray from the norm, and while I am in total disagreement with the path that he decided to take, I do admire his chutzpah. Mr. Big conforms to no one but his own ego.   **THIS** is probably why I submitted to the humiliation of having him pass judgment on my building in my presence. This would be Mr. Big talking, not the profession, and wouldn't it be a matter of pride for me to brag to everyone that "Mr. Big absolutely hated my building. What a relief that was. I don't know what I would have done if he had said something nice about it"?   **TRY** as I might to convince myself that it was Mr. Big's censure that I was after, the truth remains that I was still terrified of this man snooping around my new building. Simply put, Mr. Big, maverick or not, was a man other librarians listened to if for no other reasons than his voice was so loud and obnoxious. What if, God forbid, he did **a hatchet job** on my building for *L.J.*, like he had done on another recent prominent new library? I didn't think I could handle the humiliation. I had put five years of my life into this building project and I didn't want Mr. Big's judgment to be ringing in my ears for the next five years.   **THIS** is because the new library building was my responsibility. Against his wishes I had explained to my architect that we were not going to spend forty thousand dollars on a library consultant. That was money that I wanted to put into the building, not into a report. Also I explained to my architect that although I had little experience in the area of design and construction, I looked upon the whole project as a great big fifteen million dollar Lego set, and I didn't want some unimaginative consultant handing over a blueprint to us. Where is the fun, the romance, and the daring of putting together Lego blocks according to someone else's mediocre idea of what a library should be? That's the way I challenged the architect to stop hugging the shoreline of professional library precedent and take his craft out into the deep seas. Charting by the stars is the way I explained that we should proceed with our project.   **ABOVE** all, I wanted the building to reflect an educational mission—a traditional educational mission, a mission that would address the obvious problems of post-industrial America. The building we built therefore reflected a seriousness of purpose that I knew could be criticized as being overbearing, extravagant, and old fashioned. Our creation was not a minimalistic ticky tacky box to be filled with the futuristic toys of computer and video industries, but rather an expansive monument in which books and electronic resources were melded for a fundamentally educational purpose with the focus definitely put on youth. It was just the kind of building that Mr. Big would hate.   **THE** fated day finally came, and fortunately Mr. Big did not expect me to give him a personal tour. When he showed up at my office doorstep with Ms. Little, he said, "I have been all through your library," he said in the same grave tone that God used to speak to Moses in the movie *The Ten Commandments.*   **"YES,"** I responded nervously, "How did you like it?"   **"I** have only one thing to say to you," he replied.   **"YES,** Mr. Big, what is it?" I responded fearfully.   **"I** think you've done a great job."   **"YOU** what?"   **"YES,** I think you've done a great job."   **"WELL,** Mr. Big, thank you very much. What do you like best about the building?"   **"I** like the fact that this building appears to be easily adaptable to an office building, and that's important because with the emergence of the electronic book, that's all this building is going to be good for in ten years."

P.C. and I.F.

A couple of years ago I was working with my illustrator to finish up the drawings for a book that I was writing about the relationship between directors and trustees, and it suddenly dawned on me that all of our cartoons featured white males over forty. "We need to diversify," I told him.   **"WHY?"** he asked.   **"BECAUSE** we're going to get killed by the reviewers for featuring all white males over forty in our drawings."   **"OKAY,"** he said, "what do you want me to do? I'm quite flexible."   **"THROW** in some women and other minorities," I said. "This is the nineties. Not only do we need to promote cultural diversity, but the truth is most of the directors and trustees in our profession are women. If we were to depict every director and trustee in this book as a man, we could be justifiably attacked for being blatantly sexist."   **"OKAY,** okay," he said impatiently. "If diversity is what you want, diversity is what you'll get."   **ABOUT** six months   ★★★page 157★★★

later the book (which, by the way, I consider my best) came out and while everyone who read it seemed to like the text, they also seemed to be thrown off balance by the cartoons. A number of readers complained that we seemed to be going out of our way to ridicule women in the book's cartoons. As one woman said, "You depict women in a rather unflattering, satirical light, as though they're not quite up to the job of being directors and trustees."   **"WAIT** a minute," I responded, "Would you have preferred us to depict all the trustees and directors as men?"   **"NO,"** she replied, "you should have depicted women in a more professional and competent manner. But instead you have made fun of them by putting them in ridiculous situations."   **"BUT** wait a minute, these are cartoons. People in cartoons are supposed to look ridiculous."   **"THEN** you shouldn't have used cartoons to illustrate your book."   **THIS** was a conversation that replayed itself several times whenever I asked people for their reactions to my book. Sometimes the readers took issue to the way women were portrayed in the cartoons and sometimes they objected to the way that people of color were portrayed, but no one ever complained about the way white men over forty were portrayed.   **WHILE** all of this was going on, I began to look more closely at the way men and women and people of color were depicted on television. I noticed something quite interesting about commercials. Whenever anyone did anything stupid, it was always a white male over forty. Remember that commercial where someone backs a car right through the garage door? That person was a white guy over forty. Or how about the scene where a grown adult is sitting in the dark secretly sucking on a flavor straw? Same thing—white guy over forty.   **THIS** little revelation was actually not all that demeaning to me as a white guy over forty. I mean, for years we have been portrayed as racist, sexist, and domineering and we have, as a consequence, become quite defensive about our role in society. It's hard for us to see where we fit in when we feel that everyone resents us. Now at least we have the satisfaction of knowing that we have a role to play—the bumbling idiot.   **WHILE** this is a role that many would be insulted to play, I myself find it quite liberating because all too often in real life I do a very good imitation of the bumbling idiot. You name it—**boiling eggs in the microwave**, locking keys in the car, mixing up my socks, spilling bleach on a dark suit, running a pair of wool pants through the washer, running out of gas in the left hand turn lane, and getting lost during the A.L.A. Fun Run—I've done it. But since I'm a white guy over forty, nobody cares. It's what everyone expects of me. That greatly diminishes the humiliation. I don't have to worry about letting down my gender or my race. I can act like a klutz and feel like I have disappointed no one.   **AND** I can relate to that ★★★page 158★★★   guy in the commercial because I actually have backed my car through a garage door and, believe me, the only way you can survive an experience like that ($2,134 repair bill for the door; $978 for the car) is with humor. "Hey," I told my wife, "I'm a white guy over forty. What'd you expect? You didn't think I'd open the door first, did you?" **THAT'S** the therapeutic effect of humor. It's a safety valve. It helps us cope with tragedy. It makes the human condition livable. Think about our plight. We find ourselves **stuck on planet earth** for no apparent reason. We don't know exactly why we exist and what exactly it is that we should be doing with our existence. **AT** the very base of our existence, therefore, is this absurdity. We're here and we don't know why we're here. In fact, the only thing we can really be certain of is the fact that we're going to die, and the further absurdity of that is that none of us wants to die. In fact, we would rather endure poverty, daily humiliation, sickness, and pain than die. We don't even want to age. Think of the billions of dollars we spend to ward off aging. It's absurd. **Life's a pain**, but it's the only place we know where we can do retrospective conversions, so let's make it last as long as we possibly can even if it means not eating red meat or drinking a daily martini. **ACTUALLY** there are four ways to react to the absurdity of life. We can laugh about it, cry about it, ignore it, or rebel against it. The truth is, we do all four things given the situation that we're in. There's a time to laugh, a time to cry, a time to fight, and a time to take out the garbage. It's how we cope. It's how we get through the days and months and years. **TAKE** away any one of those coping mechanisms and you have unhappiness, which creates even more absurdity because who in his right mind doesn't ultimately want to be happy? That's what bothers me so much about the unwillingness of so many people to laugh at themselves or at the absurdity of many of the situations that they find themselves in. **WHAT** we're talking about here, of course, is the whole political correctness movement, and as librarians and advocates of intellectual freedom and First Amendment Rights, it's something that we all need to be concerned with. First, let's define our terms. Political correctness is an unwritten social rule that says that it is inappropriate to criticize, laugh at, or ridicule certain subjects or certain groups of people. The penalty for breaking this unwritten law is that you give the offended person or persons the recognized right to publicly brand you a racist, a sexist, a moral pygmy, or an intellectual Neanderthal. **THOSE** who would defend the political correctness movement do so under the justification that anything that helps eliminate racism, sexism, moral pygmieism, and intellectual stupidity is a social good even if it means putting clamps on free speech. This, of course, presents a tremendous dilemma for librarians. On the one hand, we are overwhelmingly liberal and are very seriously committed to the liberal goal of creating a gender neutral, racially harmonious, and culturally diverse society. On the other hand, however, we are equally committed to the principles of intellectual freedom and will go to great lengths to fight all forms of censorship both within our libraries and also in society at large.   **UNFORTUNATELY**, the concepts of political correctness and intellectual freedom are inherently at odds with each other. While the doctrine of political correctness seeks to limit the bounds of self-expression, the doctrine of intellectual freedom seeks to expand them, and while the doctrine of political correctness presupposes a certain set of moral values, the doctrine of intellectual freedom is value neutral. **WHAT** many good, liberal, and politically correct librarians simply do not realize is that if they truly want to be defenders of intellectual freedom, they must be willing to defend the right of a whole bunch of unsavory people—racists, sexists, pornographers, propagandists, and homophobes—to express themselves in whatever form they desire. **INTELLECTUAL** freedom, although it is our profession's holy grail, is not in and of itself a good thing. It is, in fact, a two-edged sword. It can be used for evil as easily as it can be used for good. It can spread the seeds of prejudice, hatred, and superstition as well as the seeds of tolerance, goodwill, and truth. What most librarians don't understand is that intellectual freedom is the very instrument that people like David Koresh use to spin their empires of evil. We prefer to think of intellectual freedom as something that is inherently pure and good like motherhood and oat bran muffins.   **THAT** is precisely why we librarians are much more apt to jump up and promote the First Amendment rights of our fellow liberals than we are to defend the free speech rights of people like Jerry Falwell and the dreaded Rush Limbaugh. We want to believe that intellectual freedom is reserved for the politically correct. But this, of course, is transparently hypocritical and completely unrealistic.   **LONG** before the political correctness movement was recognized and identified by social commentators, it surfaced in a very dramatic way in Detroit during the 1977 A.L.A. annual conference and, like a heat-seeking missile, it crashed headlong into the profession's commitment to intellectual freedom.   **THE** issue at hand during that long, hot summer conference was a most improbable and highly ironic one: Should the American Library Association censor a movie that it had produced on the subject of intellectual freedom? The name of the movie was *The Speaker* and it was intended for use by public librarians as a catalyst for community discussions on the subject of intellectual freedom. The wonderful irony, of course, is that the biggest discussion that it generated had to do with whether or not the movie should be suppressed by the very organization that had produced it.   **SPECIFICALLY**, the movie featured a retiring high school ★★★page 160★★★   teacher (played by Mildred Dunnock) who finds herself embroiled in an explosive controversy in her role as the faculty advisor to the special events committee. It is the purpose of this task force to invite outside speakers to the high school to talk to students on a wide diversity of subjects not normally covered in their basic curriculum, and it just so happens that one of the speakers invited is a famous scientist named James Boyd, who is notorious for espousing the odious theory that black people are genetically inferior to whites.   **THIS** invitation sets the entire community on edge as blacks and white liberals band together to pressure the school's administration into canceling Boyd's speaking engagement. Mildred Dunnock, although she finds Boyd's theories to be reprehensible, finds the community's attempts at censoring Boyd to be even more reprehensible. Finally, however, over Dunnock's objections, the school board intervenes and bans Boyd from speaking.   **THE** response of many members of the American Library Association to the movie was outrage. They branded the film as racist and attempted to remove A.L.A.'s name from it. What followed was a knockdown, drag-out fight at one of the general membership sessions that resulted in the forces of intellectual freedom winning a very narrow victory over the forces of political correctness. By the slimmest of margins it was decided that the film would continue to carry A.L.A.'s imprimatur.   **WHY** did a movie advocating the importance of intellectual freedom cause such a fury in a profession so strongly committed to fighting censorship in all of its dastardly forms? Simple. *The Speaker* showed the dark side of intellectual freedom. By making Professor Boyd and his cockeyed genetic theories the focus of the movie, the point was eloquently made that free speech and intellectual freedom can be used to espouse undesirable points of view.   **IF** the speaker in the film had been an advocate of abortion rights, minority rights, gay rights, or any other good liberal cause, the movie would have been embraced by A.L.A.'s membership with great enthusiasm, and that's exactly the kind of movie that was expected, one in which the principles of political correctness would merge nicely with the values of intellectual freedom. But such a production, although it may have been pleasing to librarians, would have been an utter failure in fulfilling its intended purpose to serve as a discussion catalyst. It would have been nice, proper, correct, and utterly boring.   **BUT** let us all be thankful that Judith Krug, the executive producer of the film and the director of A.L.A.'s Intellectual Freedom Office, had the courage to be politically incorrect. By casting a racist into the role of the victim, Krug brilliantly illuminated the difficult complexities of an issue that we librarians have always tended to see in an overly simplistic light.   **THE** fact of the matter is that *The Speaker* works brilliantly as a discussion catalyst   ★★★page 161★★★

because it promotes the right cause for the wrong reason. Intellectual freedom always produces truth, beauty, and justice, right? Of course not! The reason that intellectual freedom is such a controversial topic is that deep down inside we fear what can happen when the wrong people exercise their First Amendment rights. Librarians resented the film because it reminded them of this unsavory point. **ANOTHER** problem with the film for librarians is that it portrays censors as normal and even sensitive people who are trying to do the right thing in their communities. While this may be a fairly accurate portrayal, it is also professional heresy since we prefer to think of censors in the stereotypical terms of the intolerant, **crackpot, religious right wing**. It's much easier to be an advocate for a cause when the enemies of that cause consist solely of bigots and zealots. **TRY** as we might to paint this picture of our censors, the reality remains, however, that most censors are concerned parents (such as the ones presented in *The Speaker*) who are worried about the intellectual, moral, and social welfare of their children. It is much more difficult to condemn censorship when the censors we are confronted with are decent human beings who are as interested in promoting the common good as we are. **BUT** ultimately, what the library profession failed to realize about *The Speaker* is that although it gave some compelling reasons for the exercise of situational censorship, it still gave even more compelling reasons for the exercise of intellectual freedom. The act of suppressing speech (even hate speech) is far worse than the act of exposing free thinking individuals to ideas that are politically incorrect, because in the long run you never know what will be defined as politically correct. **FOR** instance, in Nazi Germany in the 1930s and 40s the extermination of a whole race of people was considered politically correct and those who spoke up against it were tortured and their books were burned. But you don't think that could happen in this country, do you? Of course not. Just look at how people with leftist leanings were treated in this country during the 1950s McCarthy witch hunts. The point is that the free expression of all opinions, irrespective of their "incorrectness," have a right to be aired in a free society. That's why it is the duty of the librarian to defend the First Amendment rights not only of those with whom we agree but also of those with whom we disagree. **THAT** is also why I am offended by the emotional sensibilities of certain groups of people in our society who feel they should somehow be shielded from the slings and arrows of humor, satire, and criticism, and that certain protected classes of people are off limits to these verbal barbs. If we are truly committed to the principles of intellectual freedom, then we must agree that nothing or no one in this life or this profession is ★★★page 162★★★ above ridicule, criticism, or scrutiny.

Bedtime Fables

FABLE #1—HALE AND HARDY—

Long ago and far away in the land of Biblarz, there was a little town called Hardy. Hardy, a fairly new town, was like a little brother growing up in the shadow of a much older and bigger brother named Hale. Hale, which was located five miles north of Hardy, was the biggest city in Biblarz. It had a big post office, a very large park with lakes, and a good sized public library. Hardy, on the other hand, had a small post

Long ago and far away....

office, a modest park with a swimming pool, and a teeny, tiny public library run by a **teeny, tiny volunteer librarian** named Max Merkle whose main acquisitions strategy was to pick books out of a donation basket at Shoprite, the town's grocery store. **THE** ★★★page 163★★★

people of Hardy liked Max and admired him for his dedicated service to their community and so they dropped many books into his donation basket. As a consequence, Max was able to build a library that he was proud of. His reference collection was anchored by a 1967 *World Book Encyclopedia* set that was missing only three volumes—the "T," the "E," and the "X, Y, and Z." While Max was always on the lookout for the "T," he didn't care that much about the "E" or the "X, Y, and Z" since he didn't think there were a lot of important people or subjects beginning with those letters. Max was also proud of his fiction collection which featured over 1,000 Harlequin romances, some of which were only three years old. The non-fiction collection was also beginning to develop quite nicely. Among its strengths was a recent campaign biography of who else—Slick William—the president of Biblarz. **DESPITE** Max's valiant effort, a number of people (actually a growing number of people) were not happy with the library that he had cobbled together. Some of these people were frustrated that they could not look up "xiphoid process" in the encyclopedia and others found that a **steady diet of Harlequins** was not good for their mental health. So these people got together and went to the next meeting of the Hardy city council to ask for a real public library. The city councillors listened intently and seemed to sympathize with the request, but they were alarmed by the fact that they would have to raise taxes to fund a real library, and they felt that if they raised taxes that they would not be re-elected. They thought that the main reason that Hardy was a growing community was because most of the people who were moving there were trying to **escape the high taxes** of the city of Hale.   A report of this city council meeting appeared in the *Hale Daily News*, and Siegfried Sicklemeyer happened to read it. Siegfried was, at the time, the director of the Hale Public Library. He had an M.L.S. degree and was very respected in the library profession. He believed strongly in the ideals of librarianship. One of those ideals was the importance of library cooperation.   **AFTER** Siegfried read the article, he quickly picked up the phone and called Mayor Michael Moon of Hardy, and said, "Since I hate to think that all the people in your community are without decent library services, I have an offer for you—if you allow the citizens of Hale to use your library for free we will reciprocate and allow your citizens to use our library for free." The mayor, of course, was quite agreeable. He thanked Siegfried and fought off the temptation to try to sell him some reclaimed swamp land south of Hardy. No sense in pressing his luck.   **SO**, the citizens of Hardy were very happy, and they used the Hale Public Library to their heart's content. Correct that. The ones who had the transportation to travel the five miles to the library were happy, the other people ★★★page 164★★★   (those who didn't have transportation like the young, the old, and the poor) were not satisfied. They still had to use Max's teeny, tiny library.   **THINGS** went along this way for several years, and then two things happened. First, the economy in the land of Biblarz sunk into a long recession, which meant that the tax base began to erode, which meant that funding for the Hale Public Library began to drop. Second, Siegfried Sicklemeyer retired on his sixty-fifth birthday. They had a big party for Siegfried and everyone said what a great librarian he was and how much he had upheld the principles of his profession.   **THE** new director, Petula Poundstone, was, of course, in a pickle. Because of the recession, she had to cut the library's budget. She did not think it was fair that the citizens of Hardy should be allowed to continue to use the Hale Public Library for free. She, therefore, convinced her board of trustees, to discontinue this service unless the Hardy city council was willing to compensate the library for serving its citizens. As everyone predicted, the city council was too cheap to do this.   **THE** people of Hardy became very angry. At first, they got very mad at Petula Poundstone and called her "uncooperative." She convinced them, however, that it was not fair to expect the citizens of Hale to pay for their library services. She told them that Hardy deserved to have its own library and that the Hardy city council should pay for it.   **SO** the people, having been cut off from the Hale Public Library, demanded their own library, and the city councillors all voted for it because they wanted to be re-elected.   **SOME** time later, when the building was under construction, the mayor and the city council were given a special tour. They were very proud of their new building. In fact, one of the councillors said excitedly, "We should have built this a long time ago." The mayor looked at him and said, "But we didn't need to since our citizens could use the Hale Library for free!" *MORAL—LIBRARY COOPERATION CAN HINDER LIBRARY DEVELOPMENT*   *FABLE #2—HALE BUT NOT HARDY*—Hardy Public Library director, Edweena Egglesworth, was in a bit of a panic. Her new library was scheduled to open in four months and the Hardy city council had still not given her approval to hire the librarians that she desperately needed to staff her library. **EDWEENA** had come to Hardy a year and a half ago. She was hired by the newly formed Hardy Public Library board of trustees to be the library's first library director. When she interviewed for the job, the board had been very impressed with her knowledge. She told them that developing a library in Hardy would require more than just the money that the city council had set aside for the design and construction of the new building. It would also require money for books and staff. The board ended up hiring Edweena Egglesworth because it felt that she was so smart that the city council wouldn't be able to say "no" to her. **AND** to be truthful, it looked like they were right because the first thing that Edweena did was go to the council and ask for book money. Initially the council was skeptical. "But, Ms. Egglesworth," said Mayor Moon, "for years we had a small volunteer library that was completely stocked with gifts. We didn't need a book budget because our citizens were so generous with their donations." **WITH** all due respect, Mr. Mayor," responded Edweena, "you cannot run a modern library with donated books. Look at how many people used your old volunteer library—only the ones who couldn't travel to Hale. Opening a new library with a ragtag collection of books, Mr. Mayor, is like wearing a worn out pair of penny loafers with a brand new suit." **EDWEENA** felt that this analogy would hit home since Mayor Moon owned the local haberdashery, but the mayor was not impressed. He looked up at Edweena and said, "I think that when people see the new library they will respond with much nicer book donations. It won't be a ragtag collection at all." **EDWEENA** decided to change tactics. "Mr. Mayor, I'm sure that you and the members of the city council will be much prouder to have your names stamped on new books, rather than old ones." **THIS** comment piqued the curiosity of Councillor Constance Calloway. "Why would our names be stamped on the books?" she asked. **EDWEENA** smiled at her and said, "Because each book in the library will be stamped with a special stamp that says 'this book is provided with funds appropriated by Mayor Moon and Councillors Calloway, Doberman, Freckleberry, and Sugarwater'." **"NOW** that's a nice touch," said Councillor Dolores Doberman. **"YES**, quite right," agreed Councillor Fred Freckleberry. **"I** couldn't agree more," said Councillor Susan Sugarwater. **"I** think I detect a council consensus," declared Mayor Moon. "Ms. Egglesworth, you may proceed with your plans to stock the new library using the book budget that you have recommended to us." **EVERYONE** on the board was quite pleased with Edweena's victory, and to a person, they said, "We sure picked the right person to fight our battles with the council." **BUT** unfortunately, Edweena's attempts to get her staffing budget approved were not nearly as productive. "We used volunteers in the old library, Ms. Egglesworth!" proclaimed Mayor Moon, after he had listened to her plea for staffing. **"BUT**, Mr. Mayor," responded Edweena, "a modern library needs a well trained professional staff. We need to hire at least four people with master's degrees in library science." **"WHY** do you need a master's degree to check out a book?" wondered Councillor Sugarwater. **"LIBRARIANS** don't check out books," countered Edweena, "they assist patrons with their informational needs, they produce special programs for children, and they select and catalog books on the basis of sound professional principles." **"WELL**, now," muttered Councillor Freckleberry, "I'm sure that old Miss Penelope Prosch, who lives down the street from me, could be of some assistance to you. She was the librarian at the elementary school I attended years ago. She's retired now, has been for years, so I know that she's got the time to help out down there at the library. Give her a call." **EDWEENA** was about ready to launch into a question about whether old Miss Penelope Prosch was the type of person that the mayor and council would want their names tattooed to but she didn't think that at this particular time they would appreciate that little bit of humor. **FINALLY**, Mayor Moon looked up at Edweena and said, "Maybe we could afford to give you some part time employees to help with stamping the books and checking them out, but as for these professional staff, we just don't have the money to do that." **"THAT'S** right," said Fred Freckleberry, "the *Farmer's Almanac* says that this winter will be a cold one. We've got to save up now for all the snow plowing that we're going to have to pay for in January and February." **THEN** the discussion turned to landfill sites, and the library board members looked at each other as if to say, "Maybe Edweena wasn't the right person to fight our battles with the council." *MORAL—POLITICIANS LOVE TO BUILD BUILDINGS, BUT HATE TO STAFF THEM* *FABLE #3—HARDY, HARDY, HO, HO, HO*—As far as shoulders to cry on, Max Merkle's weren't the greatest. But when you're a library director and you need someone to turn to for support, encouragement, and reassurance, your best bet is the president of your library's board of trustees, and Max Merkle, for better or worse, was the president of the Hardy Public Library board of trustees. **MAX'S** ascendency to the presidency, even if it wasn't in the best interests of the library, was at least understandable. The city council felt they had to throw him this bone after he had worked so hard for so many years providing the citizens of Hardy with his **ragtag, moth-ridden, mildew-laden volunteer** library. **PLUS**, most council watchers felt that Max was the type of person that the mayor and council knew that they could keep under control. He was, in other words, a safe person to appoint to that position. Teeny, tiny Max (he was all of five feet tall) was not the type of person to be leading any budget raids on the community's treasury. No, Max could be counted on to do the council's bidding with enthusiasm, and so he received the coveted appointment. **THAT'S** not to say anything bad about Max. He was certainly not in cahoots with the council. No, Max would never do anything purposefully to set back library progress in Hardy. The worst thing you could say about Max was that he **tended toward wimpdom**. The problem with that of course is that the last person you want leading your library board is a wimp. **SO**, Max was not a lot of help when Edweena came crying on his shoulder. "Edweena," he said, "right now the city council is strapped for cash. We can't expect them to support

library staffing above snowplowing. We'll just have to make do with part-timers and volunteers. I know it can be done. For seven years, I ran a volunteer library here in Hardy." **EDWEENA** wanted to say, "Yeah, Max, that's what I'm afraid of—that we'll get started with part-timers and volunteers and the council will never want to fund full-time, professional positions," but she held her tongue in order not to hurt Max's feelings. He was very, very proud of what he had accomplished with his teeny, tiny volunteer library.   **AT** the next regularly scheduled meeting under old business, the Hardy Public Library board discussed the staffing dilemma that Edweena Egglesworth faced. She started the discussion by saying, "When I moved my family to Hardy to become director of your library. I did it with the understanding that the board and council were serious about developing quality library services. I am now beginning to think that is not the case." **"OH,** Ms. Egglesworth, however could you think that?" exclaimed Betty Bosworth Bumpers, the board's vice president. "Just look at how beautiful that building is that's going up over on Broadway Boulevard." **"YES,"** agreed trustee Tom Tomjanovich, "and pretty soon it will be filled with all our pretty new books." **"THOSE** pretty new books," said Edweena, "can't be put on the shelves until they are cataloged and processed." **"VOLUNTEERS** can do that," said Max Merkel cheerfully. "In my old library we didn't waste time cataloging, we just arranged the books by color. It was a lot prettier that way, and we found that that's what people remembered most about a book—its color or the picture on the dust jacket. Sometimes when we had enough helpers, we did keep files on dust jacket pictures."
"OKAY," countered Edweena who was now beyond exasperation, "but how did you check them out? What system did you use?" **"THE** honor system," said Max cheerfully. "This is a small town. You can trust people. Plus I didn't think it was fair to limit our patrons to an arbitrary check-out time. We had this big old copy of *Moby-Dick* and I knew that it would take a lot more time to read that than it would take to read *Green Eggs and Ham*. So I let everyone decide for themselves what a fair checkout period would be. The only person who ever abused the privilege was Reverend Roy Riegals. He checked out *The Naked and the Dead* and never returned it because he thought **it was dirty**. He didn't want anybody to corrupt their mind by reading it."
"WHAT did you do when somebody needed help finding an answer to a question? Did you have anyone working there who knew anything about reference services?"   **"OH,** yeah," said trustee Harry Hanabrink, "old Ed Eagles used to help out quite a bit. The library was located in a little corner of the third floor and he was real good at giving patrons directions about how to get to the bathroom. It was real
★★★page 168★★★   tricky. You had to go down a flight of stairs and

then hang a left at the city clerk's office, go through a set of double doors, and then turn right at the jail." "**OH**, and don't forget about Gwendolyn Grimsley," added Max. "She used to sit in that library all day and read every book that came in. Whenever someone wanted a good book to read all they had to do was ask Gwendolyn. Why, one week she read twenty-seven Harlequin romances. She knew them by heart." "**YEAH**," said Harry Hanabrink, "it's disappointing not to get any full-time staff, but we'll make do. We've got a lot of volunteers who just love to sit in that library and read all day." **AFTER** the meeting, Edweena Egglesworth headed right for Ted Tetley's Twilight Tavern. ***MORAL—MOST PEOPLE THINK LIBRARIANS SIT AROUND ALL DAY AND READ.*** *FABLE* #4—HAIL, HAIL THE GANG'S ALL HERE—Ted Tetley's Twilight Tavern was not terribly crowded the night that Edweena Egglesworth stopped in for **a touch of Wild Turkey**. Actually it wasn't crowded at all. Ted was there and so was Ted's pet turtle, Tom, but that was it. **AFTER** Edweena ordered her drink she walked over to the jukebox, dropped a quarter in the slot and punched "E6." Suddenly Ted Tetley's Twilight Tavern reverberated with Randy Ringold singing, "I Got the Bibliographic Blues." "**PROBLEMS** down at the library?" asked Ted as he put a shot of Wild Turkey in front of Edweena. "**LET** me put it in terms you might understand," said Edweena. "I've got a state of the art sports bar with all the amenities—three satellite dishes, fifteen big screen teevees, and even a miniature indoor basketball court, but I can't afford to hire anyone to wait on tables, mix drinks, and cook meals." "**YOU** can't afford not to!" said Ted excitedly. "**TELL** that to the library board," replied Edweena. "**DO** you mean to tell me," said Ted, "that they won't give you the staff you need to run that new library that they're building on Broadway Boulevard?" "**PRECISELY!**" "**THAT** makes me mad!" said Ted Tetley. "The property taxes on my house and business went up thirty dollars a year to pay for that library, and now you tell me that I'm not going to get my money's worth? I'm angry. Who's in charge of that library board?" "**MAX** Merkle," answered Edweena. "**NO** wonder you've got problems," said Ted. "That half-pint yellow-bellied sapsucker would buckle under to my turtle Tom if Tom could talk. Don't you worry about a thing, Edweena. I'm going to make a few phone calls. Tell me who else is on your library board." **EDWEENA** gave Tom the information, finished her drink, and left feeling a bit uplifted but skeptical. What could Tom Tetley the tavern keeper do to help her? **THIRTY** days later Edweena got her answer. It was a different library board that met for their monthly meeting. "Mr. Chairman," said Arnold Applebody forthrightly, "I move that we dispense with the reading of the minutes and cut right to the quick." "**YES**," said ★★★page 169★★★

Betty Bosworth Bumpers, "I've been getting a lot of phone calls from some very angry people."   **"SO** have I," echoed Gwendolyn Grimsley. "Our citizens are upset about the city council's refusal to staff the library."   **"WE** need to get a clear message across to the city council that our citizens will not stand for second class library services in a first class library building," said Tom Tomjanovich.   **"HOW** can we best do that?" asked Arnold Applebody.   **"BY** showing up at the budget hearing in mass and letting each and every councilman and councilwoman know that the key to getting re-elected is to support the library board's budget request," replied Tom.   **TWO** weeks later all nine board members showed up at the budget hearing. Members of the city council seemed to be both surprised and a bit skittish about this show of support. "Welcome," said Mayor Michael Moon to the board, "Your participation in the budget process is always welcomed. We value the input of our citizen boards."   **"THANK** you," said board president Max Merkle, "Arnold Applebody, the chair of our budget committee is here to make a short statement regarding our financial needs."   **"MR.** Mayor and members of the City Council, I will make my remarks short and to the point," said Arnold and as he talked the rest of the library board stood up behind him in a visible show of support. "We feel very strongly that you should not even consider opening our new library building if you do not want to staff it with appropriately trained staff."   **"DO** you all feel that way?" questioned the mayor. **"YES,"** said Betty Bosworth Bumpers, "we all feel that way and furthermore we have received phone calls from hundreds of voters who do not want a second-class library operation in a first-class building." **"YES,"** said car dealer Harry Hanabrink. "It would be like buying a new Cadillac and finding out you are only allowed two gallons of gasoline a week to run it."   **"HOW** many new professional staff do you think you need?" queried the mayor.   **"FOUR** would be the minimum," said Arnold, "but six would be ideal."   **"MR.** Mayor," said Councilwoman Constance Calloway, "I move that we fund seven new professional librarians for the new public library."   **"I** second," said Susan Sugarwater with enthusiasm.   **THE** motion carried unanimously. ***MORAL—ONE POLITICALLY ACTIVE LIBRARY BOARD IS WORTH A THOUSAND POLITICALLY ACTIVE LIBRARY DIRECTORS.***

Index

American Library Association 133–136; American Library Association Fun Run 48–52; American Library Association Placement Center 52–61; Australian toaster biscuits 27   Baltimore County Library 111–114; Berlin Wall 32; bibliotherapy 121–129; book donations 35–36; book

★★★page 170★★★   reviews 8–10, 62; book selection 35–36; book selling 107–110; bookdrops 116–121 **C**atalogers and cataloging 4–8; censorship 39, 42, 62–64, 71–74, 135–136; children's services 37, 136–138, 142; Clinton, Bill 52; committees 39; computers 41 *Daddy's Roommate* 72–74; Disneyland 26–30 **F**ines 21–22; food survey 74–77 **I**nput messages 114–116 **L**ibrarian image 16, 32–35, 167–169; librarian salaries 32–35; library architecture 25–26, 153–157; library construction 92–94; library cooperation 163–165; library education 43–44; *Library Journal* 61–65; library research 44–48; Library Services and Construction Act 41; Lincoln, Abraham 29–30 **M**adonna 62–63 **O**utput measures 114–116 **P**ersonnel management 18–21, 37, 96–103, 139–140; phonographs in libraries 130–133; political correctness 157–162; popular culture 95–96; problem patrons 68–71; public art in libraries 77–91; public libraries and local politics 13–15, 39, 42, 45–48, 110–111, 165–167; public relations 17–18 **R**eference questions 16–17, 19–20; riot act 20–21; Ronald Reagan Presidential Library 30–32 **S**an Juan Capistrano Public Library 24–26; Sandburg, Carl 30; security systems 23–24; sexual harassment 67–71 **T**rustees 37, 41–42, 170 **V**ideotapes in libraries 37